Matilde Serao

In the country of Jesus

Matilde Serao

In the country of Jesus

ISBN/EAN: 9783744646710

Printed in Europe, USA, Canada, Australia, Japan

Cover: Foto ©Lupo / pixelio.de

More available books at **www.hansebooks.com**

IN THE COUNTRY OF JESUS

TRANSLATED FROM THE ITALIAN OF
MATILDE SERAO
BY RICHARD DAVEY

THOMAS NELSON AND SONS, L~~TD~~.
LONDON, EDINBURGH, AND NEW YORK

TO MY VERY DEAR SON

ANTONIO

THIS BOOK IS

AFFECTIONATELY DEDICATED

M. S.

CONTENTS.

TRANSLATOR'S NOTE	11
INTRODUCTION	13

PART I.—TOWARDS SYRIA.

I. ON THE SEA	19
II. THE NILE	22
III. CAIRO	25
IV. THE PYRAMIDS	29
V. SORIA ! SORIA !	34

PART II.—THE VOW FULFILLED.

I. IN THE TRAIN	41
II. IN THE CHURCH	45
III. THE TOMB	49
IV. THE ADORATION	53
V. DURING THE NIGHT	58

PART III.—JERUSALEM ! JERUSALEM !

I. THE CITY	67
II. THE PEOPLE	71
III. THE SOUL	76

Part IV.—THE WAY OF SUFFERING.

   I. The Mount of Olives 83
  II. Gethsemane 87
 III. The Way of the Cross 92
  IV. Calvary 97
   V. The Lament of Israel. 100
  VI. The Valley of Jehoshaphat 105
 VII. A Suffering Shadow 107

Part V.—THE IDYLL.

   I. Ephrata 119
  II. The Manger 122
 III. The Precursor 126

Part VI.—SEVEN HUNDRED FEET BELOW THE LEVEL OF THE SEA.

   I. Jericho 133
  II. In a Palanquin 139
 III. The Dead Sea. 144
  IV. The Jordan 147
   V. The Rose of Jericho 150

Part VII.—IN GALILEE.

   I. On the Road 161
  II. Herr Hardegg 163
 III. The Corn Merchant 168
  IV. Mount Carmel. 174
   V. On the Road to Nazareth 178

CONTENTS.

VI. THE STORY OF THE MADONNA	184
VII. A DAY IN NAZARETH	191
VIII. ON MOUNT TABOR	195
IX. TIBERIAS	199
X. ON THE LAKE	204
XI. THE MOUNT OF THE BEATITUDES	207
XII. MAGDALA	211

PART VIII.—ST. FRANCIS IN PALESTINE.

I. HOSPITALITY	219
II. THE WORK	223

PART IX.—THE LAST DAY.

I. ADVICE TO THE INTENDING TRAVELLER	229
II. A HOPE	233
III. ISSA COBROUSLY	237
IV. LEAVE-TAKING	246

TRANSLATOR'S NOTE.

MANY works have been written on the Land of Jesus, but few have attained the great popularity of Matilde Serao's " *Nel Paese di Gesú.*" A simple record of a journey through the land consecrated by the Life and Passion of Christ, it has in less than two years passed through thirty editions. A fervent Catholic, Signora Serao sees the Holy Land through very orthodox glasses, and unhesitatingly accepts not only the Gospels, but the ancient traditions of her Church : and in this she is most probably right, for what is tradition but unwritten history ? She makes no pretence to historical or archæological learning, but accepts all she sees and hears with the naïve faith of a true daughter of her Church. To her way of thinking there is no need to question whether the Church of the Holy Sepulchre really rises on the exact site of the Crucifixion or not. She believes implicitly in the tradition— a very ancient one, by-the-way, dating certainly from the third century—which tells her that where now stands the Church of the Holy Sepulchre Christ was not only put to Death, but also Buried : and indeed Scripture confirms this statement.

" In the place where He was Crucified there was a garden, and in the garden a new sepulchre, wherein man was never yet laid.
" There laid they Jesus therefore. . . ." (John xix. 41, 42).

And since the faith of ages has confirmed this venerable

tradition, the Tomb within the Church of the Sepulchre is, indeed, the most august of earthly relics, so that we can sympathise with the passionate reverence expressed for it by the illustrious Italian writer. Her faith is all the more welcome in this age of scepticism, because it is so honestly and so frankly expressed. Would that it were possible to transfer to our colder and terser language some of the fiery ardour of the original! But, unfortunately, much that is beautiful in the Italian of Signora Serao would sound exaggerated in English. "*Nel Paese di Gesú*" is so essentially Italian that it defies close translation. I have done my best, however, to transfer to the English version at least something of the charm of these rapidly sketched impressions of a journey undertaken by one of the most gifted women of our time to the land where Jesus was born, where He preached, and where He suffered for the Redemption of mankind.

RICHARD DAVEY.

INTRODUCTION.

THERE are three sorts of travellers: the first and the most frequently met with is that restless, energetic being, who rushes from country to country, whose face wears a look of keen interest, and who can stand any amount of fatigue. Regardless of consequences, he rushes into every sort of peril, tires out the patience of his fellow-travellers, and is the terror of the *ciceroni*. When this creature returns home from visiting the four quarters of the globe, he is perfectly self-satisfied and delighted with all he has seen, said, and done. But should you venture to ask him to give you some account of his experiences, he will assume an air of the utmost importance, and answer as if revealing some unfathomable mystery, known only to himself, that restaurants are very dear in Paris, that London has an underground railway, that you pay a penny a trip on the Grand Canal at Venice, that Russian steamers are slower than the Austrian, that there is not a drop of drinkable water in the whole East, and other like bits of trivial information which in his wisdom he has collected at vast expense of time and money. This globe-trotter is, heaven be praised, quite harmless, although, alas, his species is as countless as the very stars of heaven. In a sense he is sometimes quite fascinating, and has a charm peculiar to himself, his frivolity often being intensely amusing. He seems to me to bear an extraordinary likeness to one of his own travelling trunks, and I imagine that he curls himself up in some out-of-the-way nook or corner where, surrounded by his bags and baggage, he remains dormant until the hour arrives for him to start on a fresh voyage in search of a new crop of twaddling reminiscences.

The second, but less common sort of traveller, is he whose sole object is the search after the picturesque ; he is possessed by a mania for the discovery of exquisite views and new and picturesque colouring ; the country, the sea, the town, the churches, the people, all interest and delight him. His brain is a picture gallery and his imagination a cinematograph, the ever changing scenes of which he soon retains only a blurred impression.

There is yet a third sort of traveller who differs entirely from the two above described—the sentimentalist—who is devoured by curiosity and endeavours to extract from all he sees and hears some simple fact, legend, or historical memory, which shall enable him to discover the true character of the peoples and lands he visits. He sometimes passes over what the ordinary mortal would consider of the utmost importance, spends but a few hours in the large towns, to linger for days in some country inn, and will leave aside a renowned museum for the attractions of a village fair. What most people admire has little interest for him. He has but one object in view—that is, to lay bare the soul of the countries through which he travels. To him, the whole history of a nation may be revealed in the eyes of a woman, in the fragment of a statue, the turn of a road ; in a rusty weapon, in a flower, in a popular song, nay, even in a mere word.

I have endeavoured, in my journey through Palestine, humbly and honestly to seek out the soul of that Blessed

Land where Christ dwelt and where His voice was heard. I found it in the clear skies of Samaria, in the tiny violet and yellow flowers that bloom where once stood the home of Martha and Mary, and by that fountain at Nazareth where the Virgin Mother bathed her gentle hands. I found it on the shores of that lake of Gennesareth, on whose waters Jesus walked, and where He commanded the storm to cease ; and, indeed, in every place where the Son of God lived, suffered, and preached the words of peace and hope. I have sought to chronicle my impressions of the Holy Land even as I felt them whilst still vibrating with the intense emotions I experienced as I trod the paths He had passed along and visited the scenes hallowed by His Life and Passion.

JERUSALEM, Spring, 1893. NAPLES, Autumn, 1897.

PART I.
TOWARDS SYRIA.

I.

ON THE SEA.

THE day for departure has arrived at last, and the busy preparations for a long journey, that almost equal those of a prisoner anticipating his hour of release, are concluded. But instead of joyous expectation, a sort of chilly oppression pervades the traveller's mind, and fills him with a sense of irresolution and uncertainty. Ought I really to go? Who knows if, after all, the countries I am about to visit will realise the ideals I have formed as to their beauty and interest? Perhaps the accounts I have read of them, which have fired me with such an ardent desire to behold them, are merely travellers' tales and exaggerations spread about wholesale for interested motives by the directors of steamship and railway companies, shopmen and hotel keepers, cabmen, *ciceroni*, and others of their kind, eager to excite the unwary to visit them and spend money. Is not my own country beautiful enough to satisfy me?—that fair land of Italy where I was born, have lived, and hope to die?

In the luminous softness of a May evening, whilst the sailors are busy lifting anchor, Naples seems more seductive than ever. Thousands upon thousands of lights sparkle along the coast-line and climb the hills, studding them so thickly that one is almost inclined to think a part of the firmament has fallen to earth. The façade of a church situated on a height, brightly illuminated for the *festa* of its patron saint, stands out clearly defined in the diaphanous atmosphere; while from time to time some fireworks burst overhead and cast down glittering jewels over the city, whose inhabitants are in the full enjoyment of the delightful evening. Along the Via Marina the carriages are plainly seen, and the strident horns of the tramcars are distinctly heard; and, over all, across the deep blue vault of heaven, stretches the broad and serried band of the Milky Way.

Around our ship the disturbed waters eddy in the shade, their darksome reflections being broken now and again by the quivering red light of some passing boat, the rhythm of whose oars falls upon the ear. On board, everything is dark and indistinct, and one stumbles against coils of rope, chains, and rigging; here the crimson glow of the ship's lamp falls upon the anxious faces of a group of passengers; further on, a knot of people talk in whispers; some glide off to sit alone in out-of-the-way corners to meditate—or, perhaps, not think at all. The deck is wet and slippery, and one dare not lean over the dripping taffrail, even to contemplate the receding city. In the confusion of departure nothing is as yet in order, and it is difficult to keep one's footing—nobody can find the captain or any other officer, and we knock up against each other without apology or recognition.

As the signal for departure is given, the vessel glides slowly over the inky waters, and passes gradually out into the darkness of the night. From her deck, as she nears the horizon, the lights of the distant city, nestling amid its myrtle and orange groves, appear to glow brighter, and Naples seems more fascinating than ever in the serene beauty of the stilly night. On board all is strangely quiet. One shadowy form leaning against the taffrail watches the glittering shore, whilst another solitary traveller seated on a bench evidently experiences the first chill of the rapidly rising breeze. Then the red glow of a lighted cigar hovers about in the gloom. Suddenly a startling sound is heard, and the neighing of a horse breaks the silence; it proceeds from a big black box on the right of the vessel, which contains a solitary equine prisoner, whose head alone is seen gazing regretfully at the vanishing city. The poor animal kicks and neighs repeatedly, and is evidently suffering. By him stands another ghostly form, that of a soldier vainly endeavouring to quiet him.

ON THE SEA.

In the light wind of a bright May morning out in the open sea it would be impossible, even for the most depressed, not to experience that joyous sensation which, even if it does not entirely drive away sadness, at least alleviates it. The deep blue waters of the Mediterranean now appear as if confined in one vast bowl, across which the ship marks a broad silvery foaming line ; so still looks the water at this early hour, that one might well liken it to a stretch of shimmering silk. Meanwhile, the trim vessel, with its brasses brightly polished and the little red curtains of its portholes waving, sails on gallantly in the pleasant breeze. Now the barefooted sailors go about their daily business —washing, scrubbing, and scouring away, everything and everywhere, with that happy air which is peculiar to seamen ; whereas the passengers appear to have suddenly acquired a sixth sense, picked up nowhere else but on board ship, and which I might describe as adaptability, and are gradually getting used to a new experience—that of living on a small scale, sleeping in tiny beds, struggling in narrow gangways, and gazing out on the vast expanse of water through the smallest of loopholes. The captain, standing on the bridge in the sunlight, adds a keynote of security as he directs and commands with unfailing accuracy our onward course.

Naples, with all its familiar charms, fades from our memory as we begin to yield to that curious oblivion of time and space peculiar to life on board ship, and we give ourselves up to the mere physical enjoyment of existence. And the trim ship sails blithely over the azure sea. None the less, occasionally a sudden remembrance of home brings with it a sharp pang of regret, soon effaced by the circumscribed life we lead on board ship, in which our interests are limited to our immediate surroundings, and to observing the idiosyncrasies of our fellow-travellers, whom we shall probably never see again after we land. In a word, we have lost much of our individuality, and sail on dreamily whither the ship and the sea choose to lead us.

Day succeeds day without much variation. One day the sea is calm, and on the next you may awaken and hear the ominous roar of its waves at Cape Spartivento. On the third, we spent eight hours passing the island of Candia, its mountains, even though it is May, still covered with snow. At last, on the evening of the fourth day, we perceive in the ruddy twilight the white houses of Alexandria dotted about along a strip of yellow sand. We are in sight of Egypt, the land of Cleopatra. Later on, when the enervating effects of the journey are lost, we shall remember distinctly that first glimpse of the land of mystery—the spotless houses, the golden sand, and the first hot breath of the East as it falls on our cheeks when the crimson disk of the sun sinks below the horizon.

II.

THE NILE.

THE Nile is the soul of Egypt. That trading city of Alexandria on the sea-coast, with its busy streets in which the old and the new, the Oriental and the European, blend so strangely, will never help us to understand the true character of the land of the Pharaohs. You soon realise that the secret of its existence does not rest with the motley crowd of Alexandrian Arabs, Greeks, Frenchmen, or Italians; nor with the hubbub of polyglot tongues, nor the strident cries of the street-traders, the hundred cigarette-shops, nor the cosmopolitan bazaars. If ever you have chanced to enter a dark room at night some strange instinct may have led you to discern a person in its farthermost corner, of whose presence you were quite unaware. In the same way you are irresistibly impelled by some mysterious influence to drive out of Alexandria into the open country to look for that pale blue indefinable line which is the Nile!

It is almost impossible to control the throb of amazement which overwhelms you when you first come face to face with this most historical and wonderful of rivers, and leisurely walk along its banks—then it is that you long to understand and love it, and to yield yourself up entirely to its indescribable fascination.

THE NILE.

Every river possesses a certain poetry of its own, but none can describe that of the Nile. This is not due to its breadth, since at Alexandria it is quite narrow; nor does it arise from its rapid current, for in most places it is almost as calm as a lake; nor is it caused by the depth and darkness of its waters, for it is so mirror-like that every palm and carob tree, with its white crooked branches, every Arab hut and detail of scenery are reflected on its translucent surface.

At Cairo, for instance, in the suburb of Bulak, the Nile spreads out like a sea, whose undefined shores lose themselves in the misty distance, and impress you with a sense of indescribable majesty. If, on the other hand, you view it from below the Villa Antoniades—which is the summer residence of the Khedive, and is situated on the plain between Alexandria and Ramleh—the Nile, with its narrow banks covered with yellow blossoms, has a mournful charm peculiar to itself. When, however, you behold its waves dashing against the piers of the Ghizeh bridge, their strength inspires you with absolute fear, and you begin to understand how it came to pass that the ancient Egyptians made of this marvellous river a God of Terror as well as a God of Mercy! Out in the open country, however, this strange river lulls you with a feeling of peaceful serenity.

The Nile displays every phase of river scenery, and one is never tired of studying its varied beauties, or of endeavouring to master each of its ever-changing aspects. In this bright month of May—already full summer in Egypt—the great white *dahabiehs*, with their lowered sails, looking like so many floating houses, are moored to the banks—no one in this hot season ascends the river from Lower to Upper Egypt for mere pleasure, however charming so slow a means of travel may be. Now and again a fisher boat or a trading skiff, in the cooler hours of the morning, skims along, and as you watch them glide, you desire that you also might float upon those pale blue waters towards those wider stretches whereon are reflected the ruins of the temples of old Egypt. Sometimes you may see a group of Fellahines or Arab women, with their little bare feet peeping from beneath their great black cloaks, their faces muffled in black veils fastened to their foreheads with a metal clasp, filling their jars and gracefully lifting them on to their shoulders, whilst others wade out into the water to bend tenderly over it as if they wished to be drawn into its sacred depths. Not only is the Nile very fertile, but its waters are celebrated for their freshness and remarkable healing powers. At each bend the scene changes. Here is a small mosque, on the steps of which three or four Arabs are sleeping. Yonder is a dazzlingly white house, from behind whose closed shutters women are probably peeping: and now a group of palmettos, with their graceful fronds, comes into sight, and further on, the rose-hedge of a villa-garden is succeeded by the covered terrace of a country *café*. Presently follows a vast solitude, only broken by the undulating line of a camel caravan, led by a tiny Arab boy in a blue and white shirt. Whether it be a straw thatched mud hut, or a burnt up desolate plain, or a hamlet recently destroyed by fire, everything on the shores of the Nile assumes an aspect of mystic poesy and irresistible seductiveness, which converts ugly things into things of beauty, and vivifies with magic touch even those which are dead and corrupt.

Under the cold rays of the moon the Nile inspires mysterious and suggestive visions. A profound silence hangs over all; not a breath sways the palms, and no footstep, however cautious, disturbs the sands; only the murmur of the waters flowing on solemnly—eternally! Listening very attentively you may even hear their ripple along the bank. The air is heavy with the scent of flowers wafted from unseen gardens and hedgerows; here a great tree bends its darksome boughs over the river. Not a light is to be seen. In this intense silence the Nile alone seems to possess life or soul. It absolutely absorbs you, and you forget your sorrows and yours joys, nay, your very existence, and become lost in a sort of trance-like dream—perhaps it is the kind of dream that dilated the big soft eyes of the Egyptian idols, and imparted to the Sphinx its unfathomable gaze. Perchance it has even a share in thy long dream, O Cleopatra!

III.

CAIRO.

FROM the first moment you behold her, Cairo—clearly defined in the early morning light, with a fresh breeze blowing, and already full of bright harmonious sounds, and gay, varied and moving crowds—holds you close in her fascinating toils. You are at once seized with a wild, almost childish enthusiasm, and desire to take your share in all her life and movement. You hear the grating sounds of the iron poles, as the broad awnings are lowered to protect the curious wares in the shops from the sun. Before each of them assemble animated groups of customers, friends, and mere *flaneurs*, chattering excitedly. The soft yet sonorous tones of the Arabic, with its constantly recurring melodious syllable, *Al*, strikes the ear pleasantly enough, whilst the Greeks charm with a softer note, and the French chirp away like so many birds at sunset.

Bare-legged Arabs in white or blue cotton shirts, their fez worn jauntily sideways and entwined with small white turbans, rush by shouting. Solemn-looking Turks, enveloped in long striped silk tunics, bound round the waist with a tight belt, their heads surmounted by huge turbans, strut slowly along, or else stand motionless before some small coffee-shop. Bedouins press along with rapid stride, clothed in black and white bernouse, their long-shaped olive-tinted faces, and sweet, yet mischievous, eyes shining out from beneath the folds of the cloak which falls over the forehead and is held in its place by a golden cord. Fellah women, draped from head to foot in black, gazing with thoughtful, anxious eyes from above their veils, brush lightly past you and disappear again with their heavy burdens and water-pots ; then follow Ottoman subjects in European costumes (to which they have added a fez), hastening to their occupations in the offices of the Egyptian Government. Englishmen in cork helmets, Englishwomen, too, in cork helmets bound round with yards and yards of muslin, walk past with their easy methodical step. Greek priests with long grisly beards and meditative ecstatic eyes, wearing high, black, tube-shaped hats, proceed at a solemn pace to their churches; smart English soldiers march proudly by; the Egyptian soldiers are less elegant, perhaps, but certainly no less proud of themselves; peasants in all sorts of native costumes, consisting of many-coloured shirts and nothing more, pass and repass under the gates of Cairo, bringing their wares to sell in the bazaars and markets. Water-carriers, clanging two copper disks together, offer you fresh water; some sell popped corn; others apricots or bananas. Then come wandering coffee dealers and itinerant merchants shouting their wares in various nasal tones. Carriages pass you. In one you may see a white-bearded pasha, wrapped in his long white cloak; in another, a wealthy Oriental rigged out by Poole in unmistakable English up-to-date style, but with the addition of a fez, instead of the orthodox stereotyped silk hat. Now strings of camels laden with all sorts of goods jostle you; then long narrow carts, empty of their wares, trundle through the golden dust, conveying ten, twenty, or thirty Arabs, whose legs dangle over the sides, back to their farms. On every hand are to be seen those sweet little Egyptian donkeys, with their grey or brown coats, neat little heads, and slender legs. They never seem to hurry, but trot by with a stout Oriental on their backs: an English lady in *khaki*, a Europoean child, or an Arab with his shirt blowing in the wind. These little donkeys, or *bouricks* as they are called, are among the delights of Cairo. They stand at every few steps along the edge of the pavement, but when started they clatter like mad over the rough roadway. The donkey drivers are little half-naked brown imps, with legs as wiry as those of their *bouricks*. The fare for the unwary stranger is 25 sous, but may only be 15, 10, or even 5 sous for the more knowing. In one second the contract is made and the passenger, as he may be called, vaults into the comfortable Arabian saddle, and off goes the tiny donkey like a flash, and after it the boy, his shirt blown out like a balloon. The trotting of these dear little intelligent, untiring donkeys, and the racing of their bright quick-limbed young guides, is never absent from sight or ear. Let us hope they will never gravel the roads of Cairo, for then this charming and most characteristic feature of the place will be lost.

After mid-day things begin to quiet down. Carriages become less numerous ; the camels' heads are turned towards the gates of the city, in the direction of their villages or hamlets ; the carts jog along lazily ; occasionally a shop is closed ; another has completely lowered its awning. Everybody is asleep. It is siesta time—the hottest hour of the day. The roads are being profusely watered. The Oriental shops are left in charge of some small boy, who fans himself gently to keep off the flies. The donkey boys lightly hold their whips in their hands, and, leaning against the saddles of their *bouricks*, sleep as they stand with half-open eyes. In the Turkish or Oriental bazaar, down dark passages where the sun never enters, but where the heat is all-pervading, Turks, half asleep, move their fat fingers wearily, as they make drowsy attempts to embroider belts, or polish old silver vessels. In the great palaces the windows are all open under awnings, and the flower-filled verandahs are screened by many-coloured blinds. Punkahs are in motion, and every care is taken to admit the freshest air, whilst keeping out the least ray of sun. From every garden and courtyard we hear the gurgle and splashing where fountains are playing. It is the hour to smoke, to dream, to sleep. That drowsy contemplation, one of the strongest features of Oriental existence, overcomes you ; and although you can distinguish sounds, they are attenuated and muffled. The slightest breeze makes you shiver : the song of birds is continuous, but veiled. The ever-present tinkling of the water-sellers' disks sounds like some far-away music, and even though you may not be actually asleep, you feel so lethargic that it becomes a labour to turn even the pages of a book— it is too great an effort !

* * * * * * *

At sunset you wake up and go out into the streets of Cairo, to be delighted and surprised by their endless display of beauty and wealth. This extraordinary capital combines in a weird way the peculiarities of an Oriental and of a European city, and blends them in a harmonious whole, which is as indescribable as it is fascinating. The coffee shops, be they large or small, are crowded with Egyptians and Turks, seated motionless and silent before their tiny cups of coffee, even when in company, but invariably holding the right foot with the right hand. Beside them, also mute and solemn, Englishmen sit drinking ale. Hard by, there is the shop of a Greek confectioner, who deals in *loukoumis* and preserved strawberries, marmalade, and chocolate; and beside it you will find a French one full of "*petits fours*," "*soupirs*," or "*madeleines*." Everyone is smoking a farthing cigarette, or even one a trifle more expensive—the half-naked, proud, lithesome Bedouin, the nimble commissioner from Leghorn, the elegant Levantine, the chatterbox Greek, and the self-centred Englishman all smoke from morning till night. On the Gherizeh Road, the Bois de Boulogne of Cairo, which you reach by crossing several aristocratic streets consisting of villas surrounded by gardens, and passing over the bridge on the Nile, a scene greets you which is even more varied and strange. Here, on a vast lawn, you will see English families playing lawn-tennis or croquet; further on in the park British youths are playing polo. Brakes full of children with their nurses pass by, followed by the most elegant up-to-date London or Viennese equipages, conveying Levantine ladies in gorgeous attire, with their equally gorgeous *sais* preceding them. The *sais* is one of the most charming of Egyptian institutions, and is an Arab chosen for his exceptional grace and agility. He is always clad in white, with a jacket of scarlet or blue cloth embroidered in gold. His fez is also richly worked and enveloped by folds of white muslin. In his belt is stuck a short sword, and he carries a long thin wand in his hand. He, too, is barefooted, and flies rather than runs before the horses to clear the way. When ordered to do so, he jumps off his high perched seat with the agility of a monkey, but with a quaint look of proud indifference. Sometimes you may see two of these grand fellows, all sparkling with gold and looking mighty fine and grand, sitting immovable behind a stage coach, ready at a sign to jump down from their seat to run along in the dust. Here comes a party of ladies on horseback—*amazones*, the French call them—and following, some

British soldiers, with jaunty caps cocked over one ear: four-in-hands, carriages full of veiled harem ladies, and mingling with all these fine equipages the ever-present donkeys, scurrying off to their native villages to find a well-earned rest. Farther afield, the wobbling dromedaries undulate in long lines towards the horizon. From the open door of a wayside inn steals the guttural twang of the *guzla*, or native guitar. A host of masons and Arabs pour out of the great Gherizeh Hotel, now in course of reconstruction. In a neighbouring field a Turk, squatting on his prayer carpet, his face turned towards Mecca, salutes, for the fifth time that day, Allah and His Prophet. Presently the sun sinks quite suddenly, and instantly a delicious freshness springs up. White cloaks are put on; carriages and riders slacken their pace. In the far distance you may discern the mystic outline of the Pyramids.

IV.

THE PYRAMIDS.

IF you wish to visit the Pyramids during the great heat of May you must rise very early, and remember that early in Egypt does not mean six or even five o'clock—but between three and four—the small hours, when dissipated Europeans think of going to bed. It is already dawn when we start at half-past three: at four o'clock it is bright daylight. The air is more than cool; indeed, it is cold, but quite delightful. However commonplace a city may be, it always has a special though fleeting charm during the early hours of the morning, which is never again experienced later in the day. This charm is not without its note of sadness and mystery that contrasts curiously with the gaiety of a workaday world gradually reassuming its daily labours. Whilst driving swiftly in the early dawn towards the Pyramids, which you can now visit so comfortably, you realise more fully than ever the enchantments of Cairo. You see donkey boys with their donkeys dashing about in all directions, fellahines carrying water-jars, milkmen with their huge cans of fresh milk, and the countless little cigarette-shops opening one by one.

As you approach the Ghizeh Bridge the scene becomes more and more fantastic and animated. Our carriage gets so entangled in lines of camels laden with fruit, vegetables, coal, wood, and all sorts of odd merchandise, that it is a good half-hour before we can attempt to proceed. As to the dear, patient, silly-looking camels, they sway from side to side and apparently do not advance a step, although their drivers are swearing at them, in Arabic, I suppose. Meanwhile, the guards and custom house officers oblige the camels to cross the bridge slowly in single file, so that the congestion of traffic becomes very great and our carriage looks like a ship tossed upon a sea of unwieldy animals. Once free of them, however, our vehicle flies along the road in the fresh morning breeze, and the sense of swift motion soon dispels the memory of the picturesque but disagreeable experience we have just passed through.

It takes fully two hours at a good pace to reach the Pyramids. For a whole hour before you approach them they have been visible against the horizon, clear and well defined, for owing to the extreme limpidity of the atmosphere, even short-sighted people can see much farther than under ordinary circumstances in this peculiarly powerful yellowish light, and readily distinguish quite distant objects. And all along the high road we pass scattered and solitary Bedouins in the fields, near the hedges, and at the doors of their huts. They are the real owners of the Pyramids, for although one would naturally suppose that these sombre tombs of the Egyptian Pharaohs ought to belong to the Government of the Khedive, or, at least, to be considered as national monuments, this is not the case : they are the exclusive property of the great tribe of Bedouins, but how or why is a mystery, since these are not the direct descendants of the Rameses of the solemn eyes and closed smileless lips, or of the great Cheops of the hands that rest eternally on their knees, and whose austere clear-cut features still glow with life through their solemn masks of granite. The wild and wandering tribe of Bedouins simply came and claimed them and will never surrender their hold. No Egyptian Government would dare to dispute their possession. The dominion of the Bedouin hereabouts is secure, and extends round a circuit of several miles—wherein they have their decent dwellings and rich, well-cultivated fields. Standing by the open doors of their houses they appear to raise their beautiful expressive eyes towards the Pyramids, with a look of calm, proud proprietorship, as if they knew full well that none can ever dispute their hereditary claim.

The Bedouin of the Pyramids is generally a fine tall man with a rich golden-brown complexion—his hands and feet are perfectly shaped, his features classically regular, and he has the whitest of teeth, gleaming between his singularly flexible lips. Clad in white and wearing a great black cloak and a snowy turban, he carries his ample draperies with a proud, picturesque grace. He is generally barefooted, otherwise whenever he wants to run he has to remove his slippers. No one can rival him in untiring celerity; no one can ride better or shoot with greater accuracy. He rides without a saddle, scarcely touching the stirrup, to which is attached a small spear. He possesses a couple of sacks made of old carpet, which contain all his luggage and which dangle over each side of his horse like a pair of big bags. The Bedouin always seems to have invisible wings, so swift are his motions, whether he be running down a dusty bank or vanishing on the fleetest of steeds along the burning road. There can be no doubt, however, that nowhere else on the face of the earth are you likely to fall in with the equal of the Bedouin of the Pyramids for downright cunning dishonesty. True, the Bedouins of the mountains of Moab, on the shores of the Red Sea or on the roads of Samaria, are indeed very expert robbers. They will plunder the unwary traveller, and then disappear for a fortnight at a time to avoid being caught, but those ruffians are clumsy and stupid as compared with these civilised, gentle-mannered, most sympathetic of thieves, the Bedouins of the Egyptian Desert. When you arrive in their dominions, where the fertile country ceases and where the first streak of yellow sand becomes visible, and the Great Pyramids rise in solemn awe-inspiring grandeur on the edge of the desert, you perceive small groups of men in black and white garments mysteriously assembling and then dispersing, but invariably forming, unconsciously, lines of artistic beauty. These are the Bedouins guarding their time-honoured treasure. As soon as you alight from your carriage, accompanied by your dragoman, and are painfully making your way across the burning sand, a chief advances and salutes you with a bland and delightful smile. He bids you welcome in several languages—these Bedouins never speak less than four or five. Presently others appear from behind the Pyramids and hills of sand, smiling, bowing, and offering you every imaginable politeness. One suggests your mounting his camel to save you from the burning sand in which you sink at every step; another offers you his donkey for the same purpose; whilst a third suggests your ascending the Pyramids, for there are travellers sufficiently infatuated to try and undertake that tedious excursion. To all these offers your dragoman replies furiously in Arabic; the head Bedouin pretends to scold his subordinates, who, in their turn, make believe to excuse themselves for having ventured to take such a liberty as to address the illustrious stranger. With many protestations they disappear, only to return a few minutes later, and surround you in triumph, carrying you off against your will to the foot of the Pyramid. There, they offer you all their wares: ancient Egyptian coins, bits of alabaster, small mummies, green beetles, green sphinxes, necklaces, crystal amulets; bringing all these articles out of black leather cases hidden away in their white tunics. These Bedouins are so tenacious and determined in their advances, so sprightly and beautiful, so eager in their greed, that in a short time you have emptied your cosmopolitan pockets of all their small change: your half-francs, shillings, and Turkish piastres. The most cold-blooded rough Englishman succumbs before the insinuating manners and tricks of these delightful knaves. If you get angry, they at once look intensely pained and relapse into an offended silence; if, amused at their trickery, you

THE PYRAMIDS.

cannot refrain from smiling, back they all come again, chattering in several languages. They are so insinuating without being servile, so humble without being cringing, that the traveller is soon bereft of all his small cash, in exchange for this most amusing exhibition of deceit and play-acting, such as he is never likely to see again. Mahomed, the youngest and most agile of them, proposes to climb up and down the highest Pyramid in ten minutes. It is four hundred feet high, formed of great stone steps cut on the outside. Mahomed demanded three shillings, the usual sum, which was granted to him. Then he insisted a watch should be taken out in order to verify the exact time, and, casting off his cloak, in a twinkling he was up on the first step, his little white figure climbing higher and higher, looking at first like a white handkerchief, then a rag, and at last a mere speck. He had gained the top in five and a half minutes; when, immediately returning, jumping, stooping, gradually becoming bigger and bigger, at last he arrived triumphantly, breathless and panting, it is true, but pointing to the watch. He had taken three and a half minutes to come down—nine minutes in all! He demanded for the one minute less (and, needless to say, obtained it) an extra shilling. I gave it, asking ironically if there was nothing else he would like; whereupon, to my surprise, he haughtily told me to praise Mahomed on my return home, and never forget his feat! Saying this he threw his mantle around him with great dignity. The money, however, went into the purse of the chief, Mahomed getting about twopence-halfpenny, or a Turkish piastre, for his share. These charming thieves form a rudimentary co-operative society among themselves, giving up all their earnings, which are afterwards redivided. Each has his hours for watching the Pyramids, each one his special avocation, the younger being employed to persuade the foolish European to ascend the Pyramids. They go three at a time, thus gaining two shillings each, and the unfortunate traveller, by the time he has reached about the fourth step, becomes so giddy that he has, perforce, to beg to be taken down again—which is just what his guides want him to do, for thereby they can earn their money with little or no trouble. When they have got all they can out of you, they amiably escort you on your road, wishing you a good journey and excellent health. They hope you will return again; and having bowed low before you they throw their cloaks over their shoulders, quite satisfied with all they have done, and vanish. You look back upon their receding black and white figures, and experience no feeling of rancour against such delightful robbers. They have relieved you of your coin; but, after all, they have afforded you a charming experience. The last glimpse shows them assembled at the foot of the distant Pyramids, watching for other travellers—other uncomplaining victims!

As to the Pyramids—I think I have already remarked elsewhere that they are very steep!

V.

SORIA! SORIA!

It is without much feeling of regret that the traveller, once on board the vessel bound for Palestine, looks back upon Alexandria, and Egypt disappears from before his eyes as suddenly as its blazing sun sinks below the horizon. Its voluptuous beauty, enchanting grace and light-hearted gaiety are quickly forgotten, for they leave no very deep impressions, not having roused in him any real affection or regret. Perhaps later on these fascinating images may come back, even if blurred and indistinct, and he will be seized with a longing to return once more to the land of Cleopatra, to discern whether the eyes of the Sphinx do indeed veil some secret mystery in their solemn depths.

Even after some weeks spent in foreign lands, the feeling of regret at leaving home has only been lulled by the vision of all this new life spent among strange people, and in listening to new languages the curious attractiveness of which has merely obliterated for the moment the real object of our journey. Rushing from one hotel to another, from a steamer to a railway station, pushed, shaken, lost in a crowd, the poor traveller, worried and confused, loses. during these first days of his journey, all clear idea of its purpose. Soon, however, he remembers the real, the solemn motive that induced him to leave his home and undertake this journey to the Holy Land of his childhood's dreams, where, from the beginning of all time, God deigned to speak to men, and where the divine Son was born—that Land which shines from afar like a peerless jewel: which, like a mystic loadstone, attracts every Christian heart towards its shores.

No one on board the *Apollo* (a name of good omen, let us hope) speaks of Palestine except by the sonorous name of Soria, that poetical term for the coast of the Holy Land, which used to play such a conspicuous part in the good old Neapolitan ballads of half a century ago, that I remember to have heard my mother recite. I can only recollect a line beginning :—

"*Un mercanio lasciando Soria*"—
(A merchant sailed from Soria),

and my dear lost mother's sweet voice pronouncing ever so musically, "Soria! Soria!" How one used to love the good folk who played their parts in those beloved ballads and legends: the dear noble knights, armed *cap-à-pie*, who gave up the world to follow the Cross. They were, or we imagined them to be, so strong, so brave, and so handsome! Their warrior souls glowed with a noble ambition that led them irresistibly to the step of the Holy Sepulchre; even as Tasso describes them in his *Gerusalemme Liberata*. In later life we were, perhaps, a little ashamed to express before a modern sceptical public our admiration for Godfrey de Bouillon and the Crusaders, but now the sneering voices are far away, and the ship is approaching the very spot where the said Godfrey de Bouillon lost his life for the sake of that Tomb which perhaps to-morrow we may press with our lips.

On board our vessel, among its three classes of passengers, there are pilgrims, merchants, tourists, and business men, believers and non-believers—in fact, quite a little crowd going to the Holy Land; some drawn thither by its tender memories; others by mere mercenary motives.

Three or four lawyers from Cairo are going to Jerusalem to settle judicial or financial matters concerning the Jaffa railway. There is also a Maltese traveller, dressed like a priest, who recites his rosary, and looks lovingly in the direction of the sacred shore, with the fixed gaze of one who is habitually absorbed in prayer. There are two Ottoman ladies of Caipha—the little seaport town where people land for Nazareth or Tiberias—who have quite a European air about them. They have a hesitating, timid expression, and the clear, transparent complexion peculiar to women who have only lately given up wearing the veil. There is an entire Greek family of the upper *bourgeoisie*, accompanied by their servants, all talking vivaciously of Jerusalem, and repeating constantly the word *Panagia*, their equivalent for " Madonna." Even among the third-class passengers, small merchants, ambulating vendors, guides, dragomen, and Turkish soldiers, no one any longer mentions Egypt. Its time is over, and everybody is full of the Holy Land, where the season is just now in progress. Needless to say, the omnipresent group of English tourists is not absent, but, on the contrary, most conspicuously evident. They are all supplied with Cook's tickets. After their morning " tub " they walk the deck in bath towels until their nine o'clock breakfast ; after which they get their clergyman to read them those parts of the Bible which bear upon their journey and intended excursions. In unmusical tones they reiterate the names Jericho, Holy Land, Jordan, &c., with the everlasting exclamatory prefix, " oh ! ah ! " before each name.

The captain, a Dalmatian, and a born sailor, on being repeatedly asked if the entrance to the port of Jaffa is dangerous, answers sententiously in Italian or Greek that he knows of many worse harbours, but that as a matter of fact his ship will not attempt to cross its bar. We shall have to perform that excursion in a tiny boat which will toss us about for a good quarter of an hour, like a cockle-shell on the high crests of the waves, amid many dangerous rocks and shoals. Suddenly one's attention is riveted by a deafening noise rising from a vessel that bears down straight upon us. It is filled from stem to stern with some six hundred Mahomedans. Old men and young, women, children—dirty, ragged, and barefooted—all praying and screaming at the tops of their voices. It is a pilgrimage on its way to Ghedda, the port where they assemble to proceed to Mecca to worship before the coffin of their Prophet, which sways in mid-air in the most sacred of all the mosques of Islam. These few hundred pilgrims form but an infinitesimal fraction of the great annual pilgrimage. They are packed in their rotten old ships like cattle in pens. They bring their own provisions and cook them where they can, in some out-of-the-way corner, nothing being given them but a little water. They sleep lying on ragged mats. There is only one class on board. Out of three or four hundred thousand pilgrims who flock annually to Mecca, some forty or fifty thousand die from infectious diseases—cholera or plague, fatigue or sunstroke. But even if they should die on their pilgrimage they are happy, since they have lost their lives in doing honour to the founder of their Faith.

"Which of the Christian peoples of Europe is most readily drawn towards the Holy Sepulchre?"—"The Russian."—"But do not Italians go to Palestine?"—"Few, if any."—"Are they not believers, then?"—"Yes, they are believers, but only a few have sufficient energy, and the rest lack the necessary money to go on so long a journey; which is a pity, as Italian is the language the most spoken in the East."

It is Sunday morning. Soon after daybreak the captain appears on deck and speaks to a group of nervous travellers who could not speak for excitement, and points out to them in the distance a dark blue line in the lighter blue of the sky. The Holy Land! Everyone on board makes forward, straining his eyes to divine the distant coast. Little by little it becomes more distinct; a hill is seen—the hill where Jaffa stands amid its orchards and gardens, full of orange and lemon trees and fragrant blossoms. Its harbour is quite white with crested waves beating against the precipitous rocks. Our vessel settles slowly to a standstill. In the distance rises the mast of a Russian schooner, wrecked the year before, round which the angry waves lash furiously; those unpleasant looking waves across which we shall presently have to struggle in a fragile little boat. If you listen attentively you may distinguish the bells of Jaffa, at first muffled, but by degrees tolling more and more distinctly. All Christian Jaffa is going to Mass. Our Christian pilgrims gaze anxiously, for this is their first sight of Palestine, though as they are civilised men and women, they are overawed by the opinion of their fellows, and dare not kneel or stretch out their hands and arms in supplication towards the goal of their hopes. It is only by the pallor of their faces and the tears that dim their eyes that we realise how deep is their emotion. The long-looked-for land has dawned, and their life's dream is realised at last. The scene before them is none the less strangely familiar, as if it had been witnessed in some state of pre-existence or in a dream. Some are absorbed in thought, apparently incapable even of prayer or of making the Sign of the Cross ; others seem quite dead to all external influences, and are lost in ecstatic contemplation of the Land of Jesus, which they are vainly endeavouring to realise.

PART II.
THE VOW FULFILLED.

I.

IN THE TRAIN.

A LINE of railway now runs from Jaffa to Jerusalem, a journey which takes three and a half hours to perform, the only train starting at half-past two in the afternoon. Every vessel that touches Palestine, be it Egyptian, Austrian, French, or Russian, does so before noon; whereby travellers have barely the time, on landing, to rush up to the Jerusalem Hotel, wash hands, swallow a cup of boiling coffee, and start off again for the Holy City.

Very few people find time to visit Jaffa, and yet it is a very interesting and quaint city, whose harbour is always ruffled by crested waves. A dry sea-wind is ever blowing which carries off that unhealthy dampness that is so dangerous elsewhere in the East. The gardens of Jaffa are magnificent, and the sight of their abundance of golden oranges and pale yellow lemons, glowing amid glossy leaves, reminded me, with a sigh, of lovely Sorrento. Jaffa is a rich, prosperous city, with picturesque old streets, and rows of small, modern houses in the new quarter. The women of Jaffa, unlike other Orientals, are extremely fair; they all wear long white muslin cloaks clasped at the throat, and they are, for the most part, veiled: the more orthodox with a thick yashmac, having a pattern upon it, completely concealing the face. Some, however, who have acquired European tastes have discarded the yashmac altogether, and their dark, almond-shaped eyes glance at you with a sweet yet proud expression. But, owing to the awkward hours fixed for landing and departing, no one can see much of Jaffa. To do so one would have to remain at least a day and a night here, which very few can do; the English, having seen quite enough of Jaffa in two hours, never rest till they have started us off again. The journey, considering it is so short, is distinctly expensive, costing twelve shillings. There are only two classes, first and second, but even in the first-class carriages the seats are of unpolished wood, and there are no cushions or anything to rest your elbows on. In a word, they are a great deal less comfortable than our third-class carriages. The train starts three-quarters of an hour after time, as the Turks, never quite sure how many people may arrive, generally get confused and completely lose their heads, only to become more indolent than ever, while the passengers protest and shout in every language under the sun. At the last moment one or two carriages have to be added, and finally the train starts amid a veritable hubbub, as is always the case in these countries, people apparently quarrelling at the top of their voices. There is usually some stoppage or other on the line; we were kept, for instance, for forty minutes at Sejed, water having to be got for the engine. Once started afresh the driver had to go at full speed to make up for lost time, which was the reverse of pleasant, we were so terribly jolted. The carriages are small and badly built, and the road, always on an incline, is not much wider than the permanent way, and is flanked on one side by a steep hill and on the other by a deep precipitous ravine with a torrent dashing at its feet. The line, moreover, curves continually, and the engine and carriages jostle and sway in a most terrifying manner. It is, therefore, wiser not to look out of the windows, but to confine one's attention to the interior of the carriage and patiently await events. It is not infrequent that the train runs off the rails, but so far no very serious accident has occurred. There are five stations between Jaffa and Jerusalem, and the latter ought to be reached at six o'clock, though it is generally half-past six, or even seven, before the train runs into the terminus. Nothing can be imagined more unromantic than this railway journey, which entirely effaces all the previous pleasant anticipations, peaceful

IN THE TRAIN. 43

thoughts, holy aspirations or poetical fancies concerning the Holy Land which the sea journey had evoked. I do not mean, of course, to belittle the advantages of railway travel as a most necessary, practical and useful means of locomotion—anywhere else but in Palestine. The contrast between its practical methods and the stupendous traditions of the Holy Land is too great : and it creates a feeling of positive revulsion to see the name of the Sion of the Psalmist, the scene of the Birth and Passion, a name which should move every Christian heart to its depths, printed on a commonplace green railway ticket ! It is simply intolerable and, indeed, quite horrible to find oneself in a railway carriage full of fat, smoking, somnolent Turks, seated in their favourite attitude, with a shoeless foot in one hand ; no Turk will ever keep on his shoes a moment longer than he can help. To be driven at full speed through the beautiful plain of Sharon, where the Philistines conquered the Children of Israel and carried off the Ark of the Covenant, is positively too dreadful ; or to be " rushed " through the valley of Sorve, where Delilah overcame Samson, and whence she sent him, a blinded prisoner, to Gaza. Is not yonder the tomb of the faithful old Simeon who so tenderly took the Holy Child in his arms and then begged to depart in peace, for he had beheld the Messiah ? And is not that the Hill of Bad Counsel where the Pharisees, with Caiaphas at their head, deliberated how Jesus should be put to death ? The train goes on so fast that, although you may recognise, you cannot distinguish anything through the smoke and steam. Your eyes are tired and your spirit weary, and you sink back on your hard, wooden bench disappointed and discouraged.

By the time you reach Jerusalem you are altogether demoralised. Fancy arriving at the gates of the City of David and of Solomon at this tearing, puffing rate ! Imagine seeing the City of Jesus for the first time in all this confusion, without even having a moment to collect your thoughts and to call up the slightest feeling of devotion ! To those happy travellers who visited Jerusalem in other ages, after surmounting great difficulties, enduring much fatigue and experiencing strange adventures, it must indeed have appeared a haven of divine peace. The knights who followed Godfrey de Bouillon and fought before its holy walls saw the Holy City otherwise than we do. Even a few years ago the good people who arrived leisurely in carriages, on horseback, or on foot, could still kneel in its sacred dust as they passed under its time-honoured gates. All is changed, and we up-to-date folk dash into Jerusalem in a stuffy railway carriage, amid the oaths of railway porters and a thousand distracting sounds and scenes, just as if we were mere commercial travellers bent on the most commonplace sort of business. Thus do we pass under the shadow of the Mount whence the Light of the Cross has spread to the uttermost ends of the earth!

Oh! abomination of desolation! this horrible railway was not made for such as I, but for those who are always in a hurry, who must see everything in the shortest possible time, even the Holy Sepulchre, or the House of Mary at Nazareth. It has been made for the ever-restless Anglo-Saxons, who would only marvel at our emotion, and feel amazed that we should manifest it outwardly—since it is by them that Palestine lives, and this railway has been built expressly for their benefit. It is, therefore, under these altered and unfortunate circumstances, quite impossible to repeat, as Christians were expected to do in bygone days on beholding the Towers of David, the noble cxxii. psalm beginning:

"I was glad at the things that were said unto me: We will go into the house of the Lord.

"Our feet were wont to stand in thy courts, O Jerusalem, Jerusalem which is built as a city that is at unity with itself."

In olden times it was the rule for the pilgrim to Jerusalem never to enter any house until he had visited the Holy Sepulchre: but this can no longer be done, for now it closes at sundown, and the train only arrives after sunset! Thus we have no choice left, but must go straight to the Grand Hotel and prepare for a *table d'hôte* dinner, as if one had arrived at Monte Carlo instead of Jerusalem!

II.

IN THE CHURCH.

THE centre of Christian Jerusalem, the most modern and most essentially English centre, is the broad, populous square on which stands the new Grand Hotel, where those mighty rivals, Cook and Gaze, have their offices, and on which there are four or five large European shops and even a livery stable, situated under the Jaffa Gate! From this essentially modern centre starts the road leading to the Church of the Holy Sepulchre—a narrow alley running through one of the Turkish bazaars of Jerusalem, with little dark shop windows, in which it is impossible to distinguish the wares displayed behind them. On either side are crowds of Turks smoking their *narghilehs*, camels squatting on the ground, donkeys laden with corn, and Arabs everlastingly arranging their own and other people's affairs whilst smoking their inevitable cigarettes. Once past the bazaars the lane-like, ill-paved road makes one or two bends and then descends to a lower level by a series of very wide steps. The religious influence of the surroundings now begins to assert itself. Little shops come into sight where every kind of wax candle, bedecked with gold and silver foil, or painted blue and red, is exposed for sale ; from the slender taper costing three Turkish piastres, to the enormous candles, the weight of which only the mightiest candelabras can bear. Here also are sold cartloads of rosaries of every description and shape : from the tiny ones intended for the hand of a little child, to those made of great carved beads the size of a walnut, which a giant might use with advantage : rosaries composed of glass beads, fragrant amber, polished cherry stones and lapis lazuli. Here the dark shops are literally lighted up with pictures of Palestine painted vividly on wood, or Byzantine fashion on a gold ground like the icons of the Panagia that once upon a time blazed in Sancta Sophia at Constantinople, but even more gaudy. Sometimes the profile of the saint in these icons is outlined in the most quaint manner. All these objects, if you can believe the pale-faced shopkeeper, have touched the Holy Sepulchre and have been consecrated thereby. Now we approach the Sacred Tomb : at the fourth bend of the road, after having ascended sixty steps of the little square where it stands, the beautiful façade of the church—the only really artistic part of the ancient building —comes into view. It has two large granite Gothic doors, one of which is always shut. Above each door is a pure Gothic window, also invariably closed and choked up with creepers, among which hundreds of chattering birds have built their nests. On the little square a few poor itinerant merchants expose their wares on a strip of dirty carpet : little medals, rosaries and faded photographs. On all sides sellers of popped corn call their succulent grain, and water-carriers attract attention by the clink of their little brass disks.

The uttermost confusion of thoughts and things overwhelms the Christian at the very door of the church wherein stands the Holy Sepulchre. He has scarcely made the Sign of the Cross, after passing beneath its portals, ere he becomes aware of the extraordinary agglomeration of ill-assorted things and peoples that surround him. First of all : to your left on entering stands what may be called the Porters' Lodge, consisting of a floor, or wooden platform, covered with carpets and cushions on which are sitting, or lying, two or three Mussulmans, the custodians of the chief church of Christendom ! The Sultan has preserved his right of possession over these Holy Places, but without any show of arrogant discourtesy. These Turkish porters drink their coffee out of little cups, smoke cigars or pipes, but very rarely speak to each other, though they noiselessly and incessantly pass the amber beads of their *combolois*, or Turkish rosaries, through their brown fingers. They appear to be lost in Oriental contemplation, and look very picturesque, with their long tunics of striped red and yellow silk or satin, their feet enclosed in the whitest of socks, their slippers beside them. On their heads they wear turbans, the folds of which go twice round the fez. They

IN THE CHURCH. 47

never seem to pay the least attention to the people who enter the church, and pass their days in stolid contemplation of nothing at all ! After duly observing this group of Mahomedans, squatting at the very door of the Temple where Jesus was buried, you perceive, exactly opposite to you, the Anointing Stone, upon which the Body of Our Lord was washed and sprinkled with myrrh and aloes. Each pilgrim on reaching the Sacred Stone prostrates himself : some extend their arms in an attitude of supplication : others beat their forehead against it : others kiss it with effusion or else sit by it for hours wrapt in silent devotion. Here the varied forms of religious adoration are plainly manifest, each with a different individual manner and expression. Upon this Stone, before which every Christian bends the knee, the various Churches begin to show their curious and diverse ways of manifesting religious zeal. Eight lamps burn above it, suspended by a silver chain which is linked to two side candelabras ; of these eight lamps three belong to the Latin Church, three to the Schismatic Greek Church, one to the Armenian, and one to the Coptic. Each of these Churches belongs to Jesus and is dedicated to His service, and is a sign of His Redemption ; and each demands its share in the place where He lived, suffered, and was buried.

Anxiously we look round the Church of the Holy Sepulchre in an endeavour to seize its outline, and to impress an early, general, and enduring impression of it everlastingly on the memory and imagination. In it all kinds of architectural forms are blended harmoniously. In the centre stands a circular-shaped building which marks the crypt that contains the Holy Sepulchre, and is surrounded by a colonnade and by a wide dark corridor : on the side of the apse, which is an elongated oval, raised some three yards above the pavement on a sort of platform, stands the entrance to the chapel belonging to the Schismatic Greeks. The part nearest to the Chapel of St. Mary Magdalen, where it appears to become rectangular, belongs to the Latins : one small section, however, is the property of the Armenian Christians under the patronage of St. James. On all sides, even in the darkest nooks and corners, we perceive churches and chapels, large and small; some of which ascend to the first floor on one side, whilst others are underground. They form such a confused and irregular aggregation as to be quite bewildering and make one feel almost afraid to move. There is, moreover, a long uncovered outer gallery, where the rain comes in, and which connects the two farthest sections of this most singular church. In this half-ruined labyrinth, built in every style of architecture, and belonging to all nations, which has, moreover, been destroyed and rebuilt eight times, are united under one roof every one of the sites rendered for ever famous by the Passion. Among the different Christian sects who worship hereabouts there reigns a fair amount of good-fellowship on ordinary occasions, though sometimes it is otherwise, and the Holiest spot in Christendom not infrequently becomes the scene of scandalous disorder and riot.

In the colonnade surrounding this venerable pile may be seen groups of Coptic women, dressed in blue rags, crouching for hours on the ground with their children in their arms. They have a curious fixed gaze in their wild, beautiful eyes, which seem to watch the passer-by without quite seeing him. As you advance into the church you hear, proceeding from the higher gallery ornamented with gold and gems, the slow nasal tones of the Schismatic Greek priests chanting their rites. You then enter the underground chapel where St. Helena found the Holy Cross in a well: a dark-bearded Armenian priest, robed in black, with a hood over his head, advances and sprinkles you with holy water scented with attar of roses.

This strangest of churches is so shapeless, but at the same time so majestic, that its general outline entirely escapes you—an effect doubtless due to the confused variety of its architecture. Its mystical manifestations are so complex, it has such a varied and heterogeneous character, that the image left on the mental retina, even after many visits, soon becomes blurred. One part of it is clean and well-ordered, and another is ill-kept and almost dirty. There, it is rich and sparkling with jewels; here, poor and quite simple. In one place it is European; in another, Oriental; everything depending on the country, nation, condition, and customs of the various owners of that particular part of the building : and according to the true devotion or fanaticism, it becomes a church, a room, or a public square. On one altar are artificial flowers, whilst real fresh-cut blooms adorn another. Lights are everlastingly burning in heavy silver lamps, or in simple coloured glasses. There are shining metal balls suspended from the roof, in which your face is reflected awry ; and also big, white cocoanut mats, with knots of red ribbon and white beads, such as you see hanging in mosques. In the midst of all this medley of the beautiful and the ugly, you vainly endeavour to concentrate your thoughts on the real meaning of this holiest of Places, and seek to do homage to its Lord. The four Christian Churches have a common proprietorship in this great Shrine, and take good care to manifest their differences on every possible occasion. There are five Latin, five Greek, three Armenian priests, and one Coptic priest, sharing the same altars. You look in vain in this strange church for a controlling idea, to find only confusion, spiritual revolt and dissension.

The Holy Sepulchre itself is quite different.

III.

THE TOMB.

The flutter of wings never ceases around the façade of the Church of the Holy Sepulchre, where for generations countless little birds have haunted the great Gothic windows and doorways. At dawn their chattering is joyous enough, but at sunset, and as the evening closes in, their chirping becomes more and more plaintive and their wings fold wearily. Sometimes a little fellow, more venturesome and impertinent than his companions, will fly into the church and pipe his shrill note as he hops along the broad pavement. Then, after flying round and round for a time, he will settle on some column or niche, and, after surveying the holy place with a knowing air, blinking his small bright eyes the while, he will suddenly fly off into the open air, singing lustily. The veiled persistent song of the birds without falls on the ear of those who are absorbed in prayer or contemplation under the vaulted roof supported by the massive columns of the nave ; or in the numerous lateral chapels belonging to every Christian sect, that twinkle day and night with the lights of countless votive lamps, even as far as the steep stairway that leads to the Church of Golgotha, round which the shadows deepen mysteriously and enshrine the more sacred memorials of Christ's Passion. During the hours of Divine Service, when the hymns of Latins, Greeks, Armenians and Copts rise on all sides, the shrill song of the birds without mingles with the peal of the organ, as it accompanies the Franciscan Friars in their song of praise to the Madonna. The birds, at least, are faithful to the hoary stones of the old and grey façade, where for ages they have built their nests, and where they live as freely and joyously as in the open country. At night, when the Temple is closed and silence reigns in every path of Jerusalem, these tiny songsters, their heads tucked under their wings, sleep on carved cornices and copings of their beloved fane as confidently as they would on some flowery branch in wood and bower.

The Chapel of the Holy Sepulchre is completely separated from the rest of the Church, and has been built upon the living rock which formed the tomb of Joseph of Arimathæa, in which Christ was buried. It is still adorned with the rich marbles presented by Helena, mother of the Emperor Constantine, on whom the Christian peoples of all ages and countries have conferred the well-deserved title of Helena the Great. The sacred building measures about twenty-seven feet in length by eighteen feet in breadth, and eighteen feet high, and is raised about half a yard above the level of the pavement, four steps leading up to it. It is therefore an elongated chapel from east to west, being square towards the west, and shaped like a pentagon towards the east. The interior is composed of two little cells or chambers, almost quadrangular, joined together by a low narrow opening, through which one has to stoop to enter.

THE TOMB.

The first little cell, on entering, is called the Room of the Angel. The beloved disciple tells us that very early in the morning of the first day of the week after our Lord's death, Mary of Magdala came to the Sepulchre, to find the stone rolled back and the Tomb empty, and not knowing where they had taken and laid Him, she fell to weeping bitterly; when she beheld two young men clothed in white garments—whereat she was affrighted—who said unto her, " Ye seek Jesus of Nazareth, which was crucified: He is risen: He is not here." In the centre of the Angel's Chapel, raised on a marble stand, surrounded by a marble balustrade, worn by the kisses of countless pilgrims, is a piece of the stone which the Magdalene and other pious women found rolled back, for, as the Evangelist tells us, " it was exceeding great." This cell, which may be called the vestibule of the Holy Sepulchre, is kept in almost total darkness, save for the faint glimmer of the fifteen silver lamps hanging from the roof, which, as usual, belong to the four principal sects of the Christian Church. All the burial places of the Jews had this sort of vestibule or entrance, and the one belonging to Joseph of Arimathæa was doubtless constructed like the rest. The Sepulchre was still quite new, and had been erected by this worthy man in his garden, just outside Jerusalem, near the hillock called Golgotha. Not far from this place, in an underground corner of the church, other tombs belonging to the family of Joseph of Arimathæa have been found, the Holy Sepulchre having been isolated from the rest by Saint Helena. The topography could not be more evident, simple, or accurate.

The Holy Sepulchre is in the second small room. As I said before, the entrance to it is through an arched opening and is very low, less than a yard and a half high by three-quarters of a yard wide. One person can pass through at a time, and then only by bending nearly double. This archway is cut out of the solid rock. The cell of the Sacred Tomb is smaller than the one where the Angel appeared; it barely measures six and three-quarter feet in width, by six feet in length. It has been entirely encased in marble, for both pilgrims and tourists were in the habit of breaking off bits of the stone, which otherwise would soon have been carried away piecemeal. Through certain chinks in the slabs of marble can be seen the rock itself. The Holy Sepulchre has one long side next the wall; it is excavated in the rock in the form of an arch, measuring a little over three feet in width by six feet in length. Our Lord was placed in it with His head towards the east and His feet to the west. According to tradition, during the last days of His life, and during His agony upon the cross, He turned His face towards the west, as if He were seeking for the triumph of His faith among the peoples of the west, whilst He rejected those of the east who crucified Him. The Holy Sepulchre being raised only a few feet from the ground, it is easy for a person to kneel and kiss it ; and since there is always a priest watching, only one or two people besides him can enter at a time, and then only with difficulty. The throng remains in the church for hours before being able to enter the antechamber of the Angel—afterwards into the Holy Sepulchre itself. Every now and then, as one pilgrim comes out, walking backwards in token of reverential respect, another enters. Suspended over the Tomb from the arch are forty-three superb silver lamps burning day and night. The first series of these, and the more central, thirteen in number, belong to the Roman Catholics—that is to say, to the Franciscans of the Holy Land ; thirteen belong to the Schismatic Greeks, thirteen to the Armenians, and four to the Copts. Above the Tomb is a very dark indistinct picture representing the Resurrection, on either side of which, on two little projecting marble parapets, the Franciscans have been able to place a movable altar, upon which they daily celebrate the Mass " of the Holy Sepulchre." The chamber is light, as the Greeks made an opening in the roof at the beginning of the nineteenth century, but is blackened by the fumes of the forty-three lamps. As it is now, so has it ever been described by the pilgrims of all ages who have come and worshipped before it, and have written their impressions concerning it. All speak of the living rock encased in marble ; of the dark, smoke-blackened vault, and of the special shape of the sarcophagus against the wall. The rock of which the Tomb is made is whitish in colour and veined with red ; it is called by the Arabs *melozi*, or sacred stone. The sarcophagus was covered with marble before the thirteenth century, the walls being lined in the same way at a much later date, though otherwise everything has remained untouched and unchanged. The Tomb itself has only been opened twice. In 1501, authorised by Pope Julius II., and by Kansou-el-Gauro, Sultan of Egypt, Father Mauro, then custodian of the Holy Places, had the good fortune to be allowed to open the Sepulchre. He noticed, among other objects, a little marble tablet which he took out ; but he disturbed nothing else and had the Tomb re-closed. Four years later Father Bonifaccio, then keeper of the Holy Places, caused the marble slab to be raised, and found a piece of the True Cross wrapped in a cloth, which, coming in contact with the outer air, fell to pieces, all excepting some threads of gold woven in the stuff. He also discovered a piece of parchment, on which there was an inscription, but so obliterated by time that the words *Helena Magna* alone could be distinguished. On the 27th of August, 1555, it was closed at midnight, and has never been opened since.

The edge of the Tomb is worn away by the lips and tears of the pilgrims of all ages and nationalities. The little chapel of the Holy Sepulchre may be visited from dawn until 11 a.m., then the church is closed till 2 p.m., after which it remains open till sunset. Three Latin Masses are daily said at the Tomb, one High Mass and two Low. Whoever wishes it may remain the whole night to watch and pray in the church. The Franciscans possess near their Chapel of St. Mary Magdalene a little room set apart for those who desire to spend the watches of the night before the Holy Sepulchre, alone with their Lord, and their conscience.

IV.

THE ADORATION.

THE faithful who wish to pray before the Tomb of our Lord must wait their turn for admittance in the Antechamber of the Angel, from whence the Sepulchre is barely discernible in the twilight. Faces are scarcely distinguishable: one shadowy form may be seen bending to kiss the stone upon which the Angel is said to have stood: yet another waits leaning against the wall. The silence is only broken by a deep sigh or by the slight rustling of a rosary. Some bent, shadowy figure now and again passes out from the chamber of the Sepulchre and disappears, to make room for some one else to enter. Meanwhile, others, heavy-hearted and weary, with sad, anxious faces, glide into the chapel to await their turn to venerate the place where Christ was laid. The silent, ghost-like throng never looks to right or left: lost in earnest prayer, meditation, and sad memories, it seems oblivious of all else but its intense desire to plead, in this Holy of Holies, for pardon to the great Consoler of all the afflicted. In the gloom of the inner chapel, the thoughts of the worshipper become absorbed in such an acute sense of intense apprehension and of supreme expectancy that even identity is lost, and all things material appear shadowy and unreal.

In that inner chamber, where, wrapped in a winding-sheet, the Body of our Lord was laid to rest, and where His Mother and the holy women bathed it with their tears and wiped it with their hair, the light pours in through the perforated roof, rendering everything extremely vivid, so that the pious gathering is seen very distinctly, and you can even distinguish the nationality of each pilgrim as he passes through the low arched doorway, to fall prostrate before the august Tomb.

The worshipper enters the Tomb bent nearly double, but once within he straightens himself, and, apparently dazed by the overwhelming light, gropes his way towards the object of his veneration. Then, as his body falls in a heap before the Sepulchre, he seems to forget even how to pray, and, wrapped in a sort of contemplative trance, lacks both words and ideas wherewith to express the intensity of his emotion. Pray? The pilgrim who has come from so far, has overcome so many obstacles and difficulties in his endeavour to fulfil his ardent desire to realise this momentary contact with his Divine Master,

THE ADORATION.

has not even the strength to pray. His mind seems unhinged with excess of joy, and he cannot even control his thoughts. His head rests motionless on the sacred slab as his lips feebly press it, and he is lost in a sort of ecstasy. You may see yet another pilgrim approach the holy stone and, falling on his knees before it, burst into uncontrollable sobs, as if his heart were breaking. He beats his head and breast against it and bathes it with his scalding tears. He even tries to embrace it with his arms, and presses himself against it with the intensity of religious enthusiasm as if it were his last anchor of hope: in his desperation he seeks to become one with It, and even to expire upon It of love, sorrow, and repentance. The silence is broken only by the sound of uncontrollable, convulsive, heartrending sobbing, such as I have never heard before or since.

And it is the Latin pilgrim, whether he comes from France, Italy, or Spain, or from the distant South American Republics, who thus vehemently expresses his conviction, his love, and his tenderness.

You may easily distinguish the Russian pilgrim by his poverty and humility, by the curious way in which he makes the Sign of the Cross, widely and slowly, and, above all, by the force with which he casts his big, heavy form prone upon the ground. His cloak is torn, and his patched trousers discoloured; his bent head displays his fair curling hair, and his eyes are veiled by silent tears that trickle down his cheeks on to the pavement. His hands tremble as he grasps his old fur cap. You may readily distinguish the poor Maltese priest by his dark complexion, the strongly marked furrows on his brow, his tired look, his tattered garments, and the long continuance of his prostration. He has begged his way from his island home, has travelled third class, and said Mass daily in every town and village all along the mainland coast. You may recognise the poor Polish woman by her eyes, bright with an inward happiness, who has been on the tramp for three long months, traversing Syria on foot, living on the charity received in convents and shelters and from passers-by, kissing everyone's hand, and speaking no other language but her own. For all her sickness and fatigue, she lives on, burning with an intense longing to see, to touch the Tomb; and when at last she beholds it, she is so overwhelmed that she faints for very joy. Again, you will know the poor Greek peasant by his sunburnt hands which have tilled the ground so long that they have absorbed its colour. How those poor hands tremble as they touch the white stone, thought of in mystic dreams and reached with so much difficulty! Thus all these believers, these Christians of every nation, come from so far with such exalted, unwavering faith, each bringing that special character of adoration which is peculiar to his own land, soul, race, and temperament. In all of them you discover, as they approach the Sepulchre, the same strange expression of overpowering emotion. Each seems to think that, having worshipped before the Tomb of Christ, he may return to die in peace in his distant home, the wish of his life fulfilled. He has reached the acme of his earthly desire. There have been cases in which pilgrims have actually died of excitement within sight of the Sepulchre.

Here adoration is perpetual. The inmates of those convents which have their gratings and choirs opening into the church watch night and day. Every hour of the day foreign pilgrims are constantly joined by the Christians who live in Jerusalem itself and its environs, and by those who come from the more distant parts of Syria. Here is a woman of Jerusalem, enveloped in her long white cloak which falls over her forehead. Her veil, which is often quite transparent, discloses her dark, irregular features, and her magnificent dull black eyes: she kisses the stone with dignified reverence. Then comes the peasant from Bethany, draped in a long linen tunic and ample black and white cloak, with a handkerchief wound twice round his head like a Bedouin. Before the Tomb he signs himself hurriedly, and beats his forehead against the marble in an outburst of devotion.

The beautiful Bethlehemite woman, from the happy land where Jesus was born, dressed in a blue woollen gown embroidered in red, and wearing a white kerchief worked in yellow, blue, or red, and folded in a point over

THE ADORATION.

forehead and shoulders, bends with stately grace her noble head with its regular features, brilliant complexion, and fine eyes. Next comes the little peasant-woman from Ain-Karem, St. John of the Mountain, the land of the Forerunner, a small, thin, charming little woman, dressed in dark blue, with tiny bare feet and hands. Drawing her white, silk-like linen cloak over her brows to hide the three rows of gold and silver coins which encircle her hair, with her baby in her arms half hidden in the folds of her shawl, she bends forward, and both mother and child kiss the Sepulchre. The *beghina* of the Russian colony settled in Jerusalem now enters. She is dressed in black, and wears a large white handkerchief folded across her chest, and a tight white kerchief like a cap on her head. You can easily detect that she is a Schismatic nun by the exaggerated manner in which she makes the Sign of the Cross, and by her profound prostration.

Then follows a crowd of Turks, Arabs, Egyptians, Europeans, in turbans, fez, caps, hats, rich, poor, even beggars, the latter sometimes so horrible and misshapen as to inspire both pity and disgust. They bend over the Sepulchre, genuflect and depart. And now come members of the various religious orders: brown-cloaked Franciscans, white-robed Dominicans, Greek priests in high black hats, Armenian priests with great black silk hoods under which glitter their flashing eyes and waving black beards, the Latin missionaries, nuns of St. Joseph, European women who live in Jerusalem and lead a sort of monastic life, dressed in dark habits, throng in to venerate the Tomb of their Lord.

Mingled with these good people is a crowd of children, boys and girls, big and little, belonging to all nationalities, who approach and kiss the Sepulchre. They are especially numerous during the hours when the schools are closed, and it is a touching sight to watch these little creatures come in silently, and push their way on tiptoe through the throng of grown-up people, in their childish endeavour to kiss the sacred Stone on which they laid Him who bade little children come unto Him. I remember one day seeing a tiny brown mite in a yellow and red tunic tied round the waist by a ribbon, wearing no stockings, and laughing as he tried in vain, being too short, to reach up and kiss the Tomb. Twice he attempted to jump up and touch it with his lips, and twice fell back. At last I raised him in my arms, and he, all joyously, kissed the marble with a number of little resounding kisses. *Yalla! yalla!* (Go away! go away!) cried sharply the Armenian priest who was on watch; though I noticed he smiled all the same. And as the child with his little bare feet ran quietly away the priest sprinkled him with rose-scented holy water.

V.

DURING THE NIGHT.

DAY in the East begins at five in the morning and ends at twilight, by which time the worshippers at the great shrine have become much less numerous. Towards four o'clock the peasants from the surrounding villages begin to leave the *bazaars:* the now unladen mules are turned towards St. John in the Mountains and towards the nearer villages of Bethany and Siloam: the agrarian population round Jerusalem goes back to its homes. They all, men, women, children, and animals, disappear down the dusty road, only, however, to return next and every day, always to renew their supplications before the Holy Sepulchre. As the day declines the women of Jerusalem return to their houses, enveloped in their cloud-like white muslin cloaks, one end of which is invariably kept tightly pressed to the mouth by a brown hand. On their fingers they wear coarse silver rings, and on their slender wrist light blue glass bracelets, made in Hebron, the land of Abraham. They, too, have been upon their pious errand to the Tomb. At sunset even the sunburnt, dirty, deformed, weather-beaten Christian beggars go back to their mud huts under the shadow of the

DURING THE NIGHT.

Mount of Olives, outside the walls of Jerusalem. As they trudge along the dusty road they twist, in their dried-up fingers, the cheapest of cigarettes, their one and only luxury, without which these the meanest and poorest of human beings could not exist in this strange country. In the soft twilight hour you will see the pilgrims returning for the night from the Valley of Jehoshaphat, the Tombs of the Kings, or the Fountains of Solomon, to the Latin, Greek, Armenian, or Russian asylums. The rich European leaves the Sepulchre at sundown to rest in the English hotels. The great church becomes silent and empty. On the side of the rotunda belonging to the Copts a woman prays motionless beside some pillar, or prone upon the ground. Presently she rises and slowly departs. Outside on the square the ambulating vendors of rosaries, scapulars, little crosses, and medals in imitation silver, gather up their goods into bags with two pouches and disappear, followed by the rabble of sunburnt sellers and water-carriers. Not a soul now passes down the little stairway by which half the town of Jerusalem descends to the Piazza; no one now lingers under the archway of the Templars; the chirp of the birds is hushed. The sun sets. A dull thud re-echoes through the deserted arches and chapels of the church. The doors are closed until dawn. Within the gloomy church, pilgrims who have obtained the privilege of remaining in adoration by the Sepulchre throughout the watches of the night are left alone with their Lord.

Night gradually falls over the whole building, first effacing the marked outline of the massive columns of the rotunda, then obliterating the upper gallery, and, lastly, even the peep of blue skylight that shows through the narrow windows of the clerestory. The pillars round each chapel and all the quaint architectural features of this strange structure are soon lost in sepulchral gloom. Here and there are a few faint glimmers of light. Behind the apse, the second church, Calvary, forming part of that of the Holy Sepulchre, to which it leads up by two steep flights of marble steps, is merged in utter darkness; only the occasional flicker of a lamp lingers on that place of Golgotha where the Cross was driven into the earth. Here and there a dim light flickers in the Chapel of St. Saviour, and in the one belonging to the Franciscans, St. Mary Magdalene. The small underground chapels cut out of the solid rock, where are the tombs of Joseph of Arimathæa and his family, and where the Holy Cross was found, look like so many darksome caverns ready to engulf one. The harassed and contrite soul who has obtained permission to remain in this mysterious church through the long watches of the night realises in this weird obscurity his intense longing to converse, as it were, with his Maker and examine his conscience as, possibly, he has never thought of doing before. His senses soon become almost atrophied, and he falls a prey to strange hallucinations. Leaning against the door of the sacred building not venturing to enter or to stir a step forward, he loses himself in a profound, dreamy reverie.

The proportions of the great building seem in the darkness to expand and become colossal, limitless. If a breath of air disturbs the faint light of the lamps, the watcher fancies some spirit has passed over them and made them quiver. Is not that a step lightly treading the pavement? Who is that who sighs so deeply? Is that white figure down yonder human? Is the church really empty? Perhaps those whispers that disturb the silence are mere creations of the imagination. Be this as it may, the watcher's heart is heavy, and he fancies himself haunted by ghosts, some sad, others wrathful, that have risen from their graves to hover about the Tomb of tombs. The ear may hear nothing, but the quickened imagination conjures up strange sights and sounds, peopling the lonely church with voices wailing with sorrow or ringing with reproach, the voices of the lost ones who are gone before! Presently the darkness seems filled with hazy, vanishing figures, with livid, dying faces, and shadowy skeleton hands waving blessings or beckoning farewells. The place is indeed haunted—with memories, with sadness, with fear. The awful silence is only broken by the muttering of some bitter ejaculation, stifled sob, ay, even with the rattle of the dying!

Then, wild with horror and repentance, the keeper of this vigil staggers into the Mortuary Chamber to prostrate

DURING THE NIGHT. 61

himself by the Tomb, even as a child sinks on its mother's breast. To him this Stone is the last refuge, where he shall find shelter and love. Then the trembling, fevered lips kiss the marble, and in the dead of night repeat again and again the everlasting question that rises, during the hours of greatest exaltation or of profoundest depression, to the lips of the suffering believer, the question a son asks his father, the question a Soul asks its God—but louder, more fervent, more insistent : " Now that we are alone together in the night, O Lord, and that Thou seest all I think and feel—since I come here desiring to remain in Thy presence one night before Thy Sepulchre —tell me, oh ! tell me, what is the Truth and which the Way ? "

The Soul waits on. And here, in the clear light of the forty-nine lamps which burn perpetually above the Holy Tomb, a new-born peace falls upon the restless conscience, soothing its vain terrors. In this Holy Place all the falsehood, meanness, poverty, cupidity, false pride, and hypocrisy of the soul crumble to pieces ; like some dense wall that has kept out the light of Heaven. The heavy chain that fettered the human being to the vainglory and the pleasures of this world is loosened and the unclean spirit cast out. The Soul is freed ; for Jesus Christ, Who was buried here, desires that souls, liberated by repentance from evil, should come to Him and be healed by the touch of His Tomb. Would that the proud, the unjust, the frivolous, who live for this world only, the brutal and the sensual, could pass one night alone with Him in this sacred Spot, where stands His funeral couch, the Slab on which His Divine and Bleeding Form rested ! Then would they see light ; and the evil that binds them down would pass from them by the mere contact with the Tomb of the God of Love and unselfishness, who died that His lofty ideal of life should live and be Eternal.

Thus the Soul communes, listens, and remembers. How many profound, never-to-be-forgotten words He uttered during His Life ! Yet one, especially, vibrates here more clearly than elsewhere—" Thou dost trouble thyself about many things, Martha ; one thing only is needful." Only one ? Is it no matter, then, if our wishes are unfulfilled, if our dreams are not realised ? Does it not matter that our love should be unrequited and our hatred should be vain ? Is all this of no importance ? *No,—* or but very little. One thing *only* is necessary : He Who lay two nights in the grave has said it. Are the ties of family affection nothing ? The reverence of children for their parents : the gratitude of friends : faith and loyalty— are not these things needful ? May we not weep and bemoan the incompleteness of our work, and the scorn with which our best intentions are so often met ? Are we not to complain or trouble ourselves if our heart and mind cannot reach their goal ? If we fall fainting by the way, without wish, desire, or hope, should we seek consolation in ourselves alone ? " One thing only is needful " : the Life of the Spirit. The Soul sees and knows. He lived the great life of the Spirit, and desires that all, through Him, should also live, even as He did. All those who were suffering, oppressed, infirm, miserable, the weak on account of age, sex, or condition, women, old men, children, the sick and the poor, all received from Him those spiritual consolations which elevate and purify : those suffering from the effects of terrible misfortune, oppressed by misery, the sad and abandoned, all have felt in their inward conscience the sublime idea of a future recompense, the pure fount of all comfort. That spiritual life, which in Him assumed a Divine Form, setting aside all human calculations, pardoning all offences in pity for the humble and penitent sinner, in love for the suffering ones—He has given this boon to all who have believed or will believe in Him : this Divine gift for the cure of souls has only been granted in order to consummate the most wonderful of hidden miracles. This life of the Spirit, however humble and simple, is always consoling : it may be great and powerful, lifting men to the sublimest heights, to the ideal of heroism and martyrdom. It gives to youth its joyousness, to manhood its strength, and is the blessing of old age : for is it not the legacy of Him Who was born in Bethlehem, and died in Jerusalem ? The Soul, now quiet and calm and henceforth at peace, exclaims : " Thou hast spoken to me, O Lord, during this terrible yet glorious night, and hast answered Thy servant. I now know what is the Truth, and wherein lies the Way."

From the round space in the cupola, the light of dawn descends radiantly upon the sacred Tomb: and the bright sun enters the Temple in a triumphant burst of glory.

PART III.
JERUSALEM! JERUSALEM!

I.

THE CITY.

THROUGHOUT Holy Writ there rises a soul-felt hymn of praise to the glory and beauty of Jerusalem. The Royal Psalmist pays her passionate homage; the grand and wrathful prophets, even when compelled to curse her iniquities, cannot refrain from exalting her. All the superlative adjectives and emphatic encomiums of the most figurative of all languages, the Hebrew, are none too exaggerated if used to honour Zion. She is refulgent: her radiance dazzles: she is abounding in glory and majesty, and overflowing with riches and magnificence. Salem means peace: Jerusalem signifies "Vision of Peace." She is also styled "the Daughter of Zion," "the Queen of the Hills," "the City of David," "the City of Solomon," and the sublime dwelling-place of the Spirit. To a Jew, Jerusalem is the realisation of an earthly Paradise: whereas in the eyes of Christians she holds out the promise of another, a heavenly, Zion. Every tongue should, therefore, sing pæans of praise before her holy walls, wherein, shrouded in clouds of incense, stands the chosen altar of the world! As we gaze upon this city, our hearts are filled with anguish, and we seem to see the daughters of Zion before us, clothed in the mourning raiments they have worn ever since that day when Jerusalem slew her Lord. To the believer, the Emperor Titus, who, forty years after the death of Christ, overthrew the Temple of Solomon and destroyed Jerusalem, ought to appear as that Messenger who God ordained was not to leave a single stone one upon another in the city within whose walls the Son of Man endured His Passion and Death.

Stripping this Hebrew rhetoric of its florid hyperbole, and remembering how inflexible and obstinately conservative is the Oriental mind, I cannot help thinking that the Jerusalem of two thousand years ago was not so very different from that of to-day. The Temple of Solomon must undoubtedly have been superb, filling with wonderment the throng of devotees who kissed its threshold. On the other hand, the splendid Mosque of Omar, which has arisen on the site of the Temple that beheld the downfall of Israel's independence, is distinctly a work of genius, and may even retain in its general design some traces of the awful majesty that characterised the earlier fane, which, however, only appealed to the intellect and left the heart unsatisfied. The tumble-down houses which line the hundred lane-like streets that cover the hills of modern Zion have remained unaltered, not only here, but elsewhere in Palestine, since Biblical times. The covered bazaars and the darksome shops, illumined only by the rays of light pouring in through the narrow doorway, the very shape of the small windows in the loftier houses, nay, even the closed shutters, still endure, unchanging and unchanged, since the days of David. Doubtless, to the nomad tribes that descended from the bleak and rugged mountains of Moab and Gilead beyond Jordan : to the pastoral peoples that grazed their herds on the plain of Esdraelon, that stretches under the shadows of the mountains of Gilboa : to the agricultural and fishing folk who inhabited the gracious region of Galilee, the flowery hills of Nazareth, and the pleasant shores of Genesareth : to those rough men and women who slept under black leather tents, in natural caves, in straw-thatched cottages, or in mud huts—to all these simple-minded folk, Jerusalem, with its Temple, its priestly palaces, its gateways, arches, and tall houses, must have seemed that very " Pearl of Israel " described by the prophets. Does not the Bride in the Song of Songs sing that Jerusalem is as fair as the tents of Kedar ? And are not those precisely the same tents under which dwell the nomad tribes of our day ? I once fell in with an encampment near Tiberias, consisting of a series of low black leather tents, shining with grease and made in the shapes of animals, the entrances to which were so low that it was impossible to go in or out except by crawling on hands and knees.

It must not be forgotten that Jerusalem was the City of the Law, where Moses enshrined the Word as he received it from God Himself. Within the Holy of Holies rested the Ark of the Covenant, as well as the slab of unhewn stone upon which Abraham offered up his son Isaac. Here, too, was treasured the vessel that had contained the Heaven-sent manna, and many another famous memorial of Israel's story. Thus, the imagination of this people was in due time intensified by their constant contact with places that treasured the chief relics of their religion. What a transport of joy must have overwhelmed them when they went up yearly to Jerusalem to celebrate the Passover! Even in this matter-of-fact age, Jews from all parts of the world flock to the Holy City, abandoning beautiful and populous regions, charming and picturesque countries, great and civilised towns, for this half-ruined city, where only wretched two-storeyed houses are to be met with, except in the new quarter outside the Jaffa Gate, where the Nazarenes possess all the important dwellings—convents, monasteries, mission houses, and hospitals belonging to different nationalities and various sects of Christians. The rest of the Holy City is poor, dark, and dirty; presenting a most distressing picture of stifling poverty and oppression. It is not improbable, however, that to the Jews, who see all this misery through the eyes of the imagination, dimmed to reality by the intensity of their religious faith, Jerusalem, notwithstanding the destruction of its Temple and its desolation, still appears to them as the erstwhile sovereign City of their eternal hopes. But, even to the traveller who comes here merely to gratify his curiosity, or the ordinary tourist, Jerusalem, with its little narrow lanes, its tiny houses, and its steep paths—that take the breath out of you, and soon wear out your European boots and shoes—presents a wonderfully original aspect. The wide, unequal stone steps of its streets, which are not thoroughfares but mostly blind alleys, and its curious markets and bazaars, differentiate it utterly from every other great Oriental city—Constantinople, Cairo, Beyrout, or even Jaffa. Jerusalem, I hold, derives its peculiarity from the cosmopolitan character of its inhabitants. I am not alluding to its solitary carriageable roadway outside the Jaffa Gate, on either side of which modern Jerusalem is extending, with its consulates, hotels, and villas, some of which may be described as quite elegant, for what are they when compared with that weird aggregation of half-ruined huts in the native Mussulman, Hebrew, and Christian quarters? The Christian section of the Old City is divided up amongst the Latins, Greeks, Armenians, and Copts. In its narrow lane-like streets, crossed and re-crossed from dawn to dark by camels, donkeys, goats, and sheep, minarets rise side by side with Christian belfries. Some of the ruins that abound hereabouts date from the days of Solomon to those of Titus; others may originally have been built by Crœsus, King of Persia; whilst the greater number are not older than the time of the Crusades. In this silent city, where no carriages can circulate, every form of religion freely summons its followers to prayer; and the sharp clang of the Catholic bell mingles with the shrill cry of the *muezzin* from the balcony of the minaret. There is no display of riches or greatness in Jerusalem, but it is still surrounded by crumbling walls whose every stone has been cemented with human blood. The noblest of the City gates is, beyond question, the Damascus—sometimes called the Gate of Flowers on account of its architecture—which is not only imposing but absolutely fascinating. Jerusalem has a charm of its own which can be readily appreciated by those who love the picturesque, and to whom a saunter, especially if unaccompanied by an uncongenial dragoman, through its crowded, crooked streets, and across its sunlit spaces, can never be forgotten. Can anyone imagine a greater delight than to stop and bargain for an amber necklace, or buy for a penny or two some of those sweet, delicious little native apricots; or to watch the Mussulman workmen at their midday meal, prepared in certain outlandish little taverns, which, with their long benches and rude tables, recall those tiny Neapolitan fried-fish shops, whose quaint interiors are so dear to the painter? Then again, what can be more amusing than to listen to the bargaining of the corn merchants from Jericho, effected in that deep guttural Arabic which invariably gives one the impression that the dealer and the purchaser are quarrelling, whereas in reality both are equally calm and polite? Meanwhile, the camel on bended knees waits patiently outside for the completion of the transaction. Presently a Christian procession jostles us against the wall as we piously make the Sign of the Cross. By dint of making daily pilgrimages in the streets of this most Oriental of cities one soon becomes quite familiar not only with places, but with the people and their curious manners and strange customs. You soon perceive that, although the population is the most heterogeneous mixture of Jewish, Turkish, and European types, yet it is, in a sense, perfectly harmonious. It is very easy to lose yourself in this maze, but if you but ask your way in Greek, Italian, or French, somebody will soon put you right. It is really almost worth while mistaking your road in Jerusalem.

I remember one day, having missed my way, I found myself in the thicket of a strange deserted garden in the very heart of Jerusalem. In my endeavour to retrace my steps I fell across a plant of the identical thorn which furnished the cruel Crown that was pressed upon the Brow of the Redeemer.

II.

THE PEOPLE.

CAN it be truthfully said that there exists among the seventy thousand inhabitants of Jerusalem a distinctive people; to which can be applied the title of God's Elect, so envied by other nations, so loved by Him?

Not to the Jews, though they form more than half the population. An inestimable gift, a Divine promise, had been made to Israel, and she received the sublime realisation of the greatest of futures; but she soon wearied of piety and good deeds. From that fatal Thursday of *Nisam*, when the Jews, mysteriously roused to anger and blinded by hatred of the Nazarene, demanded that the Blood of the Son of Man should fall on them and on their children, the challenged malediction has struck them, and, being dispersed, they have ceased to be a nation. Slowly, thanks to the evolution of political and religious sentiment, and to Turkish indifference—in reality a form of pity and courteous contempt—the Jews have begun to return to Jerusalem. They arrive from the furthermost points of Europe, looking piteously pale, weary, and ill. Their habitual expression is one of extreme timidity; that of a whipped cur. They seem unable to look you straight in the face, and appear to dread meeting an enemy or persecutor at every step and turn. Silent, thoughtful, incapable of argument, they prefer to hide themselves in dark corners, in out-of-the-way tumble-down houses, or else in wretched little shops where goods are never exhibited. Notwithstanding their constantly increasing numbers, and the fact that nearly all the commerce of the town and district, both wholesale and retail, is in their hands, they have not changed their plaintive, timorous manner to become in the least degree more expansive, but remain ever crouching and seemingly unhappy, scarcely venturing to raise their heads in this, the capital of their former greatness, and the actual City of their tears and hopes! Perhaps they never will change, for time and recent events have only added to their fateful destiny.

Ah! they are well aware of all this! They know that they exist in Jerusalem only on sufferance, the effect of a generous concession, or perchance even of a mere accident. They feel that they are only temporarily settled here, and that an Imperial edict may at any moment drive them forth again. They are simply intruders with no right to enjoy in peace the fresh air and sunshine of their own Holy City. They steal along by the walls and are easily recognised by their long glossy locks, the strange cut of their garments, and, above all, by their infinitely pathetic appearance of constrained meekness and sickliness. You

THE PEOPLE.

perceive it not only in the aged, but in the adolescent and in the pale, dark-eyed little ones. The Jews of Jerusalem are engaged in all sorts of trades, selling and buying everything. They are money-changers: some, the more courageous, will even turn usurers on a small scale, but with such infinite cunning and precaution as to prevent their ever being caught in the act. One of the chief banks of Jerusalem is in Israelitish hands, though it is conducted on European lines, and is situated in the Nazarene quarter. But, for the most part, the Jews hereabouts earn their livelihood tenaciously and obstinately, by a minute sort of retail trade peculiar to the place. They cannot till the ground; their traditional pastoral occupations are, like their nationality, lost. The habits of twenty centuries of commerce, industries, and shopkeeping, however, remain with them. Their women, who are seldom beautiful but nearly always anæmic and dissipated-looking, have light wavering eyes and are never veiled: they wear, however, a kind of cap of a strange antiquated form placed crossways on the head, which entirely hides the hair. Over this they drape a white woollen shawl with a broad pattern of red and yellow flowers. They glide along abstractedly, scarcely, if ever, turning to look about them, but hastening along, as if pursued, eager to dive into the worst and ugliest hovels of Jerusalem. And this is the sort of life they lead in order to exist near the spot where two thousand years ago stood their Holy of Holies, their mighty Temple! Every Friday they flock in crowds to wait by the only remaining wall of the Temple, and they die content if only they are sure that a handful of the black earth of the valley of Jehoshaphat will mingle with that of their graves. Yet, for all this, they are not the people of Jerusalem! Neither is the ruling Turkish population. The Turks, some eight or ten thousand in number, exist here, as they do in every other land which they have conquered, calm, indolent, haughty, and unconcerned. Materially their rule in Palestine has been most fruitful; their concessions to the Christians—that is, to the Latins, Greeks, and Armenians—have scarcely ever been made through the generosity of a Sultan, but almost always for some pecuniary advantage. Every inch of the Holy Land has been acquired at the price of the tears, blood, and money of the believers. It may well be said that the Country of Jesus, impoverished through the neglect of Islam, has proved of far greater value to the Sublime Porte than its corn, wheat, grapes, and oranges. Thus the Turks exercise their gentle sway in Jerusalem. They are opportunists or indifferent, as best suits their convenience. They conquered Jerusalem and they keep it ; and treat both Christians and Jews with equal forbearance. The first Station of the *Via Crucis*—that is, the Prætorium of Pontius Pilate, from which Christ set out—is now a Turkish barrack. Every Friday the Franciscan Fathers, followed by a crowd of pilgrims, and others who join the procession probably from curiosity, start from this place the devotion known as the Way of the Cross ; whilst the Turkish soldiers watch them with a curious, mingled expression of wonderment and contempt. The guardians at the gate of the Holy Sepulchre are Turks, who pass the whole day lolling on a kind of platform covered with carpets, smoking cigarettes or *chibooques*. They neither ask for money nor take the least notice of the crowd of the Faithful flocking to the Sanctuary. In their eyes, Jesus was worthy of admiration. He was inferior to Mahomet, but quite as great a Prophet as David. They call Him *Naby Issa*, or the Prophet Jesus. They also venerate the Virgin and call her *Sitti Miriam*, or the Lady Mary. They firmly believe that the great stone which is suspended in the Mosque of Omar in Jerusalem, that great rock which was taken from the Temple of Solomon, is held up miraculously both by the Mother of Mahomet and by the Mother of Jesus. They believe, too, that forty years before the end of the world *Naby Issa*, or Jesus, will return to earth, and together with Mahomet, who will join Him, convert the world to Mohammedanism. After which, the crack of doom !

Jerusalem contains the third greatest mosque of Islam, after those at Mecca and Medina, since here are venerated the remains of the Prophets and Patriarchs, because they were quickened by the word of Mahomet. Upon the Rock which was the Holy of Holies, they venerate two hairs of Mahomet's beard. This does not, however, prevent their

THE PEOPLE.

allowing believers of other faiths to pay reverence to their own prophets, martyrs, and saints. The Mussulman leaves everyone at liberty as long as this liberty does not interfere with him or his affairs. He has, indeed, conquered Zion: but, for all that, he is no Zionite, nor does he pretend to be of Jerusalem.

None the less the Christians, or so-called Christians, do not constitute the people of Jerusalem; for, although it is true that the Latins, Schismatic Greeks, Armenians, Russians, Copts, and Maronites pretend to represent the faithful followers and soldiers of Christ, they are hopelessly divided by their dissensions and fanaticism. None but the Latins, that blessed band of Franciscan monks, the custodians of the Holy Places, together with a couple of thousand Catholic believers, who alone possess that true spirit of humility, temperance, and devotion which they have received from St. Francis, could form the nucleus of a Christian people in Jerusalem. But they are very few! As to the four thousand Greeks, two thousand Latins, one thousand Armenians, and all the numerous Christian sects, they are principally distinguished for the spirit of discord and mutual animosity which must for ever prevent their forming anything approaching unity. Unhappily, the Latin, Greek, Armenian, and Coptic Christians, and even the Protestants, live here in a state of perpetual strife and jealousy, which the Turks are obliged to quell whenever their quarrels reach a pitch that threatens the peace. These divided sects of Christianity care only for their particular Church and Shrine, and each believes itself the depository of a high and perfect spiritual mission, which exonerates its members from doing any sort of work or engaging in any industry or commerce. They never think of adding to their resources. Latins, Greeks, and Armenians live thus in the shadows of their own convents and places of refuge, from which they receive board, pecuniary assistance, doctors, medicines, schools, and all protection and help. The most complete idleness reigns among these nationalities. They follow, it is true, all the rites of their various Churches, they are very pious, even fanatical, but with them religion frequently becomes a mere question of interest. The Franciscan Fathers, with their enlightened faith, have often spoken to me on this subject, and regretted so hopeless a state of affairs. But what can they, with all their zeal, do with people who make of religion a profession, and who believe that because they have heard Mass at five o'clock in the morning they are perfect Christians? To do them justice, the Franciscans give their flock plenty of work to do, and teach them to be industrious and economical; but to little or no purpose.

Therefore, that our nation (the Italian) may exist in the Holy Land and our Faith maintain its *prestige*, we must have patience; although there is little hope that we shall ever be able to form a *people* in Jerusalem. Neither will the Jews ever form a people here; for they are no longer a nation, but a mere assemblage of persons come from the farthest parts of the earth and quite incapable of organisation and re-annexation. As to the Turks, they only remain here as in a garrison; whilst the other small, lazy, fanatical Christian sects, ever at war among themselves, are not likely to unite and conquer the foremost place in the population of a regenerated Zion. It is a curious fact, but Jerusalem seems doomed never to have a distinct people of its own like any other city. The Arabs from the plains, the handsome Bedouins from the desert of Jericho and even from Arabia Petræa, will never form the people of Jerusalem, since they only come here to buy and sell.

Possibly Jerusalem will never again have a people of her own. She was great before God, and God placed in her all His Might; but the Son of Man suffered and died within her walls, and all her glory faded. And so she lives on, in the shadow of her splendid past, fulfilling day by day the prophecy that foretold her destruction and her desolation.

III.

THE SOUL.

Two thousand years have passed, and in that long lapse of time Jerusalem has been pillaged and burnt eighteen

THE SOUL.

times; she has seen fifty different forms of government and fifty different sorts of tyranny. Her people have been exterminated, and her erstwhile flourishing country has been devastated and abandoned, and, in consequence, has become sterile. A series of unparalleled catastrophes has ruined her, and, moreover, she has experienced a Divine punishment unexampled in history. All this, however, has not subjugated, transformed, or renewed the spirit of Jerusalem, which remains unchanged; it is the same as it was when, nineteen centuries ago, Jesus came from Nazareth, and, passing through the Golden Gate, shook His Head in sadness and in disgust at the hypocrisy, the vainglory, and the unutterable degradation of her people. At that time the people of Jerusalem had long since abandoned the high ideals of the Mosaic Law, to follow a narrow and unscrupulous observance, a sort of religious sophism, from which the ardour of faith had been eliminated, leaving in its place a cold spirit of hypocrisy and deceit, which it was Jesus' mission to stamp out. The Zion of two thousand years ago swarmed with religious sects, of which the Pharisees, Essenes, and Gaulonites are the best-known because the most important of those countless parties, each of which claimed to be the true interpreter of the Law of Moses. Jerusalem was a place above all others famed for its theological differences, and in which excited argument in public frequently degenerated, even within the walls of the Temple itself, into a scene of angry invective. Indeed, the Temple had become the seat of religious strife—a place where the ostentatious display of meaningless observance crushed the pure spirit of Faith—" The letter killeth; but the Spirit quickeneth."

Who can venture to describe the wrath, the horror, of Christ for all this hypocrisy, and for these false practices that masked sacrilegious and unspeakable vices? How He must have hated those stony hearts that knew no pity and were so devoid of tenderness! With what an outburst of indignant wrath did the Spirit of Jesus inveigh against the nauseating hypocrisies, the priestly lies, the cruelty of the Levites, who from their high place within the Temple held in their hands the fate of the Hebrew people, only to bend, to crush, to trample it under foot, just as they pleased!

The spirit of Jesus changes with its surroundings. When He preaches to simple, loving hearts on the mountains, or along the shores of the Sea of Tiberias, amidst the wonderful beauties of nature, His words flow from Him like a river of tenderness; the Divine Promise of the nine Beatitudes was pronounced under blue skies on the Mount of Hattine. But once He comes to Jerusalem, His Eyes are saddened, His Soul is troubled, and His Heart is overcome with indignation. The sternest of His parables are directed against the rich, the proud, and the cruel. He threatens them with the most appalling punishments and casts out the buyers and sellers from the atrium of the Temple, exclaiming that they had converted the House of God into a den of thieves. Unchanged and immutable is the Soul of Jerusalem! It is always the city of theological argument, bitter invective, and heated discussion of the various preponderating clerical hierarchies; it is more than ever the town of sects and heresies. The one exception amidst these angry and inane controversies, stands the little Latin Church, which, whilst combating with gentleness but with the ardour of its mission received from the great St. Francis, has the moral support of all Italians. All else is tumult and strife—a seeking for mystical, theological, and temporal supremacy; a war of conventions which fills one with disgust. Who can count the various religious sects which are to be found in modern Jerusalem? The Christians of the Roman Church are divided into Latins, United Greeks, and Armenians; the Maronites of Lebanon and the United Copts; after these, the heretical Christians, that is, the Schismatic Greeks, Armenians, Copts, and Abyssinians—the latter, not more than 300 in number, have their own church. The Protestant Churches which are established in the Holy Land are also subdivided into several sects. The Lutheran Christians, or Germans, who have founded a colony in Syria, are also already very influential, especially since the visit of the Emperor. They, too, are split up into two or three divisions, one being those of the Temple, a special sect. Outside the gate of St. Stephen there is a fanatical American sect, a good deal like the Salvation Army, who call themselves the " Martyrs of the

Last Hour." Even Mormons are to be found in Jerusalem. And do you suppose that the members of these numerous sects, who, after all, *do* venerate Jesus, and have come to this place where He suffered and was buried—do you imagine that they remain quiet in the presence of the august Sepulchre ? Not a bit of it ! Each is full of envy and spite against the other, and seeks to dominate by sheer brute force, or else by bribery and corruption—and this, not for the glory of Christ, but for the exaltation of their patriarchs, clergy, and missions. They even angrily count the lamps, the candles and the prayers they have a right to offer, before that very Altar where He suffered His Martyrdom, because He wished for the exaltation of the poor, the simple, and the faithful.

The year before I arrived in Jerusalem, the Armenian and Greek priests, even in their priestly robes, rose in anger and beat each other with sticks before the Holy Sepulchre itself ! In the Church of the Nativity at Bethlehem, the Turkish Pasha is obliged to place a soldier on guard *beside each altar*, and another, night and day, before the silver star which marks the site of the place where Mary gave birth to Jesus, lest the Greeks might steal it. Three years after my journey, a poor Franciscan Father was shot dead by a fanatical Greek. A great fuss was made about it, but nothing was done. You will invariably find either a Greek or an Armenian priest in the corner of the little chamber that contains the Holy Sepulchre. He remains motionless, observes you attentively, for he soon recognises that you are not of his way of thinking, and though you have not the slightest intention of doing him any harm, he mistrusts you, for he fears you will not give him alms. If you remain longer, he begins to mutter, and at last makes signs to you to go. Paying no attention, you continue to pray : sometimes, for the sake of peace, you depart : anyhow, your prayers have been disturbed. The processions, festivals, Masses, and prayers are one continual struggle for who shall have the best places, the most pomp, the greatest number of people, and make the most noise. The Schismatic Greeks and Russians, who are very fanatical, give enormous sums to their churches in the Holy Land : they are simply "fleeced" by the priests when they arrive in Jerusalem. Everything is sold, even the dregs of the oil lamps, as if they were relics. If our Lord returned to earth again, and saw what is being sold to the poor Polish agriculturists, to the poor colonists of Little Russia, and to the poor Greeks from Macedonia and Thessaly, He would again take the scourge in His Hand and turn the sellers out of the Temple. Thus the believers of all these heresies, and the believers united to the Church of Rome but not Latins, constitute so many belligerent bands, led by their patriarchs and priests, and upheld by the Consuls of their respective countries ; so that if blood is not always spilt, it is due mainly to the wise and cautious Turkish police ; and if things assume an air of quiet for a time, it is owing to Mussulman justice. So great is the hate of these "Christians" for one another, that one is compelled to praise Mahomet in a Mohammedan country, where he alone sets an example of tolerance, wisdom, and justice. And in the midst of all this, the poor dear little Latin Church, who by herself, through her Franciscan Friars, has resisted fearlessly for hundreds of years the turmoil of all this warfare, she being the only one to maintain the *prestige* of Christian charity, the only one really imbued with enlightened piety, strong and dignified in humility, and practising an asceticism which, while not separating itself from life, ennobles and exalts it. The poor Latin Church is the only one which, since the time of St. Francis till now, has passed her whole existence in the Service of Faith and the Holy Sepulchre.

On the heights of the Mount of Olives stands a little ruined chapel bearing the inscription *Dominus flevit*, "The Lord hath wept ! "

He might indeed weep, since He has preached, suffered, and died in vain—for Jerusalem !

PART IV.
THE WAY OF SUFFERING.

I.

THE MOUNT OF OLIVES.

THE Mount of Olives, whose name evokes sad and bitter memories in those who are moved and influenced by the poetry of the Passion, rises on the western side of Jerusalem, some three hundred yards outside St. Stephen's Gate, and separated from Mount Zion by the dark and lonely Valley of Jehoshaphat. It is by no means a hill of great elevation, although from any of the terraces of Jerusalem it appears to dominate the surrounding landscape: the crystalline light in which from earliest dawn its summit is bathed makes it seem of greater height than it really is. Even when seen by night it appears to soar, clear and well defined, when the inhabitants of Jerusalem are asleep in their little white houses which nestle in the broad shadows of the Christian monasteries, of the majestic mosque, and of the dark fragment of the Temple—the only relic left to the Jews of their erstwhile grandeur. Its silhouette looms distinctly against the darkness as, when all is silent in the streets of the Earthly Zion, the stars above shed their gentle light over the hill He loved.

The Mount of Olives, with its rounded top curved towards the hills upon which the city is built, has retained a strong yet indefinable impression of the tremendous events of which it was the scene: so that he who gazes upon it in the right spirit endeavours, with all his powers of concentration, to retain an ineffaceable impression of the lineaments of a spot so beloved of Jesus, where He lived and where He prayed so often, and from whence, on that terrible and most eventful of nights, He went to His Doom. It was here that Judas Iscariot kissed and betrayed Him. Here He was seized by the soldiers. Here, too, after thrice vainly trying to awaken His disciples, He rebuked them, saying, "Sleep on now, and take your rest : behold, the hour is at hand." It was from this hillock that He started on His sorrowful way, His *Via Dolorosa*, and not from the Prætorium of Pontius Pilate where He was unjustly condemned. During the watches of the night the eyes of the believer are riveted upon the Mount of Olives, as he endeavours to recall and realise that sad procession, with its flare of torches and its unsheathed weapons, wending precipitately towards the torrent of Cedron, dragging along, like a common malefactor, the Son of Mary, the Innocent One !

The road leading to the Mount of Olives is very uneven : there are only two small paths, stony and steep, which lead up to it. Those who wish to go comfortably select for the ascent either a horse or a donkey—usually a donkey, a quiet, sure-footed little beast, who knows how to convey you safely over the mountainous roads of Palestine, that are rendered extremely unsafe by rocks, stones, and the loose earth of which they are formed. If we wish to realise truly the Mount of Olives we must proceed thither on foot, and not with the haste of a mere tourist who is ever pressed for time and eager to cover ground. After reflecting earnestly and seeking to feel the full influence of this holy place, we must approach it with reverence and try to picture to ourselves the scenes that have transpired in a spot where Christ came almost daily. Kneeling in prayer, the believer can almost fancy he is able to trace His footprints. How, indeed, can anyone who has a heart to feel fail to tread reverently, step by step, the path that leads up the Mount of Olives, where every spot, whether upon it or in its neighbourhood, is pregnant with memories and traditions that appeal directly to the emotions and to the imagination ? Here is the Garden of Gethsemane, with its eight old olive trees consecrated to love and adoration. They are the self-same venerable trees that overshadowed Him in His Hour of Agony : for tradition —whether Jewish, Mussulman, or Christian—declares, and indeed proves, that the olive throws forth new shoots from

THE MOUNT OF OLIVES.

the old root, and thus it happens these silvery boughs and these gnarled trunks are the same under which He came daily to pray and cry aloud to the Father Who was His strength and His comfort. The Garden of Gethsemane alone deserves two or three visits, for under the shade of these august trees, with their pale shimmering foliage, the great blue Eyes of the Nazarene were often raised to Heaven, seeking strength to control His natural aversion to the sins of men and of earthly things. The Mount of Olives not only contains Gethsemane, the theatre of the greatest of all soul-tragedies, but records half the latter History of Jesus and of Mary which happened upon its slopes. Half-way up the hillside a few demolished stones mark the spot where once stood the chapel known as *Dominus Flevit*, "The Lord hath wept." Here, one bright spring afternoon, Jesus looking towards Jerusalem—then still in all its pride and glory, though hardened and impenitent—wept as He foresaw her impending Doom. Here, too, forty years after the agonising Death of the Saviour, the Emperor Titus encamped and hurled against Jerusalem the vigorous blows of his Ninth Legion—and Zion fell, her people massacred, her temples destroyed, and hundreds of thousands of Jews made to realise the curse they had called down upon their own heads. Close by the Garden of Gethsemane, Mary of Nazareth, having reached the mature age of seventy-three, stood face to face once more with the Angel Gabriel, who, while gently offering her a palm branch, told her that her earthly course was almost run, and that she would soon ascend in glory to Heaven. Humbly and obediently did she bend her head, even as she had done in her girlhood when the same angelic visitor stood before her. A white rock marks the spot where, according to the legend, in her flight Heavenward she dropped her girdle, which was picked up and treasured by the Apostle Thomas. About twenty paces off there stands a church into which one descends by a wide steep staircase to find our Lady's tomb. In this chapel, which also contains the remains of St. Joachim and St. Anne, and which belongs to the Greek rite, there are unceasing Masses, sermons, litanies, and prayers. In the grotto, where nothing now remains but the grave-cloth which had enveloped the body of the Mother of our Lord, people are ever praying. On the right-hand side of the Mount of Olives, and quite close to Gethsemane, is the Cave of Agony, where He Who was to perish, that Humanity might live and be saved, bathed the ground with His Bloody Sweat. In this chapel, at dawn, a Franciscan Friar comes and offers up the Divine Sacrifice which, happily, still belongs to the Latin rite. A white stone on the hillside marks the place where the Apostles slept; and at the foot of a little pathway stands a column showing where Jesus was betrayed by Judas. Indeed the Mount of Olives must be visited slowly and several times, for the sudden shock of so many impressions is almost beyond endurance! No one should fail to visit the Carmelite Church of the *Pater* at the top of the Mount, where, for the second time—the first having been on the Mount of Beatitudes in Galilee, when He preached that marvellous Sermon on the Mount, which every Christian should know by heart, and whose sublimity all philosophers are compelled to acknowledge—Jesus, at their request, taught His disciples how to pray. Joining His Hands, He uttered that Divine supplication, the "Our Father," which makes all men brothers, forgives all trespasses done unto us and implores forgiveness for the trespasses we commit against Him! Up to a few years back this place was a desert, but the munificent and pious Adelaide de Bossi, Duchess de Bouillon, a Frenchwoman and daughter of a great Italian, Carlo de Bossi, founded this convent of Carmelite nuns, with its Church of the Pater. The courtyard is full of lovely flowers, the cloister is lined with precious marbles, and the white, silent church has the Lord's Prayer written in thirty-six languages upon its walls. On the right-hand side, in a white mortuary chapel, lies the foundress, the Duchess of Bouillon, and in an urn beside her rests the heart of her father. Behind the grating of their convent, the cloistered nuns, who follow the strict rule of the ardent Theresa of Avila, pray unceasingly; but they are never seen by the outside world. This Church of the Pater, so white, so silent, and so flower-bedecked, lends itself admirably to spiritual contemplation and abstraction.

Finally, it was from the Mount of Olives that Jesus

ascended into Heaven, thereby fulfilling the prophecies and accomplishing His Divine Mission. One has but to ascend to the top of the mountain to find the sacred spot where, as foretold by the Prophets, the Easter Mount, that witnessed His grief and humiliation, saw also His glory! Alas! the place of the Ascension is occupied by an ugly, meaningless mosque: wherein, however, with customary tolerance, the dervish who is in charge of this cold, unadorned, and unpoetical Turkish place of worship opens its doors to Christians. On Ascension Day the Franciscans are allowed to bring their altar and sacerdotal ornaments for the celebration of Mass. Backsheesh, which obtains all favours in this land of Turkish rule, enables any priest who has a portable altar to come and say Mass whenever he likes in the mosque on the Mount. In the meantime, on its threshold, the Christian, anxious to forget so ridiculous and monstrous an anomaly as a mosque in such an essentially Christian place, endeavours to picture to himself the scene of our Lord's Ascension. The Mount of Olives, which at its base was once the place of tears, sadness, and agony, is here bright with a glorious and resplendent light. Looking skyward, Heaven itself seems to bend gently over the Mount of Suffering and Triumph; the mosque behind us vanishes, and the Mount seems isolated and flooded by a shower of radiance. The ground at our feet is thickly strewn with little violet flowers that embroider with their tiny chalices this otherwise barren spot.

II.

GETHSEMANE.

No longer the enclosed, suffocating walls of a church, however magnificently they may be decorated, thanks to the piety of the faithful: no stone edifice, oppressing the heart, and limiting the gaze that seeks a wider horizon: but a garden in the free open air, full of bright flowers that cover the mountain slope, under the pure vault of Heaven, which in Palestine assumes so tender a blue as to appear almost white; a garden in the sweet light of an Oriental dawn, still glittering with the diamonds shed by the nightly dews; a garden rich with the joyous song of birds—this is Gethsemane! It is so fair a spot that it attracts you even from afar, so that you are involuntarily drawn towards it as by a magnet. Once within its enchanting maze you feel spellbound, as by some mysterious unseen power from which you cannot escape. What is this magic garden, after all? It contains eight ancient olive trees: the olive never dies but springs up afresh from the same root; so that those selfsame trees may be well said to have sheltered Jesus as He sat beneath their branches praying and teaching His disciples. Eight olive trees; but so old and imposing that two of them are as majestic as the grandest of oaks. Their trunks are enormous, one measuring nearly nine yards in circumference at the base; its widespread branches shade with their glistening grey-green foliage a greater part of the orchard of Gethsemane. Their bark no longer looks like wood, but seems rather to be made of stone, or even rock, being of the same colour and equally hard, and covered with cracks and furrows. Above these seemingly petrified trunks spread branches that are bright and fresh with ever-changing foliage. These dear old olives, which cluster together in this never-to-be-forgotten garden, still bear abundant fruit! Under them, thanks to the thoughtful and loving care of the Franciscan Fathers, the brightest and most lovely beds of flowers are ever in luxuriant bloom. And thus in this parched land the Garden of Gethsemane forms a sort of enchanted oasis, its fresh beauty contrasting exquisitely with the arid desert that surrounds it. The contrast between the sweet-scented flowers and the mighty old olive trees that afford them shade, reminded me irresistibly of childhood and age standing side by side. It is fascinating indeed to watch the shadows pass over those ancient trunks which have seen two thousand years and more; and, turning from their majestic growth, gaze down upon the little white roses with their fragile petals, the rose-

GETHSEMANE.

tinted geraniums streaked with red, the charming blue periwinkles, and the great pink lilies that bloom so stately upon their long wand-like woolly stems, and look like chalices full of sweet perfume filling the air with fragrance. The old olive trees may have endured many thousands of years—while these sweet-scented flowers live but a day! Their graceful youth, passed by the side of these ancient trees, is ever renewed. With their delightful gaiety of colour and form they seem to reverence the austere giants that so lovingly protect them from wind and sun. They have seen many strange things and heard so many heartfelt prayers! The caress of the flowers seems to cling to the aged trees, and a smile of eternal springtide to cheer their grand old age.

Daily did Jesus, followed by His disciples, abandon Jerusalem and its ungrateful and rebellious people, and, passing by the Temple (which disgusted Him, since within its walls the Law had become a mask for every kind of hypocrisy and cupidity), come unto the Garden of Gethsemane. The Prophet of Galilee loved dearly to teach His disciples very near the slopes of the Hills where His Word sounded freer and more far-reaching amid the pure beauties of Nature. Half-way up the Mount of Olives was the entrance to this orchard, the owner of which was a personal friend from whom He had received permission to enter whenever He chose. Here, during the enchanting Eastern afternoons, He was wont to come and sit under the shade of these olive trees. How often must He have raised His Eyes to Heaven, seeking through their silvery foliage for that vision of His Father from Whom He gained all the sacred fervour that inspired His teaching! Often must the joyous song of the little birds, twittering in the garden as the sun sank behind Jerusalem, have filled His Heart with infinite tenderness and compassion! With Him came Simon Peter, whom He trusted so implicitly that even his act of base denial shook not His faith in him; John and James, whom He called the " sons of lightning " because of the ardour of their apostolate, were also with Him, as well as the lesser disciples. Hither, likewise, came the holy women: Mary of Cleophas, who loved and served Him from the first moment she heard His preaching; Mary of Magdala, the impassioned sinner of Galilee, whose sins He pardoned, and in whom one of the most stupendous spiritual miracles was wrought; Mary of Bethany, sister of Martha and Lazarus, on whose soul His words fell like a spell; Susannah, the wife of Conza, and several others, so faithful, tender, and true, that they remained with Him even unto the end. To all these He spake under the wide-spreading olive trees. In the entrancing springtime peculiar to this land, which still retains the blessing of its Lord, and whose outward aspect had not as yet been altered by any catastrophe, Jesus often taught a loving group of His followers, who listened with humble and devout attention to His teaching and preaching of that higher and nobler life and future in which they hoped and believed all Humanity would share and by which it would be regenerated. There He spake those wondrous words of the Lord's Prayer. Leaning against one of those ancient trunks and looking towards Mount Zion, refulgent with the glory of David and Solomon, Jesus preached the New Law of charity and equality, a Law which, in the name of the Divine promise, strengthens souls against human misfortune. Ay! under these thy branches, O olive trees! in this quiet garden of Palestine, those sublime words were uttered, the echoes of which have spread to the furthermost ends of the earth!

The name of Gethsemane is for ever associated with the most terrible suffering that ever transpierced a martyr's heart. The dreadful night of pain and overpowering anguish spent by Christ in this orchard was infinitely harder and more tragic than the Agony on the Cross itself! He came hither on that fateful night, His Sacred Heart oppressed with grief; but His disciples understood Him not, and could therefore offer Him no comfort. He bade them wake and watch, for He was sore troubled and needed their sympathy. "The spirit was willing, but the flesh was weak," and so they fell into a deep sleep. Thus He remained in this solitary garden where He had spent so many happy hours, alone in the darkness of the night that enveloped Jerusalem like a shroud. Alone with Heaven and with the tremendous problems that moved His Spirit, He sought in prayer to unite Himself with the Father Who sent Him. Unutterable sadness and discouragement overwhelmed Him when, rising, He went and called His disciples, only to find them asleep. Bitterly He reproached them that they could not watch a single hour. They slept on. Alone, ever alone, and defenceless against the horrible mistrust He felt of men and things. Ah! during this night of gloomy foreboding, of immense uncertainty and solitude, unaided by human sympathy, Jesus saw as in an all-embracing vision the boundless misery of human nature; all the roots of unconquerable wickedness which no religious or moral teaching can ever quite eradicate; all the hereditary instincts against which there is not sufficient power to struggle; all the inherent weakness of mind and body. Himself ready to fight the battle and to offer Himself a living Sacrifice, during this long and terrible night Jesus weighed Man in the balance, only to find him so deplorably frail, so wanting in courage, so defenceless against temptation, so tossed about by every wind, so deaf to His great teaching, that at one moment He almost despaired of saving him; and at this agonising thought His human nature was convulsed in such a manner that Blood gushed forth from every pore. In this solitary orchard of Gethsemane He asked Himself that most heartrending question—whether, after all, His teaching had been in vain, or mere words wafted away by the wind. Had the seed of the Word He had so carefully sown, as in the parable, fallen on the dry rock of selfishness, only to be scattered by birds of rapine? He asked Himself whether all His earthly career, dedicated to the glorious ideal of renovating the spirit of Humanity, had been but a failure; had He indeed Lived and Suffered to no purpose, and would His Death and Sacrifice upon the Cross also prove unavailing? Thus, given over to the utmost humiliation, did Jesus meekly join His Hands and pray to the Father of all Mercies that this cup might pass from Him; and thus this garden heard the most desponding cry of anguish that ever fell from human lips. How long was this night in Gethsemane? Let us ask those who, like their Lord, have passed such nights as this, immersed in the profoundest desolation, seeing all their hopes crushed into dust beneath their feet. Let us question those who have suffered in a similar manner without light or help, their glory and fortune vanished ; or let us consult those great souls who, having passed through their night of Gethsemane, have experienced all the uselessness of their efforts, the futility of their undertakings, and the worthlessness of their works. How can such nights be measured by time ? Those few simple words of the Gospel impress one by their startling directness, as they describe the moral torments of the Saviour and the crushing Agony of His Spirit during those terrible hours spent in Gethsemane. The tragedy enacted alone, in utter darkness, was boundless, unfathomable, so that when the Son of Man came forth and offered His cheek to receive the treacherous kiss of Judas, He had won the victory, but He was already Dead.

The sepulchre of Joseph of Arimathæa did but enclose the Body ; but Gethsemane heard the Voice and saw the Tears, and is thereby rendered for us more sacred than any other sacred spot. None can pass beneath the shadow of its ancient trees without a feeling akin to fear.

III.

THE WAY OF THE CROSS.

HE who wishes to pursue the " Way of the Cross " should begin his pilgrimage, not from the house of Annas, the high priest (who deliberated and determined to put our Lord to death), or from the palace of Caiaphas (who was only an instrument in the hands of his father-in-law, Annas), but from the house, or *lithostratos*, of Pontius Pilate, the humane Roman governor, or *prætor*, whose several efforts to save Jesus were unavailing. The pilgrim who selects this path, every step of which is associated with some incident in the

THE WAY OF THE CROSS.

closing act of the fatal Tragedy, and who wishes moreover to examine and meditate on each point of interest, will have to employ rather more than an hour to reach Golgotha, the place of death in the Church of Calvary. The road is still, in many places, fairly steep, whilst in others it consists of a series of steps—as, for instance, in front of the Coptic Bishop's house, where Jesus fell under the weight of the Cross for the third time : and again, before the house of the Holy Veronica. After the fashion of all the roads in Jerusalem, it is paved with long narrow stones which make walking exceedingly irksome and tiring. The Via Dolorosa, being far more precipitous than an average ill-paved country road, takes the Christian pilgrim rather more than an hour to traverse from end to end. How much longer must it have seemed to the Martyr ! At that time it must have been much steeper than now, probably not paved at all, and, moreover, in a very bad condition, as were all the roads in those days ; and He was laden with the weight of His Cross ! He had passed the preceding days in vigil and profound emotion ; the two last nights must have been especially terrible : for He had been so lately bound to the column, scourged and outraged. His Soul was full of anguish, and His strength was failing. Death upon the Cross was one of the most awful punishments conceivable, lasting sometimes as many as three days, when the legs and arms of the condemned, if still living, were broken. Thus, to Jesus, as He dragged Himself along the cruel Way of the Cross, it must have seemed interminable.

The Prætorium of Pontius Pilate is now a Turkish barrack, filled with Mohammedan foot-soldiers. The Turks, with their habitual courtesy to those who give them money, offered no opposition to our visiting the exact spot where the Via Dolorosa, the Way of Suffering, begins. Every Friday the Franciscan Fathers, followed by a band of pilgrims and other devout persons, start the " Way of the Cross " from this point, pausing to pray before each of its fourteen " stations." A flight of twenty steps leads up to the Turkish barracks. On the door being opened, after passing beneath a broad flag bearing the White Star and the Crescent, you enter a large courtyard. In this court, which is stacked with guns, and where the soldiers clean their cooking utensils and wooden bowls, is the Prætorium, or *lithostratos*, where Jesus was condemned. Who can forget Pilate's last words after he had washed his hands: " I am innocent of the blood of this just person " ? Well, they were uttered from above the wall immediately opposite to you. It was in this very courtyard, where the guns shine so brightly in the sunlight, and the Turkish soldiers polish their buckles, that the Jews cried out tumultuously, " His blood be on us, and on our children ! " Then Jesus descends into the roadway, the full weight of His Cross upon His shoulders : the site of the stairway is marked by a white stone set in the wall, the steps having been translated to Rome, where they still stand close to the Lateran Basilica. The ascent begins : the soldiers surge round the two thieves, Cosma and Disma, while He Who has been mocked as " King of the Jews," reviving by a superhuman effort, momentarily recovers His strength. His Face is deadly pale. His exhausted Frame is bathed in sweat. Blood streams from the Wounds inflicted on His Head by the Crown of Thorns, but when He comes to the spot where the street from the Prætorium enters the Damascus road, He sinks to the ground for the first time—the exact place is still indicated by a split column. Here the road is wide and filled with foot-passengers, heavily laden camels and donkeys, and half-naked Arabs going to the neighbouring bazaar. The Martyr rises, and about a hundred yards further on a group of women come forward, among whom is the Virgin Mother, seeking her Son, Who says unto her, " Salve Mater ! " But she answers Him not, and, overcome with horror and grief, falls back fainting in the arms of the other women. This touching incident happened, according to ancient tradition, in a narrow and little frequented lane beyond which stands a small chapel dedicated to " Our Lady of the Swoon." After this meeting with His mother, Jesus' strength fails rapidly : but the soldiery are in haste to finish their appalling task : for Easter is at hand, and they wish to enjoy the feast at their leisure. Therefore, finding a peasant handy, named Simon of Cyrene, they load him with the Cross. This occurs before a grey

THE WAY OF THE CROSS.

house where the road turns: the Cyrenian lightens our Lord's burden for a little, thereby relieving His aching Shoulders. From this point onwards the road grows steeper and the steps begin: and while the Sufferer, fainting and bathed in Sweat and Blood, ascends them, at each step calling on death to release Him, a woman comes forward from her house. She is called Berenice and is a Jewess. Fearlessly the tender-hearted woman advances through the soldiers and with a cloth wipes the emaciated Face of Christ. On that linen the impress of the Divine Face still remains, and from that day she is no longer called Berenice, but *Vera-icon*, the " true image." Her little house is still standing at the top of a flight of steps under a dark archway. It is very gloomy, being cut out of the living rock—perchance some day a chapel in her honour will be built here to commemorate this tender act of charity. About sixty-six yards beyond the house of Veronica, along a street which was the Road of the Gate of Judgment, Jesus falls for the second time. A number of little white houses enclose the place; on the window ledge of one of which is a white rose bush in bloom, doubtless tended by some dark-eyed woman of Jerusalem, on whose doorstep lads are playing and chattering in Arabic. Under a shower of blows, our Lord again tries to rise: His agony excites such profound pity, that, at sight of it, a group of women standing by are moved to tears. Then the great prophecy falls from His Lips, and He exclaims, " Daughters of Jerusalem, weep not for me, but weep for yourselves and for your children." Having thus spoken, He resumes His weary journey: the road is long and steep: already the place of infamy and death, Golgotha, looms in sight: but to reach it yet another effort is needed. In our time this road is closed in by buildings of a later date: and he who desires to follow Jesus during the whole length of the way, must make several turns, even retracing his steps, in order to reach one of the last " stations "—a high platform, close to Calvary, where Jesus sinks for the third time. This place, forming the corner of the Bazaar, is one of the dirtiest and most overcrowded in Jerusalem. A sense of distress fills the heart at the thought that so sacred a spot as this, one consecrated by the last spasm of anguish He endured before He reached Calvary, should be crowded with Arabs and Mohammedans, with Copts and Abyssinians, and squalid Jews, who glare at the Christian with eyes of scorn and hatred.

※　　※　　※　　※　　※　　※

The last scene of all took place above within the Church of Calvary, opposite the rock which was to receive our Lord's body. A large stone, placed on the ground, marks the spot where Jesus was stripped, and where the soldiers cast lots for His garments. A little further on, in the same church, a square of mosaic indicates the place where He was actually crucified; a few yards beyond, towards the east, is a cylindrical hole lined with silver, which indicates the spot where the Cross was raised. It was turned towards the west, and thus the Eyes of the dying Christ were fixed upon that part of the world where His faith was to be founded.

And now the sad scene is nearly over: the seven words are spoken: He has pardoned the good thief: He has bidden farewell to His mother and to John and has yielded up His spirit to His Father. It is finished!

Here stands the altar of the *Stabat Mater*, erected by pious Christians to commemorate the place where Jesus Christ was taken down from the Cross, and His body laid across His mother's knees. Upon yon marble slab, the Stone of Anointment, His body was washed and embalmed with myrrh and aloes. Twenty paces further on is the small garden of Joseph of Arimathæa, where, in a newly-made tomb, He was laid.

Night is falling!

The Via Dolorosa is ended!

IV.

CALVARY.

The Church of Calvary forms a part of that of the Holy Sepulchre. Jesus was crucified on a hillock called Golgotha, which signifies the place of a skull; for here, according to tradition, the head of Adam was buried. The Gospels distinctly tell us that the garden in which was the new sepulchre of the family of Joseph of Arimathæa adjoined Golgotha. The Jews were well pleased that the disciples should remove His body without delay, for Easter was at hand, and they could not celebrate the Passover if they were contaminated by the touch of a dead body. The Mother of Sorrows, the pious women, the Apostle John, and the good Joseph, had not far to carry their beloved, and thus He was laid to rest not many steps from the scene of His martyrdom.

It was St. Helena the Great who conceived the idea of enclosing the places consecrated by Christ's Passion under one roof. But, in order to do this, it was necessary to cut away a part of the elevation on which the Son of Man gave up the ghost, and thus the present church was founded only on a part of Golgotha, the rest being built on an artificial mound. The Church of Golgotha lies to your right as you enter that of the Holy Sepulchre, and in the darkest part of the basilica are two steep stone steps leading up to it. It is ever enveloped in gloom, dimly lighted by the flicker of the lamps that alone gleam upon the silver and gold Byzantine icons on the High Altar; for the place of the Crucifixion belongs to the Schismatic Greeks. Underneath the altar is a silver star worn away by the kisses of the faithful, which records the place where the Cross was raised. Hard by, to right and left, are two stones showing where the crosses of the good and the bad thief were erected; and to the right, under a covering of metal, can yet be seen the wide, deep cleft in the rock that opened when Jesus, with a loud cry,

4

yielded up His Spirit and the earth was rent in twain. This fissure goes deep down into the soil, and appears to have been caused by some great earthquake. St. Matthew says, " And, behold, the veil of the temple was rent in twain from the top to the bottom, and the earth did quake, and the rocks rent."

Thank God, every memorable act in the life of Christ is now commemorated by a sanctuary, a chapel, or a memorial; but surely Golgotha might well have been left without a temple ! The little hillock which He ascended so wearily, bending under His heavy burden : where He was stripped of His garments, for which the soldiers cast lots (the coat which Jesus wore was seamless, and woven by Mary, His mother, in one piece) : where He passed three hours in agony on the Cross : where, dying, He prayed for His enemies : this mound, rather than hill, ought to have been allowed to remain intact. A plain cross would have been the noblest of temples, the most matchless of altars. The cross standing here alone under the clear, blue-white sky, which no cloud ever traverses throughout the course of the long Syrian summer, would have thrown its shadow athwart the lonesome landscape ; and even if in winter it was beaten upon by wind and rain, it would none the less have stood majestic and salient against the horizon as an everlasting symbol of Christian faith.

He who wishes to follow the rest of the " Way of the Cross " by commencing it at the very beginning of the Road of Suffering, should not start from the Prætorium of Pontius Pilate, where our Lord received His unjust sentence, but from the never-to-be-forgotten Garden of Gethsemane, where He endured His bitterest agony. The pilgrim can thus traverse the road He passed along amid the glare of smoking torches, abandoned by nearly all His disciples, for only two or three followed Him afar : whilst Judas Iscariot, upon whom He had steadily fixed his tender, luminous blue Eyes, had fled, carrying with him the price of his treachery—a purse of thirty pieces of silver. He may now ascend, even as Jesus did, to the beginning of the Valley of Jehoshaphat, which lies between the Mount of Olives and Mount Zion ; can cross, as He did, the little

CALVARY.

stone bridge over the torrent of Cedron, and toiling up the same steep steps leading to Sion and to the house of Caiaphas, thereby realise every scene in the heartbreaking story of the Passion, from the night passed at the house of Annas to the scene in that of Caiaphas, when Simon Peter, whom He loved so well and in whom He had placed His trust, thrice denied Him. Kissing each of the " stations " of the Via Dolorosa, the pilgrim at length reaches the hillock upon which the awful drama came to its appalling close at the ninth hour of a Friday in *Nisan*. Here a cross, and a cross only, would have sufficed to afford him a vision of that supreme moment when, by reason of so much injustice and cruelty, the very earth was shaken to its depths. The white calcareous rock, with its red veinings, should have remained as it was, so that our wondering eyes could have gazed upon the enormous mass of stone rent throughout its entire length.

Of what avail is a small, dark chapel in which even the Latin rites are not performed : where one cannot see and can scarcely breathe : wherein the wondrous scene of Golgotha is completely obliterated from the mind ? Those who in fervent faith come from all parts of the Christian world to prostrate themselves here, could surely not have worn away an entire hill, as it was feared they might have done the rock of the Holy Sepulchre. God has not said that prayer is heard only within the narrow walls of a church. It is so good to pray in the open air, under the ancient trees of Gethsemane, beneath whose shadow Christ so often prayed : or on those flowery banks of Jordan in the fields He loved so dearly !

One day, by the well of Samaria, a woman ingenuously asked Jesus whether it were best to pray in the Temple, as the Jews insisted, or upon the mountain top, as said the Samaritans, and He answered her that from henceforth people should no longer pray exclusively in Temples made by hands, or on the mountain tops, but in any place where reigns the Spirit of Truth and Light.

Oh ! if only Golgotha had remained as it was—bare, austere, and tragic : not narrowed in and filled with darksome icons enclosed in silver frames blackened by the smoke of many lamps : while the marvellous crack in the rock is hidden under a coating of wax, dripped from the tapers the pilgrims press down upon it, in their endeavour to obtain a better glimpse of the fissure ! Oh ! how the heart would rejoice if, under the clear heavens, without having to be challenged by Turkish custodians and soldiers, it were possible to contemplate in the freshness of dawn, in the tender warmth of twilight, the place where He ended His life ! How rejoiced thereby would be the restless soul, that only longs for the clearest and most direct impressions.

The faith of St. Helena and of her time was so fervent, so loving, so pure, so perfectly simple, and, at the same time, so luxuriously pagan, that it could only be satisfied by the erection of a magnificent building, rich in marbles and precious stones. St. Helena had thirty-three temples built over the Holy Places : how, therefore, could she dream of omitting Golgotha ? Later on, these basilicas were destroyed and again and again rebuilt, but no one imagined that Calvary ought to be left a barren hill, adorned only by a cross, a cross that might have been seen from the hills surrounding Jerusalem, and on which no eye could gaze without tears ! Down below in the Church of the Holy Sepulchre, on the left-hand side, is a small iron grating surrounding a stone. About forty or fifty paces from it, and opposite Golgotha, stood the faithful and sorrowing women, tearfully watching their dying Lord.

They at least could see Him, but we cannot even behold the symbol of His suffering : the gloomy chapel with its smoke-blackened icons but vexes the spirit and limits the power of the imagination.

V.

THE LAMENT OF ISRAEL.

As I have already said, every Friday a procession of Christians, starting from the Prætorium, passes through the

THE LAMENT OF ISRAEL.

streets of Jerusalem, kneeling and praying at every one of the fourteen "stations," and thereby performing what is known as the "Way of the Cross." At each "station" they recall the heartrending episode it records; the fateful dialogue between Pontius Pilate and the surging mob of angry Jews, "What then shall I do with Jesus which is called Christ?" And they answering said, "His blood be on us and on our children." When Pilate again exclaimed: "I am innocent of the blood of this just person." And thus is fulfilled every Friday throughout the year this Jewish imprecation with deepest and saddest testimony. By a strange coincidence, too, on Fridays, the Jews who inhabit Jerusalem, about thirty thousand in number, close their shops and places of business, lock up their dwellings and quit their malodorous quarters, and the city, except in the Christian districts, is deserted. The markets are closed: the last camels, with empty sacks across their humps, have gone home towards Bethlehem, Jericho, or St. John-of-the-Mountain. The ancient Solima, the city of David and Solomon, is wrapped in silence: the breath of Israel seems to have swept its streets: the small Nazarene quarter, that of Jesus, is entirely overrun by the Jews in the performance of their rites. Whither have the pale-faced, thin, violet-lipped, the sad, proud-eyed people of Zion fled? The Christians returning from the Via Dolorosa regain their hotels or the Franciscan convent, to rest after their exciting pilgrimage of the "Way of the Cross." Later in the afternoon they are reminded by their faithful guides that they should go and witness the most pathetic of sights, the "Wailing of the Jews." Every Friday the Jewish population, which throughout the rest of the week works so hard, bargains so fiercely over a matter of half a *piastre* (rather more than a penny), or over a Greek *parcà* (rather less than half a farthing), which feeds so sparingly, sleeps so little, is so silent, obstinate, ever increasing in numbers and wealth, abandons business and trade to give vent to its pent-up feelings by weeping and wailing before the walls of its erstwhile time-honoured Temple. There is no stranger, sadder, or more moving sight on earth than this weekly "Wailing of the Jews" of Jerusalem.

A wall! Not an ordinary wall, but a lofty, overpowering mass of Cyclopean brickwork : is all that now remains of the Temple of Solomon ; of the Seat of the Mosaic Law ; of that Temple whose grandeur and majesty fills the Scriptures. Only a wall—but so magnificent, so colossal, that the sonorous descriptions of it do not appear exaggerated; and the eye raised to take in its height is quickly lowered, as if humbled by the spectacle of so much might and strength. The stones of which the wall of the Temple is made are long, wide, and thick, and are more like huge slabs, evenly placed one above the other, forming a sheer rock, square, polished, heavy, and overwhelmingly strong. All else has been demolished : did not Jesus say that He could destroy the Temple and build it up again in three days ? Nothing remains of its rich inlaid woods, ivories, and precious stones, which made it so bewilderingly bright and lovely : only this wall is left standing to show what the Temple must have been, and the power of the Hand which crumbled it to dust. These huge slabs alone bear witness to the past glory of Israel, and, in order that the curse might seem the more tragic, Fate has decreed that this wall, which testifies to the greatness of Moses and Solomon, to the pride and splendour of a nation, should now be the support of the left wing of the Mosque of Omar !

The Turks, during the reign of Omar, made use of the foundations of the Temple to build a magnificent mosque, the most important in Islam, after the one at Mecca, which contains the Prophet's tomb, and that of Medina. The wall, which was covered with costly woods, carbuncles, and emeralds, and inlaid work of gold and copper : the sacred wall which had witnessed the solemn rites of the Law of Moses has now become the prop of a mosque, whose only ornaments are straggling Mohammedan inscriptions and a series of blue and yellow tiles running along the great cornice of its interior. The wall looks on to a narrow, dirty alley, where its huge grey stones contrast strangely with the neighbouring small houses and squalid huts. The glory of Solomon has vanished ; the greatness of the Jewish people is no more ; that sacred wall which heard the Judaic prophecies and prayers, which was the

THE LAMENT OF ISRAEL.

ideal cradle of the Law, is now polluted by Mohammedans. The Jews who come every Friday to wail and weep, never enter the Mosque of Omar, which they hold in horror, for it is said that the Book of the Law was buried underneath the peristyle, and they fear to enter lest they might, inadvertently, tread it under their feet. They cannot, moreover, bear to see the Crescent shining over the place where the Ark of the Covenant once was venerated ; or to see the *mirhab* on the site of the Tabernacle. Every Friday, women, children, old men and young, set out for the narrow lane where King Solomon's mighty wall still endures. The women wear a kind of toque of silk or wool over their hair, and above it a light woollen shawl with a flowery pattern, in the folds of which they hide half their faces. The Russian and Polish Jews wear a fur cap ; others, the French and English, a black silk cap; and some still wear the real old Hebrew *Zimarra*. Along the houses opposite the wall of Solomon there are stones and benches upon which the old people and children sit, praying and reading their holy books. And all along the wall itself, with their foreheads pressed against it, is a crowd of women, their shawls thrown back from their heads, with shoulders bent, weeping in silence ; and thus the cold, smooth wall gradually becomes saturated with tears. Two or three hundred people at a time, men and women, congregate there, remaining ten minutes or a quarter of an hour, sobbing silently. When they have finished their wail, two or three hundred other people take their places, beating their heads against the stone, praying and weeping; and as they do so they recite, in a dismal monotone, a doleful yet touching litany that begins thus :—

> " For our destroyed Temple—Here we come and weep.
> For our fallen glory—Here we come and weep.
> For our exterminated people—Here we come and weep."

The rabbi, or some other ancient, pious and fanatical servant of Israel, says the first part of this dreary dirge, to which the mourning people make answer. And as the narrative of their misfortunes continues and all the fulness of the misery of the Jewish race, with no fatherland, no nationality, and no king, is unrolled in one great lamentation, the wailing increases: since nothing now remains to Israel of her vanished glory and prosperity but these rocks, piled one upon the other to remind her that she was once the chosen people of God. To these poor souls this fragment of the wall of their Temple is a sort of huge sepulchre in which their nationality, their pride, and their history lie buried! If a Christian approaches they never turn round to look at him, and he, amazed and touched by what he beholds, pauses: then, reverence taking the place of curiosity, he passes on his way, anxious not to disturb the mourners. Barely an hour ago he recalled the fierce words of the assassins of Jesus: the Blood which they shed has sown the seeds of war, fire, disease, and persecution, and now nothing remains to the Hebrews of their mystical inheritance but this poor remnant of a crumbling wall—and even this is no longer theirs, since it belongs to Mahomet!

Out here, in the cold open air, in a narrow, filthy alley, their feet in the mire, looking like so many whipped curs, they kiss these stones and weep over them in the presence of a crowd of unfeeling onlookers, Turks and Christians. They endeavour to stifle their sobs, but, none the less, the air is filled with the sound of their wailing and with the rhythm of their sighs. Phlegmatic English tourists watch them through their eyeglasses, and when I was last there an impertinent, obstinate old lady, riding donkey-back, insisted upon inspecting the entire line, thereby greatly disturbing their piteous lament.

Strange and touching spectacle! Weeping is surely contagious, and in this dark alley tears seem bidden to flow almost involuntarily by the subtle hypnotic influence of Solomon's wall, where the Jews grieve over a real woe, whilst expiating the greatest of all crimes. They only find in religion a fresh source of sorrow; even as we discover therein our chiefest consolation! How can anyone deride them? True, they killed the Lord; but they are so wretched, so abject, notwithstanding their stubbornness, so forlorn in spite of their courage. In the presence of this public expression of their trouble the sense of the immensity of their punishment is quite overwhelming. They are hemmed in

THE VALLEY OF JEHOSHAPHAT.

by a cruel destiny, and this, their weekly wailing in the presence of the ruins of their Temple, is marvellously significant. After a lapse of two thousand years, the Jewish people are still expiating the Curse !

VI.

THE VALLEY OF JEHOSHAPHAT.

As you drive out of the Holy City towards the bright little town of Bethlehem, you catch glimpses of the dismal Valley of Jehoshaphat ; and if you ride to the fresh, shady, happy village of St. John-of-the-Mountain, where the Baptist was born, yet another dreary expanse of this same valley overpowers you with a sense of inexpressible sadness. So, too, when you leave Jerusalem on horseback to undertake the venturesome journey to Jericho, the Dead Sea, and the Jordan, ere reaching Bethany, the funereal and silent Valley of Jehoshaphat again spreads before you. Throughout the wearisome journey to Jericho this same dreary vision haunts you, as, indeed, it also does every time you ascend the Mount of Olives. Should you, perchance, seek to evade it, your officious dragoman, each time you pass by or near, is sure to remind you of its presence and inform you that you have it still to visit. In vain you struggle against the depressing influences and try to resist the fascination of its mournful associations. The less impressionable side of your nature makes unavailing efforts to overcome the spell cast by this black, lonesome, desolate valley, where, notwithstanding the deep blue of the sky and the brightness of the sun, you feel an overwhelming sense of melancholy ; an irrepressible longing to give vent to these pent-up feelings takes possession of you, as, with a heart full of sad memories and your imagination filled with images of horror and despair, you descend into the Valley of Jehoshaphat.

Do not imagine that this valley is of vast extent, since its greatest length is but two and a half miles, its width about two hundred and twenty yards. But what matter in this case paltry measurements and details ? As you slowly descend by a narrow, steep, and stony pathway into its depths you seem to lose sight of every joy and charm of life, and to be entering the kingdom of everlasting darkness. No trees, flowers, or grasses grow in this arid vale : no sort of vegetation mantles its stern rocks and rugged stones. Its entire western side is filled with Jewish tombs, so numerous and closely packed as to leave no room to bury any more of the dead sent here from all parts of the world. The dreariness of the darksome valley is not, however, due to this mighty agglomeration of nameless tombs. They do not give one the impression of a cemetery, and, moreover, a burial-ground is not necessarily dismal, but often has something definite, precise, and limited about it which prevents the mind from wandering into those regions where the dreary breath of death alone reigns. A funereal silence ever broods over it. Its sides rise like the walls of an abyss, where not even the soft radiance of the stars can penetrate. The little daylight that reaches it is pale and cold, and seems to have lost all brightness. The sky appears so distant, motionless, and white, excluding every ray of hope or aspiration, that, looking up, the eyes are glad to turn from it to seek the darkness below. Not a soul passes this way. Far away, towards the Pool of Siloam, a peasant girl, laden with her pitcher, moves slowly on, seeming rather a shade than a living thing. Solitude here becomes eternal, both as to time and space. Perhaps no living soul dares venture into this gruesome pit, where Christian imagination has fixed the scene of the Last Judgment. A kind of awesome spell possesses the traveller when he has entered this haunted region, and binds him, as it were, by some dread incantation to the stone upon which, tired out and exhausted, he has cast himself. No bird soars over the heights above : the buzz of insect life is hushed. Three huge, weird monuments stand out distinctly among the countless tombs : they are those of Absalom, David's unworthy son ; the tomb of Zachariah, the son of Barachiah ;

and the tomb of St. James the Less. Each has its own peculiar style: that of Absalom seems to emerge direct from the bottom of the valley; those of Zachariah and St. James the Less lean against the rock of which they form part. These three tombs rivet the attention. The Valley of Jehoshaphat is cold and dumb, as though its silence had not been broken for thousands of years, and is more dreary than any other place on earth! He who has obeyed the fatal impulse to descend into this vale of terrors and rest in its colourless atmosphere and dim light amid its unchanging gloom, feels as if no gay colour could ever again gladden his eyes, or perfumed flower delight his senses: the joys of life have no further existence for him! He loses all count of time, forgets the caresses of his children, the smiles of his parents, the soft light in the eyes of his friend, and is lost in a desolate wilderness, which the final Crack of Doom alone can waken into life!

He is indeed bold who descends here—for Jehoshaphat is truly " The Valley of Death!"

VII.

A SUFFERING SHADOW.

I HAD the great happiness of being in Jerusalem on Corpus Christi Day. To those who have spent their childhood in our beautiful Southern clime, where religious sentiment so often finds vent in manifestations of joyous enthusiasm, this festival recalls many a cherished memory. In the sunny South, the Feast of Corpus Christi is ushered in by a merry ringing of bells, for it is the day that divides spring from summer: and remembering it in after life, one thinks of a canopy held up by golden poles, a shower of rose petals falling from every window and balcony, of a sunshine saturated with the odour of fresh flowers, laden with song and with the pungent fumes of incense. The graphic brush of Francesco Paolo Michetti has depicted the brilliant colouring of this great holiday, and many who have become cold and indifferent to religious influences have been deeply touched by his glowing presentment of a cherished event of their youth. Once upon a time this festival was a sort of summer Christmas, or birth of summer, held in the open air in the sunshine, amid the flowers and the smiling faces of women and children: and if customs fade and die, and we perceive with dismay that the rising generation is out of touch with these sweet influences, we of the elder cling all the more tenderly to old forms and recollections.

I was, therefore, delighted to be present at this festival in the modern Zion, the city which, of all others, should be entirely given up to prayer, to the singing of hymns, and to the praise of the Lord, and so I thought to myself how singularly bright and happy Corpus Christi Day should be in the dear land of Jesus. Ah me! I had forgotten that in Jerusalem we were under Turkish rule! I do not mean to insinuate that the Turks in the slightest degree oppose any of the outward manifestations of Christian worship; on the contrary, they reverence the great Prophet Issa and approve of all the Christians do in His honour. Still, Jerusalem *is*, after all, Turkish, and, therefore, solemn Catholic processions are impossible in Mohammedan or, even worse, Jewish quarters. Jerusalem belongs to Mahomet, and the Mosque of Omar, built upon the ruins of the Temple of Solomon, is larger, and, æsthetically speaking, far finer than the Church of the Holy Sepulchre!

The Latins, therefore, hold their modest procession on Corpus Christi Day within the church, though it is none the less carried out in a spirit of intense devotion. The whole Franciscan community take part in it, and last year Father Luigi, of Parma, the very small friar who is general of the very great Franciscan Order, joined in it, quite unobtrusively, taking his place humbly among the other monks. The Church of the Holy Sepulchre, as I have already said, is very large—in fact, enormous—quaint and unique. It consists of seven or eight churches linked

A SUFFERING SHADOW

together, some lofty, others low, square, round, subterranean, Latin, Greek, Coptic, Armenian, light, dark, dim, gloomy, all of them connected at a given point by an uncovered corridor, open to the rain ! This weird aggregation of churches cannot be fully appreciated until after it has been visited several times, though even then one carries away but a vague notion of its dimensions, and it defies you to form any definite idea of its proportions. To specify a few points : in the Church of the Holy Sepulchre, besides the sacred building which contains the Tomb, there is the underground chapel, comprising the remaining sepulchres of the family of Joseph of Arimathæa ; the subterranean chapels of St. Helena, of the Invention of the Cross, and the small chapel of the Tomb of Jesus ; then the chapel of the Easter morning Apparition to Mary Magdalene ; that of the Flagellation ; the Anointing Stone, which is close to the entrance of the principal church ; the Church of Golgotha, which also contains the chapel of the Nailing to the Cross, the Mortuary chapel, and the one where the Body was deposited. Have I omitted others, or are there too many ? No ; Christian piety during the first centuries loved to multiply these memorials, the better to impress the image of the Divine Martyr upon the hearts of men.

I have enumerated these churches and chapels, for the Latin procession has to pass, chanting and praying, through them all. It was to start at three o'clock, and I was already in the church at half-past two. Even then it was full of people, of Christian women from Jerusalem, wrapped in their white muslin cloaks, and often carrying a baby inside, sheltered as in a niche ; of Bethlehemite women, with their refined faces ; of European ladies, so strangely attired ; of English Catholics, with their queer cork helmets bound about with a white muslin handkerchief ; of beggars dressed in dirty rags ; and, above all, of children of all ages and both sexes, for Zion seems to be singularly happy in adding to the human race. The Church of the Holy Sepulchre presented on this high holy day its usual surprising appearance, its strange blending of the mystic and the profane : of fanaticism and indifference :

of the beautiful and the ugly: and was at once squalid and rich, revolting and touching!

The Latin procession started at three o'clock precisely from the Church of St. Mary Magdalene, belonging to the Franciscans. First came the *kavass*, or armed guards of the convent, magnificently attired, and carrying great wands with gold knobs, with which they struck the ground at regular intervals; then the clergy, followed by half the Franciscan community; then the canopy, and under it the Host; and again the rest of the Franciscan monks, a file of children belonging to the Franciscan girls' school, who are taught by the nuns of St. Joseph, came next, and lastly the faithful of all sorts and conditions. This immensely long procession wound with great difficulty through the labyrinth of chapels, amid the mighty pillars, and in and out of the upper and lower sanctuaries. The monks and clergy chanted, and the responses were sung by the nuns and children. At the first halting-place, which was before the Holy Sepulchre, the sun shone down from the high windows, through a cloud of incense, for the day was gloriously brilliant, the charm of the sunny atmosphere enhanced by the voices of innocent children, of fervent monks, and of pious nuns.

Ah, those nuns! Four or five among them dressed in grey with white caps, quietly active, superintending the movements of the children and seeing that they knelt or stood at the right moment and said the responses properly. They moved so noiselessly that they scarcely seemed busy, but went about murmuring prayers all the time. There was one sister, still young and rosy, but more staid than the rest, with such a charming, peaceful expression. She may have been about thirty, and was ever flitting about looking after everything and everybody. With the children, though a little behind them, was yet another nun, who instantly attracted my attention, for she was not dressed in grey like the others, but in black, with a tunic and a *pazienza* similar to that worn by the Carmelite nuns, the daughters of the great St. Theresa of Avila; but her tunic and scapular were black, whereas those of the Carmelites are brown. Her headgear had not the wide, white flaps worn by the Sisters

A SUFFERING SHADOW.

of Charity, but was white and closely fastened under the chin. To what order could she belong? Certainly not to a cloistered one, for her veil was thrown back and hung somewhat limply over her black habit.

This nun, who belonged to no community known to me, was tall and thin, so thin that the folds of her dress floated loosely about her. Her slow walk clearly indicated her prostration, for at each step she was obliged to pause as if she could go no further. Each time she moved on a little she seemed as if about to fall, not abruptly, but gradually fainting and fading away. Her face and hands only were visible. Such a young face—she could not have been more than two-and-twenty—but so thin and transparent that every kind of human suffering seemed to be written upon her pallid countenance. The dark eyes, full of unutterable weariness, looked around without seeming to observe anything: her glance was vague, melancholy, and her eyes were suffused with tears. Her pale lips had a quite heart-rending expression. One hand hung, white, thin, and almost lifeless, down her black dress, the other could scarcely steady the tiny taper it held. Hers were the diaphanous, purple-veined hands of a woman who has wept and suffered much.

How came it about that all of a sudden the procession of Corpus Christi faded from my mind; and that, as soon as my prayer before the Tomb was finished, my whole attention became riveted on this vision of grief? Why could I not remove my eyes from that fragile figure that could barely drag itself along? I cannot tell. I was overcome by a mixture of pity and curiosity and fascinated by the mystery of this silent, suffering nun. Who could she be; from whence did she come; what cause had she for so much woe? I was in the midst of the devout crowd; she among the singing children.

The procession was extremely lengthy, and, moreover, paused continually before each church and chapel, when everyone knelt, prayed, and sang for at least a quarter, or even half an hour. This woman could scarcely be said to kneel, poor soul, but rather to fall prone upon her knees, her head bowed, and quite unable to hold her taper upright.

She looked like an inert mass of black cloth, from which her white and bloodless face was uplifted from time to time as she panted for breath. It was a fearful effort for her to rise, and twice I noticed her turn paler still and close her eyes as if she were about to expire. Those long stations upon her knees must have completely exhausted her failing strength, for at the third chapel she had to lean against the wall for support. Poor, poor thing! Two or three times she even tried to add her feeble voice to the joyous song of the children; but no sound came from her suffering lips, and tears filled her beautiful dark eyes. Once or twice the nun who busied herself with the little girls smiled at her from a distance, and she tried to smile in return—but, oh! how sadly, how wearily! The kindly nun's smiles were encouraging, but the poor sufferer did not seem to gain much comfort or strength from them—she became paler and paler yet, and great dark shadows settled beneath her eyes.

She must be dying, I thought to myself, trembling as if I were battling with a nightmare.

Indeed, it all seemed like a dream: the slow winding procession of monks, clergy, and lay-brothers: the swaying canopy: the files of little children, with gentle, happy eyes, and open lips and throats swelling with song. All this holy mysticism, blended together under the vault of this august temple, wherein the Son of Man was Crucified and was Buried, seemed to me a vision of peace and prayer—whilst through it all flitted the shadow of this poor nun, nursing in her aching heart all the anguish, torture, and misery of the human race. That nun, so frail, so delicate, lost within the dark folds of her habit, her tiny face so worn and drawn by terrible illness (was it of mind or body, who can tell?): those piteous eyes: that tender mouth with the blue lips: those hands so pure and white, falling so listlessly: that nun seemed to be an emblem of all that Human Nature, so limited in its joys, so immeasurable in its suffering, can endure!

The little sister who was minding the children went up to her, speaking in a low tone. She listened with closed eyes, but did not answer: twice she shook her head feebly.

Maybe the words of the nun had given her renewed vigour. At all events, when the procession started off again to enter another chapel, she suddenly rose, and taking a rosary out of her pocket and pressing it to her lips held it there as if it gave her fresh courage and comfort. When she descended to the Church of the Invention of the Cross I felt truly alarmed. To enter this chapel one must go down a long flight of uneven, slippery steps, fifteen or twenty in number, and without a handrail. The long procession wound slowly down towards the Altar of St. Helena, the monks chanting all the time. She apparently could venture no further, but remained kneeling and leaning against an architrave above, under an archway at the top of the steps. I can see her still, her face as white as her coif, her eyelids closed over her dear, sad eyes, her mouth half open, breathing with difficulty—oh! what suffering was here! And see, the hands which hold the taper and the rosary, how they tremble! She was not able to ascend into the Church of Golgotha. The Church of Calvary is situated on a higher floor, and from a balustrade one looks in upon that of the Holy Sepulchre: this is ever steeped in mysterious twilight, for the rays from the candles do not quite illumine it, but merely sparkle on the silver and gold ornaments of the Byzantine icons. A steep, narrow, marble flight leads up to it, so that only a part of the procession was able to enter the very small Chapel of Golgotha. I could hear the voices singing up on high round the gemmed and gilded ring where the Cross had been planted: they reached me—those of the monks, deep and sonorous; those of the acolytes, young and silvery; and those of the children, sweet, quavering, even slightly strident.

The nun did not move. I saw her attempt to do so, but in vain: at the first step she gave way. Strange to say, for a moment her face became suffused with colour, and biting her lips she seemed to be stifling a sob, a sigh, or a cry. Then she appeared to be waiting in agony of suspense for something horrible to happen, her eyes full of fear and wide open, clearly denoting her intense anxiety. Up above they still prayed and sang. Then, by degrees, her face lost its flush, the blood retreated from her cheeks and forehead, leaving her even more ghostlike than before. I noticed from my place behind a pillar two great tears roll from under her lowered lids. Silently, in the gloaming, with bowed head, she wept on : great tears coursed down her thin cheeks from under the dark lashes, falling upon the black dress : she never wiped them away, but let them flow freely : her hand now no longer raised the rosary to her lips, and the taper she held between her fingers was almost burnt out. The little sister, busied with the children, then came to her, and pausing close to the poor sufferer, looked at her anxiously, saying nothing, but taking a handkerchief from her pocket, in a gentle caressing manner wiped away the poor nun's tears, and she, raising her head, thanked her, but only by a slow inclination of the eyes and movement of the lips.

Now the procession had only to pray before the Anointing Stone, where the body of Jesus was embalmed. Millions of kisses have not yet worn it away! Above it burn fifteen silver lamps, and both on entering and leaving the Church of the Holy Sepulchre, everyone prostrates himself upon this sacred stone, touching it with brow and lips. The whole procession surrounded the Stone, bending over and kissing it in turns, under the glow of the ever burning lamps ; firstly, the Franciscan Fathers, one by one, then the clergy and the children, and lastly all the devout crowd—a continual bending and stooping down : some kept their lips pressed longer than others on the marble, others kissed it passionately, quickly. The nun, with closed eyes, remained outside, leaning against the wall of the vestibule waiting for the procession to pass by, before she, in her turn, ventured to kiss the holy relic. She glanced around her anxiously to see if she were alone. Then, not kneeling, but falling with outspread arms, in a paroxysm of passion she kissed the Stone convulsively. Here she remained prostrate, a dark inert form worshipping the Stone upon which Jesus was embalmed by the holy women.

Later, I learnt the history of this nun. Consumptive and in a dying condition, she had been sent, at her own request, to the Holy Land, to see whether a miracle would be worked in her favour. Sometimes the sun in the East

A SUFFERING SHADOW.

aids the Divine will. But she herself had not wished for this. She only longed to pass away where her Saviour had suffered. This was the last festival in which she ever took part. When I left Galilee, she was already united to her Lord, even as she had desired.

PART V.
THE IDYLL.

I.

EPHRATA.

I APOLOGISE for using a Hebrew word as the title of this chapter; Ephrata, the ancient name for Bethlehem of Judæa, signifies "the fruitful," and, therefore, expresses perfectly the true significance of the village where the Saviour first saw light. We might, indeed, even prefer it to the more familiar Bethlehem but for old and tender associations; we learnt that name at our mother's knee, and have in our turn taught it to our children. Bethlehem —the fruitful: the place where, from that first happy Christmas Day onwards, the seed of its fields, the grass of its meadows, the intelligence of its men, the beauty of its children, the virtue of its women, and the venerable age of its old people have prospered exceedingly under beneficent spiritual and material influences. Possibly few, if any, of my readers remember the ancient name which so faithfully describes the characteristics of the Land of Judah, but surely no one can ever forget the prophecies connected with this dear land, which was to be the birthplace of the Saviour of Mankind. The prophets foretold that Bethlehem would not be the least among the cities, and bade her rejoice since the Light of the World was to issue from her gates. And so it came to pass that in Bethlehem on a cold December night, "the Word was made flesh" in a stable hewn out of the living rock. The stars glittered in the clear sky above, and even domestic animals had sought shelter from the frost without, in the humble lodging of the Madonna and the new-born Babe. By whom can it have been named

Ephrata? What prophet gave this most appropriate title to the grey walls that rise on a hill-side whence vineyards descend into the green plain below, from beyond which the shepherds came to worship a little shivering new-born Child wrapped in swaddling clothes? When at dawn the little One lifted His tiny Arms towards the blue heavens from whence He had come, Mary lost all thought of her suffering and poverty as she beheld the Treasure nestled in her arms. Then was the high destiny of Ephrata realised, and Bethlehem became a name for ever blessed and to be repeated with the tenderest significance.

This charming little town can be reached in an hour from Jerusalem, for, wonderful to relate, a good carriageable highway leads to it—a rarity, indeed, in the Ottoman Empire. At a turn in this road, as you approach it, Bethlehem comes suddenly in sight, with houses set in the midst of rich fields, vineyards and the apricot orchards, for which it is famous. The main street is long and narrow, but through the open doors you get glimpses of cleanly interiors, exhibiting an absence of that malodorous, smoky dinginess so general elsewhere in Palestine. The inhabitants of Bethlehem at present number about 8,000 souls, whose chief pride consists, not in the fact that their famous village has risen from an insignificant hamlet to be almost a town, with its fine stone quarries and general prosperity, but because they are nearly all Christians.

That predestined land, where the Divine Infant was born, could not be peopled by Jews and Mohammedans, and, therefore, to the Bethlehemite the title of Christian is his most precious possession. He is naturally industrious and loves work, one of his chief occupations being that of inlaying mother-of-pearl into objects of devotion, especially rosaries; and ornaments chiselled out of black volcanic stone brought from the Dead Sea. These people also use amber, the wood and kernels of olives and the stones of fruit, which they carve or make into rosaries and necklaces. The Bethlehemite is a great traveller, and goes far afield with his pretty merchandise—to Rome, France, and even to America—living frugally by the way and learning with singular rapidity the languages of the

EPHRATA.

countries he visits. He is shrewd and observant, and is distinguished by the pleasant, courteous manners for which his native place is famed. Those who do not travel cultivate the fields, and when the wanderers return, the profits of agriculture as well as of commerce are mutually shared. They are not grasping, and their chief pride is to keep their houses neat and tidy, and unlike those of other villagers in these parts, their children are kept very clean. At Christmas, pilgrimages from all parts of the Holy Land come to Bethlehem to assist at the celebration of the great feast in the Church of the Nativity. The Bethlehemite, although exceedingly jealous, is proverbially a good husband, and never treats his womenfolk with the contempt which is so general in the East.

The Bethlehemite woman deserves to be loved, respected, and even merits the compliment implied by jealousy. She is, above all, wonderfully beautiful, not a brunette, but with a bright, warm, clear complexion ; her eyes, large and rather wide apart, have a frank look, and her perfectly shaped mouth gives her a proud and reserved expression, though she rarely smiles. (Most of the women in the East glance sideways through half-closed eyes, and their mouths are large and ill-formed.) The women of Bethlehem carry themselves so admirably that they appear taller than they really are. They are generally plump without being fat, and their hands and feet are exceptionally small. The costume they wear is strikingly picturesque, consisting of a long, narrow tunic of dark blue cotton, hanging from the throat to the ankles, raised slightly at the waist by a cord like a blouse. Over this tunic they wear a double stole of a dark blue woollen material, embroidered in red. Only the girls wear a ribbon in their hair, over which is draped a large white cotton kerchief or veil, the border of which is richly worked in red and blue worsted. The married women, on the other hand, wear a kind of cloth cap adorned with gold and silver sequins, their only dower. These sequins are pierced and fall one over the other, like leaves, so that a great number can, therefore, be sewn on to the headdress. The Bethlehemite woman wears her veil with delightful grace and dignity, and is unlike her indolent, languid-eyed sister of Jerusalem who spends all her time squatting in church mumbling prayers she does not understand, with her infant in the folds of her veil, and three or four other children grouped round her; moreover she works hard in her home, sells fruit and corn, and even finds time to inlay ornaments with mother-of-pearl. In the absence of her husband she looks after his house, teaches her children, and contributes her earnings to the family hoard. It is a goodly sight to see these women going down to Jerusalem with their flasks of oil or baskets of fruit, their veils thrown back from their faces and falling in graceful folds around them, with step so light they scarcely seem to touch the ground.

Then, in the afternoon, their day's work ended in prayer before the Holy Sepulchre, they return to their homes in groups of four or five. Reserved and dignified, their beautiful lips are silent and they pay no attention to the passers-by.

All the good fortune and virtue that attend them the inhabitants of Bethlehem will tell you are gifts of the Divine Child.

II.

THE MANGER.

EVERYONE knows that our Lord was born in a *khan*. A *khan* is not an inn, but something much more lowly. It is generally a roughly constructed building, more often than not erected in the open country, surrounded by rough walls and without any roof: sometimes, however, it is built up against a rock or a cave. Occasionally the superior kind of *khan* may be half roofed in, thus affording shelter for horses, mules, and donkeys, the mangers being invariably filled with hay and barley. There is always plenty of water at hand, so that the animals can quench their thirst. As to the *moukres*, or horsemen, they may merely lie down on

THE MANGER.   123

the ground in the courtyard, with their heads resting on their saddles, sleeping under the light of the stars, or even in the hot sunshine. The wayfarer may sleep, if he likes, on his carpet or cloak, outside on the bench which serves as a stepping-stone to mount the horses. Unfortunately, however, he can only obtain a drink of water, unless, indeed, the *khan* is exceptionally important, when he may even get a cup of coffee. The place is generally tenanted by its owner and a couple of youths who help to do the service, but if it be situated in a deserted or otherwise dangerous locality, the Turkish Government supplies a soldier or *zaptieh* to keep order.

At the time of the Nativity, these *khans* must have been even more primitive than at present—probably mere prolongations of natural grottoes. Bethlehem certainly possessed a small inn in those days, but Joseph and Mary were unable to find a lodging within its walls, as it was full. Cyrenius, the Governor of Syria, commanded, by order of Cæsar Augustus, that all should be taxed, everyone in his own city, and therefore much confusion reigned throughout the land. Joseph, notwithstanding his humble trade of a carpenter, was a descendant of David, and was, therefore, obliged to go up to Jerusalem to declare himself. It took six or seven days to go, by short stages, from Nazareth to Jerusalem, by the way of Nahim. Bethlehem was one of the last halting places on this road, and Joseph and Mary arrived here, very tired, on the night of what is popularly believed to have been the 24th of December. As they only intended to remain a few hours in Bethlehem, hoping to reach Jerusalem the following morning, Joseph and Mary were constrained to stay in the *khan*, where the Virgin Mother, who, according to tradition, was at this time only fourteen years of age, was seized with the pangs of childbirth, and, in this cold and wretched stable, brought forth a male Child, whilst the cattle, so says the legend, seeing the little shivering Babe in the manger, drew near and warmed Him with their gentle breath, as He nestled in the Madonna's arms. And high above, in the frosty heavens, glittered that star which had guided the three Kings on their way to adore Him. One came from Persia, another from India, and the third from Ethiopia, each bearing his offering of gold and spices to present on bended knees to the new-born King, the light of whose infant Eyes was to enkindle a flame of love throughout the world!

What good would it serve to describe in detail the splendid church erected above the place of the Nativity? The churches of Palestine were, for the most part, erected by St. Helena, and have, in the course of ages, been either partly or entirely destroyed and rebuilt five or six times over, and their history is, therefore, extremely complicated. Here, in Bethlehem, notwithstanding the many vicissitudes it has undergone, the grotto where the Divine Infant was born has remained unaltered. You descend from the upper church, by the light of a small taper, twelve steep steps cut out of the rock, and, walking along a very dark subterranean passage, at length emerge in the cave of the Nativity, to be dazzled by the reflection of the lamps on the gold and silver ornaments with which it is adorned. It is a natural grotto cut in the calcareous rock, but covered in by an artificial vault. Its length is nearly thirteen and a half yards by three or four in width: there are three entrances, but no light penetrates from the exterior. Fifty-three lamps burn continually: the floor is paved with white marble, whilst the walls of the rock are not only encased in costly marble, but covered with magnificent hangings of stamped leather. A few steps to the left, after entering, you find yourself in a tribune, under which is a circular opening through which you perceive a bluish jasper-like stone. Here is a marble slab fixed in the pavement, with a silver star in the centre, round which are the words: "HIC DE VIRGINE MARIA JESUS CHRISTUS NATUS EST."—" Here Jesus Christ was born of the Virgin Mary." In an angle in the side of the grotto is a small chapel that marks where stood the manger or crib. Here it was that the shepherds who were watching their flocks on that cold December night came and knelt, even as the angel had bidden them: "Fear not: for, behold, I bring you good tidings of great joy, which shall be to all people. For unto you is born this day in the city of David a Saviour, which is Christ the Lord. And this shall be a sign unto you: Ye shall find the Babe wrapped in swaddling clothes, lying in a manger." In this hallowed spot, the magnificent church above fades from the memory. Unhappily, however, here, possible more than anywhere else, the fanaticism of the Schismatic Greeks is most evident, and the Turkish Government is obliged to station a soldier beside each altar in order to prevent a repetition of the outrage which took place here in 1847, when the Greeks stole the star of the Nativity, and thereby brought about the Crimean War of 1854. You now no longer think of the soldiers, the Greek and Armenian priests, the magnificent lamps, the costly marble altars, or the ancient tapestries, or the pictures, but only remember that here that Child was born towards whom, for nearly two thousand years, myriads of Christian children have extended their tiny hands. Here was the crib where He was placed by the caressing hands of His young mother, and where she lulled Him to sleep with her sweet Hebrew lullaby. This, then, is the *Presepio* that so many endeavour to reproduce at Christmas time, and before which the most disinterested prayers are offered. It is, therefore, impossible to think of anything when beneath its roof, unless it be the touching mystery of which it was the scene. Let us ponder well beside this poor manger, for although, on our return home, many who suffer and struggle to resist temptation will question us about Golgotha, the Holy Sepulchre, the Mount of Olives, and Gethsemane, there will be still greater eagerness, especially among the children, to learn all about the Stable of Bethlehem, with its mystic memories.

Children understand nothing of the Suffering of the Passion, but they are sure to be interested in this cold cave, surrounded as it is by a lovely landscape full of trees, meadows, and green lanes.

The little ones' hands tremble with delight as they carry their tiny waxen Child Jesus and place Him in their toy stable. Surely their innocent prayers addressed to the Infant Saviour will be the most acceptable of any ? We must not fail to tell these babes, with the great, sweet, inquiring eyes in which shine the light of faith and intelligence, that the Stable of Bethlehem is even as they imagine it to be—merely a little thatched grotto, where meek-eyed cows and white-faced donkeys watch the Madonna as she bends over the Infant nestling in her arms, whilst a crowd of simple-hearted folk kneel by the door. Who can possibly forget that living rock and that silver ring which marks the spot where first beat the Heart of Jesus? It will certainly return to our memory when we relate to our little friends at home all about the Divine Infant and the Stable and tell them how well He loved them, for did He not say, " Suffer little children to come unto Me, and forbid them not "? They, listening eagerly, will be so happy to think their illusions need not be destroyed. Let him who tells them of these things speak the simple truth—just that— no more.

NOTE.—In this chapter Signora Serao alludes to the custom among the Italians, especially in the South, of making a *Presepio*, or Crib, of Bethlehem. There is scarcely a Neapolitan family that has not its *Presepio* at Christmas time, in the arrangement of which the children take the greatest interest. Illuminated by many tapers, it generally occupies a conspicuous place in the family sitting-room or even in the shop. Of an evening the children kneel before this representation of the Infant Saviour in His Crib to say their prayers before they go to bed—a sweet and pretty custom, if ever there was one.—TRANSLATOR.

III.

THE PRECURSOR.

No place can be imagined more charming than the little mountain village of Aïn-Karem. The houses stand in groups of two or three, facing the rising sun, and straggling about half-way down the green slope. They are surrounded by well-cultivated orchards and flowering gardens, and in front of them stretches the wide valley of Karem, which gradually fades away between the mountains. The air is full of sweet scents, and is refreshed by three or four clear brooks, one of which supplies the three stone basins of the principal fountain of the village, which is shaded by a huge old tree. Resting beneath it for a while you may watch the pretty, delicate-looking native women filling their stone jars with water, or engaged in washing their linen. They are generally small and slight in stature, and their brown faces are partially hidden by their tawny locks. Their mouths are singularly small, and their lips, full and red, look like rose-buds. They have, moreover, extremely small and shapely hands and feet. Their costume consists of a dark blue woollen gown, and over their heads they wear a diadem of black ribbon, to which are attached a number of gold and silver coins, which constitute their dower. A large white kerchief, with a red and blue border, embroidered in a quaint design, covers them from head to waist. Sometimes they carry a tiny brown baby that peeps out smilingly from between the folds of their cloak. Aïn-Karem, cosily niched on the hill-side, is, therefore, full of a sort of sylvan poetry; it is, moreover, protected from both the heat and the cold winds, and, unlike most places in Palestine, is well watered by limpid streams. The women, as I have said before, are fascinating, industrious little creatures. In June, when the pilgrimages are over, many people from Jerusalem come here to pass the summer months, and, if a house is not secured early in the season, it is difficult to find a lodging. The sick and the convalescent are sent here to gain strength and be cured. Aïn-Karem takes about two hours to reach by carriage from Jerusalem, and is so charming and peaceful that those who visit it, if only for a day, long to remain to enjoy the murmur of its brooks and its invigorating air. Aïn-Karem is the Arabic name, but it is commonly called by Christians St. John-of-the-Mountain. Here was born the Precursor, the son of Elisabeth and Zacharias.

The aged Zacharias was the owner of a house here, in which the Baptist was born, and that can still be reached by a narrow lane bordered by trees. The Franciscan Fathers have built an oratory over it, but the two little rooms retain their original idyllic simplicity. Zacharias and Elisabeth were already so advanced in years when their renowned son was born that they had abandoned every hope of having a child ; but this humble nest at Aïn-Karem, nevertheless, sent forth its eagle. It was before the birth of St. John the Baptist that Mary of Nazareth came from the far distant hills of Galilee to visit her cousin Elisabeth in the land of Judah. Who can forget the account in the Gospel of that charming meeting between these two holy women, who were destined to become the mothers, the one of Jesus, the other of John ; or the humble words of Elisabeth as she bowed low before Mary, although she was so much younger than herself ; or how, upon the threshold of this humble dwelling, the fair daughter of Sepphoris and the aged woman of Aïn-Karem magnified the Lord ? In this peaceful abode Mary dwelt for three months : the village well is still called after her, whither she came daily to fetch water for the household, with that customary simplicity which she preserved throughout her life. The traveller, as he sits by this venerable well which stands by the road-side, can conjure up in his imagination the young girl, as she came lightly down the hill in the golden light of sunrise, balancing the graceful amphora of water on her head, and wearing the blue mantle and the red and blue skirt for ever associated with her in countless pictures ; and he can venerate her far better here than he can in even the most sumptuous of the countless temples dedicated to her honour. The idyllic companionship between Mary and Elisabeth lasted three months ; but from the day Mary left the hill of Aïn-Karem, in the blessed land of Judah, everything in her existence was overshadowed by that gloom which darkened the life of her who was destined to become the Mother of Sorrows. According to tradition, the Precursor was born two or three months before Jesus, and Elisabeth was obliged to hide her infant in a cave to save him from the persecutions of Herod. The stone upon which the child rested is still shown, but it is being slowly worn away by the kisses of the faithful. And thus Aïn-Karem—St. John-of-the-Mountain—retains, after all these ages, its erstwhile peaceful aspect. Its waters still flow in soothing rhythm to cool the parched lips of the wayfarer, and its fruit trees and flowers flourish as of yore and

THE PRECURSOR. 129

perfume the air : the idyllic charm of this place, together with its tender memories, rises clear above the dark valley which vanishes into the desert beyond.

John left the paternal roof while still young to dwell in a lonely cave, in which he began his life of prayer and mystical contemplation. The beauties of nature and the charm of women had no influence upon one whose soul was ever turned heavenwards. Whilst the Redeemer passed these same years in the obscurity of the carpenter's shop at Nazareth, John had already yielded himself up entirely to his lofty ideals ; so that the fame of his austere life had spread over all Judæa. In Jerusalem the Pharisees hypocritically enjoyed their clandestine pleasures, though they outwardly pretended to observe the Law. John, who only loved solitude and the wide horizon of the desert, never even entered Jerusalem, scorning all contact with human life, which he deemed disturbing to his meditations. Never again was he who leapt within his mother's womb at the approach of the Virgin Mother of Jesus to take up the thread of that fair existence which in boyhood he had led in Aïn-Karem : never more was the dark thin figure of the Precursor to be seen ascending the narrow road that led to his native village ; nor were his parched lips ever more to be refreshed by the waters of its fountain. Never again were its hills to overshadow that ardent spirit which longed only for solitude. The fair maidens with the sparkling, dark eyes never beheld him more. He disappeared from their midst. Later it became known that, in the burning desert of Jericho, which lies between the Dead Sea and the Jordan, a loud voice was awakening the echoes of the dread plain. The prophecy of Isaiah concerning " The voice of one crying in the wilderness, Prepare ye the way of the Lord, make His paths straight," was fulfilled. For many years John dwelt in the accursed plain, where nature seems dead, where the stealthy jackal glides under the salt-covered bushes, and where the curse of a God who would not temper justice with His mercy still weighs upon the parched land. " His raiment was of camel's hair, and a leathern girdle was about his loins. His food was locusts and wild honey." He was a true son of the desert, full of ascetic mysticism. The fame of his piety and austerity spread far and wide, into remote villages, and even to Jerusalem, where the Tetrarch Herod, the spouse of Herodias, trembled as he heard of the man who was denouncing in the wilderness the eternal iniquity of mankind, and uplifting his arms in supplication to the God Judæa had denied. The humble and penitent flocked to hear him preach and to crave baptism at his hands. And the thin brown hand of John poured the water of Jordan on their heads, and they returned comforted to lead the higher life. At last, on one ever memorable day, the fair-haired Prophet of Nazareth came down into the burning plain of Jericho and humbly asked to be baptised of the Precursor ! Thus, after thirty years, even as their holy mothers had met and embraced long before, so did the sons meet on the shores by the sacred waters of Jordan, in fields which must ever be favoured of God, since they witnessed so memorable a scene. John, vibrating with joy, but deeming himself unworthy, did not at first venture to baptise Jesus ; but the Galilean gently insisted, and bent His fair Head under the trembling brown hand of the austere man of Aïn-Karem ; thus did He receive the regenerating waters, who was Himself to give His life for the Salvation of the World. With this great incident closed the history of John the Baptist. His sacrifice of youthful joys and passions met its full reward when he baptised his Lord !

Salome, the daughter of Herodias, may now dance voluptuously before the Tetrarch and demand the Baptist's head as her prize. In his prison at Machærus he will behold without fear the executioner enter to claim him ; his mystic destiny is fulfilled !

PART VI.

SEVEN HUNDRED FEET BELOW THE LEVEL OF THE SEA.

I.

JERICHO.

JERICHO! Jericho! Jericho! is the word you hear repeated from morning to night soon after you set foot in Jerusalem. It reaches your ear in a variety of languages, with a lighter or heavier inflection on the first or the last syllable. Travellers from every part of the known world may be heard repeating it, generally at the breakfast or dinner table. Jericho! Jericho! He who has visited the Holy Sepulchre, who has ascended the Mount of Olives, and descended into the so-called Tombs of the Kings, who has been to Bethlehem and to Hebron, the city of the Patriarch Abraham, has seen nothing to boast of, since he has only followed in the track of all the guests of the Grand Hotel in Jerusalem. It is Jericho which is really the point of interest: not on its own account, however, for of the once famous Jericho nothing now remains but eight or ten houses, among which are a small hotel and a Russian refuge, and a few furnished apartments. Jericho in itself is nothing, but it is the starting-point of the Jordan and Dead Sea. It is merely a place to eat and sleep in—if anyone can be found who can eat and sleep seven hundred feet below the level of the Mediterranean, where the air one breathes is like molten lead, and whence after one has eaten and *not* slept, and has been devoured by the smallest, whitest, and most fearful gnats on the face of the earth, one sets out for the salt lake which covers the site of Sodom and Gomorrah, or for the river Jordan, with whose clear waters the Baptist baptised Jesus. Many people do not visit Samaria, though it is one of the loveliest places in Palestine, and, dreading the fatigue of the journey, do not even go to Nazareth of Galilee, or to Tabor, Tiberias, the Lake of Genesareth, and Capernaum, where the Saviour passed His youth and where He first preached. No one, however, can possibly leave Jerusalem without visiting the Dead Sea and the Jordan, for to do so is an absolute point of honour with most travellers, and weighs upon them like a nightmare until they have actually been to Jericho and returned from it.

So soon as the ingenuous traveller announces his intention of going to Jericho, his troubles begin, and he is bound to listen to the following sort of dialogue.

" Going to Jericho ! I suppose you know that the journey is very dangerous ? "

" Why dangerous ? "

" On account of the Bedouins."

" And what may they do ? "

" They sometimes rob people and even murder them."

" Do they, really ? "

" Quite true."

" And what about the Turkish police ? "

" Oh, it arrests them, but invariably *after* the deed is done."

" Ah ! indeed."

(After this the wretched tourist falls into a profound reverie, which ends in his asking someone else all he knows about Jericho.)

" Jericho ? Yes, the journey is occasionally rather dangerous, but nothing unpleasant has happened for some time past."

" Since when ? "

" Oh, about three months ago there was a little trouble, but it was said to be merely a matter of private revenge."

" But are the Bedouins robbers ? "

" Of course they are, but the Turkish Government has a contract with them, whereby they may not attack travellers."

" Is this a fact ? "

JERICHO. 135

"Certainly."

"Then I suppose it is possible to reach Jericho in safety?"

"With *absolute* safety, no."

"What do you mean?"

"Oh, in these countries, you know . . ."

(The traveller becomes still more thoughtful; then, taking courage, he puts the question to some people who have actually been to Jericho.)

"Jericho? We did not see any Bedouins by the way."

"You were, then, quite easy in your minds?"

"Well—not quite. At a certain point our escort told us to hurry, as brigands were known to be on the other side of the mountain."

"A little blackmailing trick, eh?"

"May be."

"Going to Jericho?" (asks someone who has just returned from that unpleasant place). "You will surely take an escort?"

"Of course. But of what must this escort be composed?"

"An armed Bedouin on horseback will do. You pay him about 12s. 6d. This is a kind of tribute to the chief of the tribe at Aboutis, a village situated on the confines between Jerusalem and the land of the Bedouins."

"Oh! that's all right then!" (says the traveller, greatly relieved). "And with this escort and tribute money we may get along safely enough, I suppose?"

"Pretty nearly."

"How so?"

"Well, at times there are other Bedouins belonging to more distant tribes over whom the *sheikh* at Aboutis has no control."

"What happens then?"

"Your escort decamps and leaves you in the lurch."

"Then, it seems to me, this escort is pretty useless."

"How can you say such a thing? Why, you simply daren't start without one!"

"But if it runs away?"

"So they say. But, still, you must have an escort,

otherwise the chances are ninety to a hundred that something horrible will happen to you."

"And having one?"

"Ninety-nine chances to one that nothing will happen."

"Is the road to Jericho good?"

"Not so very bad."

"Did anything happen to you?"

"Nothing whatever!"

(The traveller, who may be likened to a sort of Hamlet of the Holy Land, is overcome by one last lingering doubt, and asks timidly.)

"But, tell me: how long is it since anyone was murdered and robbed on the road to Jericho?"

"Quite an age; but, anyway, you'll take a dragoman and an escort, won't you?"

"Certainly."

"Have you secured an armed Bedouin on horseback?"

"Yes, I have."

"If you possess any firearms, you had better take them with you."

"I have a revolver, but I am always afraid it might go off in the portmanteau."

"Never mind: take it all the same."

"Then is the road to Jericho so *very* dangerous?"

"No."

"Then why all these precautions?"

"In case of any unforeseen accident . . . you understand . . . in the East!"

Then the chorus continues thus.

"The road to Jericho is the dreariest and most desolate in the world."

"How long does it take to reach?"

"Seven hours to the first stopping-place, two to the second, and three to the third."

"And the return journey?"

"The same as the outward one; you must allow three days to go there and back, as the animals must have a rest."

"Is the heat in Jericho so very intense?"

"Beyond description!"

JERICHO.

"But I come from the South."

"That may be. But Jericho is the lowest spot on the earth's surface: it is literally impossible to breathe there."

"You think of going to Jericho? It is late in the season, and the Jordan hotel is shut, you know, and so is the Russian hospice: but there are a few furnished rooms."

"What are they like?"

"Oh, well! they are kept by Russian women: they are *fairly* clean."

"Only *fairly*?"

"You know all goes by comparison in this country."

"Jericho? I suppose you know there is nothing to eat there?"

"I shall take my own provisions with me."

"There is no one to cook for you."

"My dragoman must do the cooking."

"You won't think of drinking the water, will you?"

"Is it best to drink wine?"

"I should suggest tea."

"Jericho? You must leave Jerusalem at dawn, even as early as three o'clock in the morning: you will thus get there by ten o'clock. It will be very hot, but still you will not suffer much during the first hours."

"Very well; I'll start as you suggest at three o'clock."

"Have you a very broad-brimmed hat?"

"No; only a small straw one."

"That will never do. You have, at least, a *koufia*, or silk handkerchief?"

"Yes, I have."

"Then wind it round your straw hat."

"I will."

"You would do well to put a linen handkerchief over your head first."

"Why wear so many things?"

"The more you cover your head, the less danger there will be of sunstroke."

"Very well."

"You would do well to wear a helmet."

"Oh! not a helmet, please!"

"Do you think that so very strange in the East? It is the greatest safeguard against sunstroke."

"I don't possess one."

"What a pity!"

"And if I had one, I wouldn't wear it!"

"Anyhow, be sure to thoroughly cover your head."

"Thank you, I will do as you say."

"Jericho? I suppose you'll start in the afternoon?"

"Not at all; I shall start at dawn."

"You make a great mistake."

"Why?"

"By starting in the morning you face the sun for at least five hours, and this is a terrible ordeal, I assure you: I tried it once, and had all the skin burnt off my face!"

"When would *you* advise starting?"

"At half-past one; you will then have the sun at your back all the way. Thus, whether you are on horseback, or in a palanquin, you will not suffer in either case."

"But I shall arrive so late."

"What does that matter?"

"But isn't it dangerous?"

"Just listen to this: you are not sure of meeting thieves, but you are certain to get sunstroke."

"Is the sun so scorching, then?"

"Terribly: and then there is the dust: be sure to take some brandy with you, your throat will be always parched."

"I shall not forget."

"And don't drink any water by the way."

"Not even that of the Jordan?"

"Only if it has been filtered."

"Jericho! A very dangerous journey, I assure you. Moreover, exceedingly tiring and expensive."

Here the unfortunate traveller asks, in a moment of profound dejection: "Is it really worth while going to Jericho after all?"

Four will answer *no*, three will say *yes*, and one will answer evasively *yes* and *no*.

Notwithstanding all this, not a single traveller in Palestine, be he young or old, man or woman, ever fails to go to Jericho!

II.

IN A PALANQUIN.

EVEN the most energetic traveller would never dream of visiting Jericho, with its ten houses and twenty huts, buried as it is in the suffocating plain of Rihah, if it were not the chief resting-place between Jerusalem and the Dead Sea, as well as the starting-point for the idyllic region of the Jordan. Otherwise, nobody in their senses would literally " go to Jericho " if they could help it, for it is about the most loathsome place in the world. When at length one does reach it, and finds one's self in a vile sulphurous sort of pit, where breathing is difficult, and the sky above seems to be receding, it is with a feeling of absolute terror that one realises the fact that here is the lowest spot on the earth's surface. Anybody who has spent a night in this dismal abode, vainly endeavouring to sleep—a feat rendered impossible, thanks to the attentions of the most abominable little white gnats—is never likely to forget the unpleasant experience, and even the least imaginative is apt to dream of imprisonment in a deep pit filled with acrid vapours, and rendered hideous by the rustling of venomous and mysterious snakes ! Jericho is situated more than seven hundred feet below the level of the Mediterranean. The two nights spent in Jericho, in the little refuge or house kept by two silent old Russian women, return vividly to my mind, and I remember that I felt as if I were doomed to die of suffocation. My nerves became unstrung ; and even now, when I remember the detestable food which tasted of cinders, and the brackish water it was impossible to drink, I feel a sensation of absolute loathing. I experienced a keen desire to rise from my uncomfortable couch and fly from the sickening, suffocating place at any risk. I would have done anything to get out of the town, to the Dead Sea, the Jordan, or anywhere else, provided I could but get away from Jericho, even to the mountains of Moab, at the risk of falling a victim to Bedouin bandits—anything rather than remain in a place where I likened myself unto a wretched fly struggling vainly to escape out of the neck of a bottle.

Flight! The miserable little house, built of wood, bricks and mortar, where I paid three shillings to spend the night, was situated at the end of a long valley, and was so silent and so lonely as to be quite uncanny. The two strange-looking old Russian women, dressed in grey, and wearing narrow white nun-like caps and large white collars, who kept the place, did not speak a word of French, Italian, or Greek, and moved about noiselessly. The lower floor creaked in a ghostly fashion. Impossible to find out who my neighbours were. My sleeping-room was on the ground floor, and opened into the lane; the windows overlooking the country were barred. The bed was enveloped in such a thick mosquito net that it might have hidden a corpse—like the one in Ann Radcliffe's *Mysteries of Udolpho*. My dragoman, faithful companion, guide and friend, slept on a couch in the dining-room, but so far off that he could not have heard me even if I had called him ever so loud. The Bedouin escort, *moukre*, or horseman, and his boy slumbered in a stable at the end of the lane. Here I passed two nights: and though I opened all the windows, I could not obtain a breath of air. I walked out into the lane and gazed at the stars through the trees, and even then I felt as if I might, at any moment, encounter some awful apparition! No, I shall never forget the two sinister nights spent in Jericho!

It takes six hours to get to Jericho from Jerusalem on horseback, four more to visit the Jordan and the Dead Sea, and yet another four to return to Jericho, besides, of course, the six back again to Jerusalem—in all twenty hours' hard riding. I selected a palanquin. It seemed a more comfortable as well as a more practical means of locomotion, less fatiguing, and, moreover, less commonplace. The palanquin of the East is a sort of wooden litter, open in front, having unglassed windows on either side. The interior is stuffed with horsehair, covered with grey linen, and as it stands very high from the ground it has to be set down to enable you to enter it. The four poles before and behind pass through strong iron rings attached to the saddles of two sturdy mules, one in front and the other behind. Once the palanquin, with its inmate, is raised, it starts off with a gruesome undulating motion that sets you thinking unpleasantly of a sea voyage, though, thank Heaven, without its attendant results. A journey in a litter in search of the footprints of sacred history, even to the riverside where Jesus received baptism, can never be forgotten. We left Jerusalem at half-past one in the afternoon; already a fresh breeze was blowing, and the sun was at our backs. The little caravan opened with the palaquin, in which reclined the author with all her bags and baggage, books, rugs, and cloaks—the nights are cold—parasols, and silk handkerchiefs, for protection against the hot sun. A big bunch of pink oleanders was stuck into one of the windows. All this miscellaneous paraphernalia swayed continuously from side to side. My dragoman, Issa, proceeded on horseback, and guided and guarded the jaunty little vehicle; while the escort, a slim, brown, silent young Bedouin, named Ahmed, mounted on a fleet Arab, and armed to the teeth, rode on in front, smoking cigarettes incessantly. John, the *moukre*, with his boy Joseph, followed on foot at a sauntering pace, leading a sleek donkey laden with provisions; the two Arabs, who occasionally chattered together, but who habitually dozed on the donkey's back, which they rode in turns for about an hour at a time, closed the cavalcade. Occasionally the Bedouin and his steed would remain as motionless as a statue of a horse and his rider, waiting for the rest of the caravan to join them, and their well-defined silhouette would stand out clearly in the diaphanous Eastern atmosphere, in the most picturesque manner conceivable.

I passed the long hours in my travelling prison in a sort of delightful reverie, which enabled me to indulge in all sorts of fantastic dreams as I was borne along in the gently swaying litter by sure-footed mules. The country, seen through the windows, appeared to unroll itself swiftly, like a panorama, occasionally a trifle blurred by the motion. The bitter almond blossoms and the oleanders that lie fading in the May sunshine fill the palanquin with delicious odours. The dreary road between Jerusalem and

Jericho winds in and out of the arid yellow hills and descends precipitously, the rugged mountain sides appearing interminable, especially when viewed from the narrow boundary of a palanquin; none the less, it affords a sort of pleasurable, dream-like sensation of undulating to and fro in mid-air.

We passed the high mountains whence Zion once cast her radiance around, and Bethany, the home of Martha and Mary, and entered a hilly, stony region, where even the greedy jackal finds no food, and thus descended by rocky paths into the beds of rivers, into gullies formed by winter torrents, and finally ascended the arid and gruesome mountains of San Saba, once upon a time a resort of hermits and penitents. The dragoman, the escort, and the boy went quietly on their way, never for a moment losing their patience, but ever exhibiting that wonderful self-control that enables the Arab to overcome every obstacle. The lithe Bedouin, with his daggers crossed in his belt and his gun slung behind his shoulders, rode on in absolute silence. I never dreamt of even opening my book, but yielded myself to the mood into which I had fallen: and thus those six hours passed swiftly enough, in a sort of dreamy enchantment. I at last became so absorbed in my strange environment, every inch of which is associated with events and scenes of the utmost historical importance, that presently I lost all sense of the actual, and could think of nothing but the wide expanse of desolation through which I was passing. I felt I was no longer myself, but a disembodied spirit that had lived and suffered long ago. Even now I have only to close my eyes, to vividly recall the never-to-be-forgotten palanquin, the scent of the oleanders, and the dry, sun-beaten road; and I fancy I can still feel that swaying motion, and even see the dreary yet fascinating country through which I passed from Jerusalem to Jericho!

My night journey in a palanquin was, indeed, a remarkable experience. The dragoman came at three o'clock in the morning to knock at the door of my little room; and in utter darkness, amidst the flitting of ghost-like shadows, the caravan again started off, this time towards Jordan. Everything was enveloped in gloom, but there was no need to be afraid, for the mules are wonderfully sure-footed, and so on went the palanquin, descending, swerving, and ascending, brushing aside tall bushes heavy with fragrance, pressing on further and further into the darkness : a stretch of starry heaven is now alone visible above. This nocturnal journey through unknown regions, performed in a sort of box or cradle, seemed so mysterious and dream-like that I could scarcely believe myself awake, and sometimes wondered if we had lost our way—if there were indeed any road at all. It was of no use looking out of the windows of the palanquin to verify things, for we were moving in absolute darkness. I began to think this uncanny night would never come to an end, and that I should go on for ever in my wooden box with the ship-like motion ! By the time this feeling was becoming unendurable, the thick veil of night began to lift, and gradually the shadows faded ; black turned to grey, and the cool morning breeze—that veritable caress of the East—refreshed us as we continued to advance into the light of the new-born day. This was indeed an exquisite moment ! On the great salt-covered plain which lies between Jericho and the Dead Sea dawn breaks with none of the sadness which marks the awakening of another day of toil in a great city, but is a delicious renewal of life, flooding with a glorious light the plains as they unroll at the foot of the mountain where Jesus was tempted of Satan, even to the margin of the accursed lake that engulfs the cities of the plain. Everything reappears gradually in the light, and what was shadowy an hour or so before becomes distinct, and the wilderness where John preached stretches out before us in majestic grandeur. The people one meets by the way seem, in the dimness of dawn, so many shadows that still retain in their languid looks traces of the dreams from which they have so recently awakened. The sun rises at last, and we behold lying in front of us a vast and colourless expanse of waveless water—the Dead Sea !

III.

THE DEAD SEA.

THE Dead Sea, at least thirty miles away from Jerusalem, lies 1,308 feet below the level of the Mediterranean. This vast expanse of motionless water is shut in by two barren mountain ranges, the chain of Judæa and the table-land of Moab. Its shores are as parched as the surrounding country, and bear no traces of vegetation or of the existence of man. The whole place has the sinister appearance of having been, at one time, upheaved by the hand of Titans. The extreme width of the Dead Sea is between nine and ten miles, and length *circa* forty-six miles: its greatest depth is nearly three miles. The metallic rigidity of its waters and their unchanging tints, which, unlike those of other seas, do not reflect even the blue of the sky, are such that the eye meanders vaguely across its immensity, and it appears to the imagination like a bewitched and stagnant lake over which no vessel dares venture. Notwithstanding a certain degree of transparency, it is impossible for the eye to penetrate the waters of the Dead Sea beyond a few yards, beneath which they look as if mingled with asbestos or some other opaque mineral. It may be well to caution intending bathers in the Dead Sea that, unless a slanting posture is assumed in swimming, the body bobs up to the surface like a cork, face downwards, and that it is, moreover, absolutely necessary to wear a complete bathing costume on account of the mineral qualities of the water, and to put on a straw hat to protect the head from sunstroke. If the water gets into the eyes it acts like tobacco smoke, making them smart painfully, and when the bather comes to land he is covered with salt crystals, as indeed are all objects which have been plunged into it. It contains quantities of sodium, magnesium, calcium, potassium, bromide, and lime; but especially magnesium and sodium. The temperature is warm but variable: often a stream of cold water is found running

THE DEAD SEA.

between two of hot. No fish can live in the exceeding salt of this singular sea, and only occasionally is it skimmed by some melancholy aquatic bird.

Three rivers empty themselves into the Dead Sea, the impetuous Jordan, the Callirhoe, and the Arnon, but their waters do not increase its bulk or alter its level, and the phenomenon of evaporation adds to its general aspect of solemn mystery. For three or four miles inland the surrounding earth is white with salt, into which the horses' hoofs sink as though it were sparkling snow. At a considerable distance from the shore grow a few gnarled dwarfed shrubs that bear a strange fruit, which, when fresh, has a nasty bitter flavour, and when dry is filled apparently with ashes. This is the Dead Sea fruit or Sodom apple, the sole and truly emblematical product of an accursed vegetation.

This waveless tide, which is never ruffled by storm or wind, looks at dawn like a sheet of unburnished steel : at midday sparkles like molten silver. In the presence of so weird a sea even the frivolous is awed into silence : for what matters it if the handle of a parasol which has been steeped in the saline liquid be instantly covered with crystals, or that the Arab lad who has just emerged from his bath looks a very pillar of salt ? Who cares whether yon island be one or two miles distant, or if an Englishman lost his life in an attempt to reach it by swimming ? Here vain curiosity is silenced, and the Arabs, with their ardent faith in Divine intervention in human affairs, assume an expression of awed respect—even of terror—as they gaze solemnly at this sinister stretch of ill-omened water. An irresistible impulse induces you to dismount from your horse and bend over the water, with an intense gaze even as Dante endeavoured to peer into the dread abyss, and to seek therein traces of those five cities of the plain which perished in a rain of fire and brimstone. Their punishment was an awful example of the implacable vengeance of an outraged Deity who refused to temper His justice with mercy, at whose bidding the Dead Sea extended over the adjacent villages, once so full of life, and covered them with its acrid boiling waters.

Not a stone has been left one above another, not a trace exists of Sodom, Gomorrah, Adama, Segor, or Soboim. The fact of their punishment spread throughout the land of the Patriarchs, and still, after a lapse of ages, dominates these regions like some awful spectre that seems to be for ever pointing downwards towards the gulf wherein the sinful cities lie buried. The dread of the punishment inflicted upon their inhabitants, among whom not ten just men could be found, has disturbed the rest of impious kings and troubled the dreams of wicked princes. Countless pilgrims have beheld these deadly listless waters and have endeavoured to divine their secret, but vainly : and home returning they can never banish the memory of the Dead Sea and its lesson from their minds.

Nowhere else on the face of the earth has symbolism been so graphically and dreadfully illustrated as here. Sodom and Gomorrah have disappeared for ever, and no human power can call them back. This immense desert, where no grass grows : this sea without waves or tide, whose sulphurous vapours ascend night and day towards Heaven : this lake of metal, in which the most opposite elements harmonise : this stone-like colouring and, above all, the absence of men, fill with gloomy foreboding all who behold them, and who realise their true significance, which is proverbially shown in the only plant that grows in the vicinity, the Sodom apple, that when it looks its ripest proves to be a mere casket of bitter ashes ! Everything hereabouts seems to refer to the soul—with its struggles, its sins, and its punishment. And the man who has degraded himself by sensual pleasures : who has worshipped the shadow instead of the substance, the flesh instead of the spirit, and who has sacrificed his highest aspirations to his lowest instincts, must, in the presence of this mysterious evidence of Divine wrath, be penetrated with a sense of fear that he too may one day be stricken in his pride, even as those cities were, never to rise again.

IV.

THE JORDAN.

By degrees the arid clods of earth coated with saline deposit, with which the turbid evil-smelling vapours exhaled from the Dead Sea have strewn the Desert of Jericho, disappeared, as did likewise the black, sandy, stony soil so tiring to the horses' feet : the air becomes free from that grey, almost metallic, mist that oppresses the sight along the shores of the bituminous lake, and presently the pure, tender blue sky of the East reappears in all its charm and beauty. The caravan continued slowly on its way, the horses and the mules with their quiet regular step, and the high palanquin undulating as usual. Soon, in the fresh morning air, clumps of grass, sprinkled with dew, were hailed with pleasure as an agreeable surprise. A sweet light trill struck the ear and filled us with delight : it was the note of one of those small native birds that live in the grass, hopping about gaily and fearlessly close to us. Vegetation increased and the verdure was studded with those little white, yellow, and mauve flowers, peculiar to these latitudes, whose dainty cups trembled in the slight breeze created by the motion of our caravan ; strange to relate, I never saw any red flowers growing in this part of the world. The grass became thicker and the pathway meandered between hedges of flowering and prickly shrubs, and the horses bent their heads every moment to nibble at the tufts of aromatic herbs.

The interior of the palanquin was filled with delicious perfumes, and I eagerly bent forward to catch a glimpse of the verdant scene through which I was passing. The view of the great flowery plain, however, was somewhat impeded by the oscillating movement of the vehicle, which made the landscape seem like a waving sea : and all I was able to realise of it was a vague notion of its bright, flame-coloured breath, animated by the warbling and chirping of thousands of birds. At last I heard a slight rustling and tapping against the sides of the palanquin, as a way had to be cleared for its passage through the thick undergrowth, and we presently proceeded under a gentle shower of flower-petals sprinkled with dew. This lovely, flower-laden verdure, and this freshness and gentle rustling of branches and leaves, coming after the parched, stony, suffocating, accursed country we had just left, afforded me a most delightful experience. I was passing through the oasis of Palestine into the fields beloved of Heaven—when, lo! the Jordan is in sight!

Not far from the right bank of that famed river the caravan halted and was unpacked: in a few moments the palanquin was set on the ground, the horses and mules were let loose, and shawls, bags, rugs, and sunshades scattered all over the flowering clumps. The sun, which was still low, bathed all the right bank with bright light, whereas the left was still plunged in the twilight of dawn: amid this characteristic contrast the sacred river flowed clear and rapid, its tiny grey waves gaining colour as the sun reached them. The men of the caravan, lying on rugs, ate but sparingly: the Bedouin escort smoked his eternal cigarettes: the dragoman inspected the sacks of provisions, and spread out the carpets, whilst I was left in peace to enjoy my first glimpse of the Jordan. It is impossible to describe the wonderful beauty and fascination of this lovely river, flowing silently as it does, overshadowed by great trees and amid luxurious vegetation. Its banks are studded with flowers, and are gay with the chirping of birds and the hum of insects. The beauty of the scenery did not diminish as we ascended the river, but became, if anything, more and more enchanting as we advanced.

The clear roll of the Jordan becomes, at times, agitated and forms into a thousand rippling rings which, collecting further on in a different shape, glide on smoothly through the willows. A feeling of absolute enjoyment pervaded my mind, and the very memory of the tiresome and fatiguing journey I had undergone vanished, and, for a time, I forgot Jericho and the horrors of the Dead Sea.

The Jordan flows on swiftly, and he who has made this long journey to reach it realises an intense longing

THE JORDAN.

to throw himself into its waters and feel their vigorous embrace. He wishes to pay homage to this great river, so loved of God, praised by the Prophets and blessed by the Apostles. Standing on its bank I felt spellbound by the heavenly beauty of the scene, with the tender delicate plants reflected in the water, the lovely flowers exhaling their morning perfumes, the grand old gnarled trees, and even with the little white and coloured pebbles that pave the shores.

The traveller is only allowed a brief hour in which to enjoy it : and memory is so evanescent ! Although the wonderfully beautiful does leave a deep impression, it is impossible that time should not eventually somewhat lessen its effect. Lying down by the banks, the pilgrim feels the very cool waters of this most holy of rivers caress his hand, as he turns his face towards the grass, whilst scattering the white pebbles, and yielding himself, body and soul, to the charm of the hour. The tragic emotions experienced in the land of Christ's Martyrdom seem already obliterated, as are also the horrors of Jericho and the Dead Sea, which, for the time being, have faded into the mists of the past. The Jordan is the symbol of prayer unmingled with sobs or tears. Heaven smiles upon this loved river, and it seems to echo back joyously the Divine greeting. The gracious vegetation, the luxuriant grasses and shrubs, and the noble trees which enrich its shores, are full of song from dawn to sunset. The rapidly on-flowing waters reflect the azure blue of the sky above and retain a limpid loveliness that can never be disturbed. The heart, no longer afflicted by the memory of the great Tragedy which still saddens millions of Christians, yields itself up to thoughts of love and peace and of an unquestioning Faith, strengthened by Hope and tempered by Charity. These mystic waves renew the miracle of that noblest of all baptisms, purifying and regenerating the heart. The sweetness of the flowers, the clearness of the quick-flowing stream, the serenity of the brilliant sky, pass as by magic into the soul of him who has made this pious pilgrimage. For here, one day in Springtime, under the shadow of these trees, Jesus bent His Sacred Head to receive the regenerating waters from the hand of John: it was the shores of this fair river that witnessed the great scene of supreme love!

V.

THE ROSE OF JERICHO.

WHEN you are setting out on a journey, there is sure to be someone tiresome ready to damp your enthusiasm by belittling the attractions of the countries you propose to visit. He delights in depriving you of faith in your poetical legends, and in pulling down bit by bit all your air-castles to the realisation of which you so eagerly look forward. In April, I remember, I had the weakness (or, it might be called, overweening pretension) to announce that I was going to Palestine: the journey was subsequently ·delayed about three weeks, and I was, therefore, unable to escape the sceptical, sarcastic friend, and prevent his scoffing at the Holy Land—at Jerusalem, the Gospels, in fact, at all the mystic and memorable things which so especially attracted me to *Soria*. He begged me to write to him the exact dimensions of the Valley of Jehoshaphat; he asked me to send him in an envelope a lock of Absolom's hair, and to seal it with Solomon's great seal. He wished me to report whether Sodom and Gomorrah were visible under the Dead Sea, and insisted upon my bringing him a photograph of the submerged cities; he advised me to re-christen the Jordan, if that little stream really existed, and so on, all through the entire gamut of the idiotic remarks a would-be witty but by no means bad sort of fellow knows so well how to invent. His fixed idea was to possess a rose of Jericho. At the very last moment he entreated me not to forget the coveted flower; although he declared it to be non-existent. I was to be sure and find it and bring him a living or else a dried specimen. I was not to deceive him. He wanted the real authentic rose of Jericho, unto which

THE ROSE OF JERICHO. 151

women's beauty is so often compared in Holy Writ. If he could but see the flower, he said, it would at least give him some idea of what those far-famed beauties were really like.

I questioned all those who had undertaken the fatiguing and perilous journey to Jericho about this rose, but I invariably received the most contradictory and unsatisfactory answers.

One had never heard of the said rose; another had always considered it to be a mere figure of speech; a third had, indeed, looked for, but had failed to find it (but this may have been because the season was already too far advanced and the roses were over); a fourth declared that the people of Jericho had assured him there never had been any roses in their country; a fifth, and last, asserted that this flower was only to be found in the most inaccessible altitudes, which was obviously a misstatement. In the midst of all this uncertainty and controversy my faith in the rose of Jericho began to waver. We have all of us felt, at some time or other, a return of the bitter feeling we experienced when some of the poetical fancies of our childhood were ruthlessly shattered. It is no great sorrow, but none the less a keen sense of loss, the fading away of yet another delightful illusion. Could it be true that no one had ever seen this sweet, mystic, exquisitely-shaped flower, whose perfume, together with that of spikenard and cinnamon, impregnates so many pages of Scripture with the sweetest aroma ? Could no one tell me where to look for it ? Was it a mere Biblical image—a name and nothing more ? And yet it had received the great honour of being compared to Mary of Nazareth ! Was it possible, therefore, that it had been swept away with so many other things in Palestine—cities, towns, villages, nay, even Jericho itself, with its stupendous walls ? If the rose of Jericho had, indeed, never existed, then those tiresome scoffers and third-rate sceptics were in the right, and all those to whom travel is hateful, especially in countries possessing legends, traditions, poetry and the ideal, must learn, once and for all, that the rose of Jericho is but a flower of speech. " Mind you bring back a bunch of these roses and lilies of the valley," said my friend, mockingly, and, as usual, determined to be sarcastic, whereas in reality he is very inoffensive.

Do not imagine, reader, that I for a moment gave up all hope of finding this famed rose of Jericho. As I intended to spend two days in the hamlet where that town once stood, I determined to pass a part of my time in searching for this mysterious flower. I resolved to make some excursions in the neighbourhood in quest of it, and I, therefore, induced my dragoman to help me in the search, and to climb some of the surrounding hills, even the Quarantana Mountains, where Jesus after His baptism passed forty days in prayer and fasting. This mountain is yellow, arid and stony, formed of steep rocks; from its summit one looks over the great plain of Jericho, stretching to the Dead Sea, and the Jordan. Here Satan tempted our Lord, offering Him all the kingdoms of the world if He would but deny His Father in Heaven. It is a much more difficult and perilous ascent than that of Mount Tabor; but I was particularly desirous of attempting it, not only because I wished to visit all the places where Jesus passed, but also to discover the coveted flower. If I could not find it after all, well . . . there would be nothing for it but to own that nowhere under the blue of Heaven, amid the cooing of turtle-doves, neither in the time of the Prophets and Patriarchs, nor during the lifetime of Christ, or in our own days, never, never, had there existed a rose of Jericho!

One of the first excursions to be made, after having explored Jerusalem, is that to Bethlehem, which lies about an hour-and-a-half's drive from Zion. One day, as I was waiting for my dragoman to escort me outside the town, I entered a shop where such fancy goods were sold as finely incised mother-of-pearl shells representing some scene of the Passion, rosaries of all sorts and prices, small wooden or ivory crosses, necklaces made of curiously stained wooden beads, paper-cutters in mother-of-pearl, ash-trays formed of the Dead Sea blackstone, and numerous other small keepsakes in which deal the ever-active and business-like Bethlehemites. As I had made some small purchases and was about to leave the shop the tradesman asked me abruptly whether I would like to have a rose of Jericho!

THE ROSE OF JERICHO.

Quite taken aback by this unexpected request, I replied that I certainly should; whereupon he handed me what looked like a very dry bunch of shrivelled-up twigs, to which a few seeds were still attached.

"Is this withered sprig the rose of Jericho?" I queried.

"Yes," he answered, "it always looks like that."

"But," I objected, "have you none more freshly gathered?"

"The rose of Jericho is never fresh," he replied, phlegmatically.

"Perhaps this is not the right season?" I persisted, not at all impressed with this very withered specimen.

"That has nothing to do with it. Besides it performs its miracle all the same."

"What miracle?" I asked, more astonished than ever.

"If you soak it in water it opens, and its little branches spread out, giving signs of renewed life."

"What then?" I ventured to remark.

"It dries up again. But be sure you entirely cover it with water," he added.

On being told that it cost but a halfpenny, I purchased three of the yellow sprigs, which looked as though they might fall to pieces at any moment, and walked off, much elated at having obtained the rose of Jericho so cheaply. I smiled to myself as I thought how triumphantly I should now be able to refute my scoffing acquaintances. Still, I was not altogether enthusiastic, for it was depressing to think that the lovely flower so lauded by the Psalmist could never be obtained except in this withered form, instead of a rose with gloriously coloured petals, exhaling the most delicious fragrance. It is true that when plunged into water it did really expand and seemed even to sprout in places, but none the less I still felt secretly disappointed. That same evening, at the *table d'hôte*, I sat next to the secretary of the French Consulate and showed him my acquisition. He was, however, positive that it was not a real rose of Jericho, saying that such specimens as this were sold all over the place for a trifle.

I confessed I had only paid a halfpenny for it, and

asked him whether he had ever seen a genuine Jericho rose.

He answered that he had not done so as yet, but then he had only lately arrived in Palestine and had plenty of time before him in which to make his researches. He had been informed that either Jericho itself or the Quarantana Mountains were the most likely places to find the said flower.

" I will hunt for it there," said I, more to myself than to him.

The following day at two p.m. I started for Jericho. The first hour was passed entirely in the mountains, as Zion is over three hundred feet above the level of the sea. At that time it begins to get cool in Palestine and the sun was behind us. The beginning of the journey was therefore delightful; but, as I have already said elsewhere, the road presently begins to descend and continues doing so between arid hills. The sky recedes further and further as the traveller sinks deeper and deeper into what appears to be a narrowing, hot, and suffocating pit.

. Night was beginning to fall. The air was quite unbreathable, as with its three or four houses and twenty or thirty huts Jericho loomed in sight.

The temperature both in winter and summer hereabouts is such that, even were the surrounding lands fertile, very few people could live here on account of the heat, and, moreover, as the dragoman reiterates, it is the lowest spot on the face of the earth! At this statement, what little breath one has becomes quite spent. It is almost impossible to believe that on this site once stood a large and prosperous city, which was flourishing at the time of Christ, when it was called Rihah and was famous throughout Palestine for the quality of its bread. The question presents itself, how was it that so many farmers and merchants could have managed to live here? It was, no doubt, owing to some great seismic disturbance that the entire surface of the surrounding country has changed and that vast regions have been desolated and great cities annihilated. The Gospels speak of the Horns of Judgment

THE ROSE OF JERICHO.

being alone powerful enough to overturn the impregnable walls of Jericho—and now only this miserable group of hovels remains and not a living soul is to be seen! Where could we find a place in which to sleep? The small hotel had been closed on account of the heat since the end of April. The Russian refuge, where pilgrims of all denominations find room, is shut after the fifteenth of May.

One must, therefore, pass the night in the little house kept by the two old Russian women already described, and where, on payment of three shillings, you can get a room for yourself, while your dragoman is allowed to sleep on a couch in the dining-room, and the horsemen on the ground in the stable. I knocked at the gate. It was eight o'clock and already dark. No one answered. I knocked again. At last one of the two old women appeared with a lantern. The dragoman spoke to her in Arabic, and presently she gave us a rather surly reception. Once the horses were safely stabled, we proceeded along a garden path. Looking upwards we perceived the stars visible through the branches, and notwithstanding the darkness we realised the existence of luxuriant vegetation: but the atmosphere was so oppressive it was nearly impossible to breathe.

After about a quarter-of-an-hour the sense of suffocation was such that I opened each of my windows in turn, and at last went out into the garden. The stars were shining, but there was not a breath of air. I perceived something showing white under the trellis, and discovered it was a dear little convolvulus plant. I heard all sorts of strange rustlings and noises. I re-entered my room and tried to sleep, as it was already two o'clock in the morning, but the heat was so intense, my head seemed bursting; and, moreover, the mosquitoes stung me frightfully, so that I felt convinced that I was doomed to pass the night in a house of evil omen, teeming with venomous reptiles.

In the morning, before starting for Jordan, I made my dragoman ask the old Russian lady if there were any roses in Jericho: she answered that there certainly were.

By the light of dawn the house looked quite neat and

clean: and presently the old lady approached me with a smiling countenance, and bringing with her a lovely rose.

The dragoman, interpreting, asked her whether this was the real rose of Jericho: she said yes, and declared she knew of no other, although she had lived in Jericho twenty-eight years.

I, therefore, carried off my rose in high glee. It was a lovely, fresh, bright-coloured flower, much like our own rose of May, though smaller. I carried it with me to the Jordan and the Dead Sea, and thought of it continually during my long silent journey. On my return to Jerusalem, as it was beginning to fade, I placed it carefully between two sheets of cotton-wool and put it in a big book, saying to myself that if the cheeks of the Hebrew women had had that lovely tint and their breath had been as sweet, then in very truth was the psalmist right.

At dinner that same evening, my friend the young French Secretary introduced to me the Doctor of the Consulate, a most charming and clever man, who had lived in Palestine for eight years.

"Well, madam," he said, "did you find the rose of Jericho?"

"Indeed I have! I have brought it back with me."

"On the Quarantana Mountains, no doubt," he observed.

"It was needless for me to make that ascent, for I found it in the garden of the house where I passed the night."

On this he looked very sceptical and, shaking his head, murmured, "Strange!"

When I asked why he thought it strange, he said that the rose was seldom found, and then only at great altitudes. He begged to see it, and I acquiesced, bringing the book in which I had placed it, though already the lovely colour was gone.

The learned Doctor told me it was only a simple May rose, and was surprised I had not recognised it, since, he said, there must be plenty of them in Naples. When I pointed out that this particular one actually came from Jericho, he replied that no doubt it did, but, for all that,

THE ROSE OF JERICHO.

it was not the flower mentioned in Scripture. Seeing my profound disappointment, he consoled me by saying that he had three or four genuine specimens and would make me a present of one.

When I returned to Naples, I carried my real rose of Jericho in a little box, together with its scientific description. It is a tiny, dry, horn-shaped flower, about the size of a finger-nail : it has small withered branches, which spread out the moment the stem is placed in water, though the colour does not return. This is the scientific description : " It is a plant belonging to the Composite Family : is grey in colour and woolly in texture, and spreads out widely at its base. The sheath of the dry leaves presents noteworthy hygrometric qualities to which M. de Saulcy was the first to call attention. This plant, which is known as *Astericus acquaticus*, is also termed *Saulsya igrometrica*. The *Anastatica antherocuntica*, or false rose of Jericho, is found abundantly in the plains of El Zelzyd : but this plant lacks certain qualities which the *Astericus acquaticus* possesses ; so that both de Saulcy and Michon consider the latter to be the rose of Jericho known to the ancients. Moreover, they have called attention to the fact that many families which trace their pedigree back to the time of the Crusades have a rose which exactly resembles the *Astericus acquaticus*, and is not the least like the *anastatica*, on their escutcheons : the true rose of Jericho grows all over the Quarantana Mountains."

The one I possess does indeed open out when placed in water, but otherwise it remains dry, grey, and woolly. Such is the rose of Jericho !

PART VII.
IN GALILEE.

I.

ON THE ROAD.

ALTHOUGH, according to the maps, the distance between Jerusalem and Nazareth seems trifling, eight days on horseback are, however, needed to accomplish the journey overland, by crossing half Judæa, all Samaria, and a part of Galilee. This journey is most fatiguing, and is only undertaken by natives or by those most dauntless of all pilgrims, the Russian peasants. Another way of reaching this interesting town and region is *via* sea to Jaffa and Haifa, and thence on to Nazareth by carriage; the roads are, however, bad, and the conveyances detestable. There is really no road for a great part of the way, and one seldom passes any other vehicle, and is beset by many dangers, some real and others imaginary, though none the less terrifying. The choice generally settles upon the sea route by way of Jaffa. The absurd little railway already described takes you from Jerusalem to Jaffa in three and a half hours, say on a Tuesday evening. On Wednesday morning an Austrian Lloyd steamer carries you to Haifa, which you reach on the evening of the same day. On Thursday morning you take a carriage to Nazareth, thus accomplishing the whole journey in two days and a half, with many changes and much fatigue, it is true—by train, sea, and carriage, sleeping at Jaffa and at Haifa, and snatching a meal whenever an hour can be spared for the purpose.

One willingly undertakes to encounter all these difficulties in order to reach Galilee, which has so many irresistible attractions. When you have seen the localities that witnessed Christ's Passion and Death ; when you have experienced so many heartrending emotions, you will find the utmost consolation in visiting these peaceful scenes where His youthful years were spent.

As you approach the coast of St. John-of-Acre and behold afar off the snow-capped peaks of Mount Hermon, the treacherous Syrian Sea becomes bluer, and the coast line, as seen through a slight mist, is less angular, assuming a sunny green tint which soon effaces your recollection of the tawny, sterile land of Jericho. The little industrial town of Haifa, the seaport of Carmel, which seems in perpetual adoration before the great Sanctuary of the Virgin, towering above it, bids you a pleasant welcome to its hospitable German hostelry. The people, nay, the very air, strike you as gentle and beneficent.

At dawn next day the German coachman, George Suss by name, knocked at my door. His little cart, with its big, powerful horses, was already waiting outside. Suss was a good honest Westphalian, settled in Haifa, and moreover a member of a very industrious German colony. He was the happy possessor of several carriages, but, for fear of accident, drove me himself to Nazareth. The journey was begun in the freshness of dawn, and we passed through cornfields, beds of rivers, and by the side of very steep precipices. The carriage flew along, but with a rather uncomfortable swaying motion. Occasionally a halt was made in the deep shade of some fine old tree to enable us to refresh ourselves with wine and biscuits. The scenery was quite enchanting in its rural simplicity. As we traversed the well-cultivated fields of the rich plain of Esdraelon, the mystic charm of the country became more and more apparent. At every turn of the road, sometimes near and sometimes far off, Mount Tabor, the Mount of the Transfiguration, stood out round and green, like an immense mound thrown up from the flowery plain at its feet. Swarthy farmers, clad in blue cotton shirts and trousers, greeted each other pleasantly in Arabic as they passed by on their way to work. Now and then, a cart laden with wood or stones trundled along the road. A spirit of exquisite peace and calm pervaded everything. The curtains of the little cart were stirred by a gentle breeze, whilst overhead stretched the clearest of blue skies. Although Nazareth was still far off we were in no hurry to reach it, feeling quite happy in the enjoyment of the delightful country we were passing through. In what did this peacefulness consist? Could there be something more besides the fact that Galilee was, above all others, the land of Love? Undoubtedly my feelings had undergone a marked change since we landed at Haifa, and I was filled with a strange sense of tenderness and joy, for is not Galilee the land in which Charity and Mercy are best illustrated in the material and spiritual beauties of the landscape? When you first behold Nazareth from the surrounding hills, the truth dawns upon you in its sweet significance. Galilee is not only the Land of Jesus, but it is also the Land of Mary.

II.

HERR HARDEGG.

THE Hôtel Jerusalem at Jaffa is always crowded with people, although no one ever stops there. The reason is simple: Jaffa being a seaport town, French, Austrian, Russian, and Egyptian steamers call to take up tourists and pilgrims for the Holy Land, and discharge cargo, and arrive and leave with the utmost punctuality on fixed days and at stated hours; consequently, the pilgrim knows the exact day and hour when he will reach Jaffa, when he will be able to leave it, and, therefore, can arrange his plans accordingly. These facts explain why the hotel is always by day full of travellers, and empty of them at night. The busiest time is from nine in the morning until two p.m. every day. Then there is a continuous string of carriages, cracking of whips, and tinkling of bells all the way up the dusty road which leads from the commercial city through the scented orchards of the suburbs, to the clean white quarter inhabited by the German colony, of which the Hôtel Jerusalem may be called the chief monument, and its proprietor, Herr Hardegg, the principal inhabitant. It is one perpetual procession of porters laden with baggage, for the most part belonging to English travellers, plastered all over with the labels of half the hotels in the world. Then follow animated discussions and shouts from beneath the flower-covered pergola in front of the hotel door; there is a noisy going up and down the wooden staircase, screaming voices from open doors, demanding hot water and cups of coffee, or asking the hour of breakfast. There is an everlasting hubbub, keys turning in locks, upsetting of chairs; in short, all the miscellaneous noises that accompany unexpected arrivals and departures. Suddenly the breakfast gong sounds; and, notwithstanding their British phlegm, which requires three bells to sound before they obey the summons, the stalwart tourists from old Albion rush headlong downstairs. There are never less than twenty or thirty people at breakfast: Greeks, Egyptians, Russians, Germans, and, above all others, English. The meal is abundant, and fairly good, and no one complains, even the fastidious English eating it without grumbling. People hastily drink their wine of Hebron, which costs a franc a bottle, and devour their food without as much as glancing at their neighbour; scalding coffee is gulped down, and the bill is paid in such haste that it is not even looked at. At two o'clock another noisy crowd arrives: but by half-past two a conventual silence envelops the Hôtel Jerusalem, broken only by the rustling leaves of the orange trees in its garden.

It is quite worth while remaining a day or two in Jaffa, both going to and coming from Jerusalem. The town itself is pretty and quaint, and deserves visiting, as also do its monasteries and churches, and, above all, its gardens, which are famous all over Syria. Then again, the Hôtel Jerusalem, together with its proprietor, Herr Hardegg, would alone merit a short stay. The Herr is a thin wiry little man, quite wonderful for his age; has short grey whiskers, and an expression of placid serenity. He invariably wears a pair of grey trousers, a black overcoat, and a velvet skull-cap covers his bald head. Herr Hardegg is always rigidly correct in manner, and flits silently about like a shadow. He is not only an hotel keeper, but a Christian, and, above all else, a moralist and philosopher. It would be impossible to discover all these intellectual qualities at once, as he rarely speaks : indeed, he never deigns to hold any conversation with the travellers during the three or four hours of tumult, when he will suddenly appear at some door or on the stairs, casting a cold glance here and there out of his steely eyes, but never opening his thin lips to utter a word. Those who only make the usual brief halt at Jaffa do not, probably, notice that instead of a number being affixed to each door, as in all other hotels, at the Jerusalem this number is replaced by the name of a patriarch, prophet, or some other great man of the Old Testament, such as Abraham, Jacob, Ezekiel, or Elias, and then a little further on, David, or Dan ; the door opposite mine bore the name of Melchisedec, and my own of Joshua.

Few travellers will, I fear, find time to study the strange book, printed in English, German, and even Italian, which is placed on the table in the middle of every room. The cover is embellished with symbolic signs—beasts representing the seven deadly sins, dragons of the Apocalypse, and seven-branched candelabra. For this reason, although Herr Hardegg, host, Christian, philosopher, and moralist, is not above accepting the cash of his guests, since he cannot improve their morals, he rather looks down upon them. Only those who stay for a day or so under his roof have a chance of coming under his evangelising influence.

You are sure to meet the Greek Consul at the Hotel, as he lives there ; also Cook's representative, with his wife and daughter ; and, at the time of which I am speaking, there was a tall, handsome Turkish official, a nephew of the Sultan, and *aide-de-camp* of the Governor of Jerusalem, a most cultivated man, one of those refined Mohammedans who have served in the Embassies either of Paris or St. Petersburg. Sometimes, too, a whimsical traveller will remain, either from curiosity, because he is weary, or for some other physical or moral reason which determines him not to go on to Jerusalem that same day: these people—perhaps some six or seven—dine and chat together. The dinner is excellent—Herr Hardegg loves the traveller who stops and whom he hopes to convert, so he feeds him well: but for the others, who just come and go, he cares not at all. He even condescends to be present at the evening dinner, though he does not eat. One wonders *when* he eats: he probably often fasts, from religious motives. But, oh! wonder of wonders, he actually speaks to those guests who elect to stay the night, and finds them, moreover, very interesting, and even willing to read his book. After a little conversation, we retire to our rooms, to read a bit, or write a letter or two, when, attracted by the serpents, wolves, tortoises, and pole-cats on the cover, we proceed to dip into Herr Hardegg's moral treatises, and find they consist of a most curious blending of passages from the Bible, and of strange fragments from the writings of the Early Fathers, together with weird commentaries by Herr Hardegg himself. Maledictions, prophecies, ejaculations, mysteries, and fearfully complicated phrases run through the volume, the main idea of which is that not a step can be taken in life without falling into sin. A cheerful thought for a traveller! I could not, however, refrain from perusing this book, wherein Tolstoian philosophy, especially that of the "Kreutzer Sonata," was curiously transcribed. Herr Hardegg is particularly bitter against matrimony, which he considers a most criminal state; and he, therefore, vigorously inveighs against husbands and wives. He is capable of pouncing upon you suddenly: as, indeed, he did upon me, when, on coming upstairs from dinner, about nine o'clock at night, the first evening after my arrival, I found him standing close to my door.

"Are you married?" he blurted out, without even looking me in the face.

"Of course," I replied, much taken aback.

"Then read my book," he added, and immediately disappeared.

The following day, just as I was about to enter the

carriage, he came up to me and asked severely, " Have you read it ? "

I answered, humbly, that I had.

" And have you understood it ? " he said, in a tone charged with threats of Divine retribution in the event of my not agreeing with his philosophy.

" I hope so," I replied, quite abashed.

He was evidently entirely satisfied with me, for the following day I found an Italian copy of this moral treatise on my table. In the afternoon, about six o'clock, as I was sitting close to the windows in a rocking chair, smiling to myself while reading his dreary meditations, I saw him walking up and down outside. He looked up at me and nodded his head approvingly. I evidently appeared to him a good subject and was apparently in great favour, for the waiters hastened at my summons, and my letters were brought to me with lightning speed : the housemaid did my room twice instead of once a day, and my unfinished bottle of " Hebron " wine was carefully preserved till the next meal. During these days the only subjects for Herr Hardegg's evangelisation were myself, a Russian suffering from lung disease, and an English lady : the Greek Consul, Cook's representative, and the Turkish official appeared to be deaf to Herr Hardegg's teaching. But I was the special object of all his attentions, and, in his pride as a philosopher, when I was leaving for Jerusalem, he said he hoped we should meet again. Six weeks afterwards, on my road to Galilee, we indeed did so. The hotel was so quiet and fresh, owing to its pleasant-scented garden, and the sea-breeze was so delightful, that I willingly passed two days there. Before me on the table lay the precious volume, and Herr Hardegg may have imagined I was taking notes from it, for during those two days he smiled at me from afar. When I finally left for Galilee he actually had the condescension to open the door of my carriage, and remain leaning against it while the luggage was stowed away.

" You must read my book when you get home," he proudly observed, with a placid smile.

" I will do so, most certainly," I solemnly promised.

" And make your husband read it also. Here is

one for him," and out of his pocket he pulled yet another copy.

"Many thanks," I murmured, composedly.

"If you meet with any difficulties in understanding it, write to me. People consult me on moral and philosophical questions from all parts of the world."

"Herr Hardegg, you are quite an apostle," I said, with conviction.

"Yes, madam, I am," he replied, taking off his black velvet cap as I drove off.

For all that, Herr Hardegg's bills are scarcely what most people would consider *moderate*.

III.

THE CORN MERCHANT.

THE Austrian Lloyd steamship *Achilles* left the port of Jaffa at midday, and was due at Haifa at seven o'clock in the evening. It had taken in passengers at Alexandria, Port Said, and Jaffa, and was accomplishing its journey along the coast of Egypt, Palestine, Syria, and Asia Minor, as far as Constantinople, loading and unloading wherever it put in. The hum of voices, rattling of chains, and general hubbub of men and things were only in a measure hushed during the hours of the night. Father Marcello of Noilhac, Father Joseph of Naples, and myself, got on board at Jaffa to land at Haifa, a short passage, but there were many who had been on board three weeks and more and were quite at home and familiar with all the customs of the vessel.

Father Marcello, a Franciscan, and Superior of the Convent at Nazareth, was still quite young, charming, thoughtful, and somewhat of a mystic. Father Joseph of Naples, on the other hand, was a good, burly friar, with a black beard tinged with grey, and was the most popular

Franciscan monk in the Holy Land—clever, amiable, and so active as to be almost restless. He still retained a slight Neapolitan accent, and those qualities of quick perception and intuition so characteristic of his native place. He knows and does everything—is a diplomatic agent, and a most pious man; a cheerful and shrewd traveller, and understands Jews, Christians, and Maronites, as well as any farmer's wife does the four-and-twenty hens of her poultry yard. When we got on board, Father Marcello sauntered off by himself to read his breviary: Father Joseph, however, was immediately surrounded by a crowd of people—the captain, ship's doctor, the Austrian Lloyd agent, and five or six more. I placed myself near enough to catch his familiar accent, suggestive of dear Naples and the first time I had heard it since my arrival in Palestine, and naturally it quite touched my heart. I was feeling rather sad at the thought that I should never again press my lips on the cold stone of the Holy Sepulchre, that I should no more behold Jerusalem, or see the sun rise above the Garden of Gethsemane. The second part of my journey to Galilee appeared rather colourless as compared with the stirring emotions of the first. All the time Father Joseph was going backwards and forwards, laughing, arguing, shaking his head in the odd manner so absolutely Neapolitan: always in motion, shaking hands first with one and then with another, but never unduly exciting himself as so many of my compatriots are wont to do. Just now he was surrounded by the children of a French *employé* in the service of Turkey, who had been ordered to leave Alexandria for Constantinople, and was going to pass a couple of months at Cyprus before settling down. With these children the good Father was chatting away in French. Then, all at once, he disappeared. Meanwhile, I went and sat down at the prow, partly to watch the track we were making—a favourite pastime of mine, as I can imagine so many things in the long line of white foam—and partly to read a book. Suddenly Father Joseph appeared beside me, followed by an Eastern gentleman wearing black trousers, frock coat, and red fez. He was a man about fifty, of middle height, stalwart, cleanshaven, and had very bright, merry eyes.

"Allow me to introduce Ibrahim Effendi to you," said Father Joseph, addressing me.

I wondered why he presented this Ottoman to me, for, unlike a Mohammedan, he did not put his hand to his forehead and heart, but stretched it out frankly to meet mine.

"The Custodians of the Holy Places have no better friend than Ibrahim," continued Father Joseph.

Thereupon I observed the new comer, who blushed at the praise of the Franciscan and vainly endeavoured to put in a protest. Then I stupidly remarked, it was a fine thing for a Turk to venerate the Holy Land and her monks; whereat Ibrahim turned pale and a look of pain overspread his features.

"I am not a Moslem, madam," he murmured in a sad tone. "I am a Christian."

"I beg your pardon—so much the better," I remarked, quite overcome with mortification.

"And, moreover, a good Christian!" asserted the Neapolitan father, emphatically.

Thus conversing, I learnt by degrees who Ibrahim Effendi really was. It appeared he was a very rich corn merchant of St. John-of-Acre. He had come from Lebanon to the coast, and was a man of strict morals, who divided his time between his great corn warehouses and the numerous religious exercises his piety obliged him to pursue, and which absorbed his whole attention. He carried the same devotion into his commercial transactions that he did into the prayers he repeated at intervals throughout the day. He was more than devout—I should describe him as a positive enthusiast—for his faith was something so impetuous and spontaneous, so apparent in every word and tone, that it put our own lukewarmness to shame, and excited my sincerest admiration and even envy. Ibrahim spent large sums of money in charity and had erected, at his own expense, a church in honour of St. Louis, King of France, who had ardently wished to die in the land of Jesus. He assisted generously by his liberality the Custodians of the Holy Places, for, unfortunately, Italy gives nothing towards the maintenance of the Franciscans, who are an Italian order of monks: and

Ibrahim has always successfully intervened in the settlement of any disputes which have arisen between them and the Turkish authorities. It may well be said of him " that his left hand knew not what his right hand gave ! "

It was during his travels, however, that his religious zeal showed itself in the most remarkable manner. He went to Europe every spring for three months to visit all the noblest Cathedrals and most famous shrines. He would wander from Cologne to Loreto, from St. James of Compostella to Lourdes, or even to the valley of Pompeii : in short, to wherever there is a beautiful church, an important shrine, or place of pilgrimage. During those three months this otherwise practical man of business was absorbed by religious fervour ; and he had thus travelled for eight or ten years past, caring little or nothing for the cities and their monuments. Uninterested in contemporary life, his whole mind was rapt in the contemplation of the pictures of the Madonna and the saints. He cared nothing for those things which form the chief attractions of travel to the ordinary mortal, but if you asked him who was the famous French preacher at Notre Dame des Victoires, he could not only give you the name but tell you the subjects of his sermons. These three months were full of infinite happiness to this worthy man and gave him the necessary courage wherewith to cope with shrewd Jews, obstinate Mussulmans, German freight agents, Arab porters, and all the fighting, screaming gang with whom he had to deal during the remaining nine. His piety was wholly free from ostentation or self-righteousness.

" Where have you been this year ? " I asked.

With an expression of intense satisfaction depicted in his face, Ibrahim informed me that he had been to Italy, France, and Spain.

" Ah, you went first to Italy ? "

" Yes, dear madam. What a wonderful country is yours ! "

" You went there on business, I suppose ? " said I, unable to forget the corn merchant.

" Not at all, not at all. I visited Italy for St. Mark's at Venice, the Duomo at Florence, for St. Peter's at Rome, and for the matchless Madonnas painted by your incomparable artists! I dream of them all when I return to St. John-of-Acre. This year I had indeed a happy experience in Rome!"

"You saw the Pope, did you not?" I asked, appreciating the nature of the man for the first time.

"Yes, I saw the Pope," he replied, in an awed whisper.

"And what did you think of him?"

Ibrahim answered in an undertone: "I can scarcely tell you. I had been waiting for an audience for more than a week and was so much excited I could no longer eat or sleep. When I did get inside the Vatican I was kept waiting three or four hours. During the last hour I could scarcely control my impatience. At last he appeared, that little, frail man all clad in white, with the waxen face and hands. I fell on my knees before him. Shall I ever forget it? I could almost feel his presence as he came forward and spoke to my companions. When at last he reached me I was well-nigh breathless at the thought that Pope Leo XIII., the representative of Christ upon earth, was standing close to the poor corn merchant of Acre!"

"And did he speak to you? and what did he say?"

"Yes," answered Ibrahim, in a tone of profound emotion. "He said, 'Are you an Oriental Christian?' I shall never forget that voice as long as I live!"

"And you. What did you reply?"

"Scarcely anything. I just said, 'Your Holiness, I am a Maronite of Lebanon,' and nothing more. I might have said a hundred things. I would have offered my fortune, my very life, for Christ's sake and His Church, but I had not the courage. I merely gazed at him with tears in my eyes; and he, who is the head of the Church, the spiritual ruler of millions of Christians, who has the power to bind and to loose, looked at me so tenderly that I could say nothing to him."

"He is sure to have understood you," I said.

"Yes; I believe he did," Ibrahim answered, with conviction.

After this we were silent. The *Achilles* was in sight of Mount Carmel.

THE CORN MERCHANT.

"I also went to Naples not long ago," said he, after a pause.

"Oh, did you—to Naples?" I asked, quite interested.

"I always go there when I am in Italy. There is no place where faith is so ardent. Religion is as it should be there. The churches are always full on Sundays, and even on week-days they are far from empty. I kissed the reliquary that contains the blood of St. Gennaro. What a glorious church is Santa Chiara! I could not keep away from it. But how is it that the façade of your cathedral is unfinished?"

"For want of funds, dear sir; the Neapolitans, though believers, are very poor."

"Never mind, never mind. God will provide."

"Why don't *you* complete the façade for us yourself?" I asked.

"Would that I could, and many other churches besides. But it would need greater riches than I possess. I give what I can to the poor, to the houses, and to the servants of Jesus. I give a good deal in Naples because I love it, with its churches, where I go to confession and to Holy Communion, and to recite my rosary among the pious people. Your people will have all the graces in heaven and on earth!"

"The fact is that, although poor, they are a very contented people."

"God bless them! I also visited Pompeii and my favourite Madonna of the Rosary, and found her more beautiful and rich in gifts and offerings than ever. The miracles which take place at this shrine are beyond count. I remained three days at Val de Pompeii, and hope to return several times before I die."

"You will end by becoming a monk," I said, smiling.

"Oh, no. I am too independent and self-willed. I must travel, and say my rosary in all parts of the world. Besides, I am obliged to look after my business. The poor need money, and Christ has given me so many to care for. How could I be a monk? Time is short, and though I am a corn merchant, I am also a humble servant of God, trying to do my duty, though not belonging to any religious order.

Do you think I am mistaken ? Do you think life in the world must necessarily be sinful ? "

" I am sure I cannot tell," I said, thoughtfully. " Maybe it is selfishness to leave the world, and maybe not."

He gazed at me anxiously. It was easy to see that even he had often asked himself questions which occasionally torment every Christian conscience.

As the *Achilles* neared the promontory we became silent. The day was waning when Ibrahim pointed out Mount Carmel to me, suggesting we should recite the " Ave Maris Stella." Then falling on his knees, with myself and several others, Ibrahim, with bent head, prayed, and his face wore a touchingly serene expression, while we all recited the Mariners' Hymn.

IV.

MOUNT CARMEL.

THOSE who quit Egypt for Syria, passing by way of Port Said, which is always more or less in a ferment, need a deep sense of mysticism in order to fully appreciate the Holy Land, the first sight of which is Jaffa, seen through a mist that envelops its grey and white houses, making them all look one colour, and blurring the rich tints of the verdant orange groves. Jaffa, with its dangerous bay and white-crested waves, looks both charming and original, with its line of new houses extending along the yellow-sanded coast to right and left of the ancient Oriental city, but it affords no definite indication of being the Holy Land where Jesus Lived, Suffered, and Died. Nothing in either its outline or colouring awakens emotion in the pilgrim, who vainly looks for some evidence that he is approaching the sacred region, and it is, therefore, within himself that he must seek that spiritual enthusiasm which dims the eyes and makes the heart beat.

MOUNT CARMEL.

The traveller from Italy, Germany, or France arrives in Palestine from Smyrna, after regretfully leaving Beyrout, the Pearl of the East, coasts Syria without touching at any place on the way, and enters the harbour at Jaffa in the early morning hours. He is sure to find the prospect of the gentle curve line of the coast and the ancient fortified town of St. John-of-Acre, together with its neat little seaport, Haifa, extremely beautiful. But his interest, however, is not alone attracted by the graceful outline of the shore, seen in the limpid morning air, dotted with large and small towns, some with a glorious past, but fallen into decay, others new and flourishing : but by two magic words spoken on board, which have brought everybody up on deck, and compelled even the most indolent to quit his deck-chair, and the invalid his berth—" Mount Carmel ! "

The great promontory advances out into the sea, curving round and forming the bay, with its blue still waters : the Mountain of Mary rises to the left, covered with verdure, trees, and grass to its summit. The dazzling white church stands out, clearly defined, against the deep blue, seeming to watch over the waves, which during eight months of the year are never at rest.

Pious pilgrims who pass beneath the shadow of the mountain where Mary prayed and where she appeared after her Assumption, look up at its Sanctuary, so far above them and apparently so much nearer to God, with feelings of mystic emotion evoked by this first glimpse of the land of the prophets and patriarchs. They humbly sink upon their knees and stretch out their hands towards the mountain where Mary in her girlhood was wont to accompany her mother, and they murmur quietly the " Ave Maris Stella." For here, more than elsewhere, is the Blessed Virgin the protectress of the seafarers who implore her aid, as she looks down from the verdant Carmel on all the bread-winners who risk their lives at sea, as well as on all the countless pilgrims who make this journey of love. According to Hebrew tradition, on this mountain, where the angry tones of the Prophet Elias were heard, St. Anne and St. Joachim, the parents of Mary, who were fairly well off, possessed both land and cattle. Every year they left the fair land of Galilee and the heights of Sepphoris and Cana, near the happy vale of Nazareth, and, crossing the wide plain of Esdraelon, came, accompanied by their daughter, to Carmel. Those scented paths where the pretty yellow daisies grow have, therefore, often been pressed by the little feet of the purest of women and the most sorrowful of mothers. How often must she have sat on these rocky heights to gaze with her sweet thoughtful eyes over the expanse of blue waters, and thus became the bright " Star of the Sea." As we approach the Mount of Mary we indeed realise that we are in sight of the Holy Land.

An excellent road with many a pleasant curve, rich in verdure, ascends the sacred hill and leads to the Sanctuary of the monks of our Lady of Carmel. It is one of the few good roads in Palestine, and even the indolent traveller can indulge in day-dreams as the carriage leisurely makes the ascent, which is quite easy to perform on foot. The drive passes between hedges of the sweet-smelling herbs from which the monks make their famous elixir. At every turn the blue-grey expanse of the Syrian Sea greets the eye, and far off is seen the bay of St. John-of-Acre, with the white houses of Haifa nestling at the foot of the mountain. It is an enchanting sight, but for some unaccountable reason has nothing Oriental about it, for Carmel recalls other sanctuaries nearer home by the shores of the Mediterranean wherein I have often prayed. It requires quite an effort of memory to realise that this beautiful convent, with its well-cultivated grounds, is not situated at Sorento or at Francavilla in the Abruzzi, and that it is the promontory where, in the days of the prophets, Elias lived as a hermit in a cave and from whence he preached and foretold the future to the expectant people. Here Mary of Nazareth tripped with light step along the herb-covered paths. Every sailor, be he from Constantinople or Beyrout, Piræus or Latakia, Alexandria of Egypt or Cyprus, turns his eyes with loving gaze towards this famed spot. It is almost impossible to believe that this neat-looking convent is that same Carmel which my good townsfolk invoke every hour of the day as they ask for protection or help in the trials of daily life. Oh! dear, dear Lady of Mount Carmel, whose scapular covers many a

MOUNT CARMEL.

brave heart in far distant lands, thy dwelling is indeed beautiful, with its flowers and its sweet-scented herbs, and the very road to it is so easy that the most inactive can reach it. But thou didst love simple rural scenes, vast horizons, and noble solitudes!

In the convent garden, the monks, who are all Frenchmen, are rather silent and distant in manner, but kindly withal. They distribute medals, rosaries, and printed prayers in honour of our Lady of Mount Carmel, in exchange for which you make a small offering. These Barefooted Carmelites wear the white and brown habit of their order. They have, for the most part, received their education in this far-distant land. They sell the balsam called *Eau de mélisse des Carmes*, which is excellent in cases of paralysis, heart failure, or even ordinary indigestion. The large bottles cost half-a-crown, and the small ones half that price. It is through the sale of this liqueur and the offerings of those who visit it, that the magnificent convent and its splendid grounds are kept up. There were two Russian pilgrims in the parlour, in their moujik's dress, with long, fair locks and dust-covered shoes. They had, no doubt, come on foot overland from Jerusalem, and had been at least a week on the way. They both looked weary and ill, and were standing silently beside the table where bottles of *Eau des Carmes* were exposed. A Carmelite, silent and patient, waited for them to speak. The Russians had already bought scapulars, rosaries, and medals, and had made their small offerings. They evidently wished to purchase the elixir, but since they only spoke Russian and the Father only French, they could not explain what they wanted. So great, however, was their longing to possess the cordial that the wish was expressed in their eyes, without any need of words, for it was quite evident they imagined that the water was miraculous and expected no one knows what wonders to be worked by its agency. They looked anxiously at the monk, and, by signs on either side, soon made out the price. This done, they looked very dejected, for they had so little money. The monk, absorbed in meditation, waited on patiently. I, close by, was much affected by their distress.

At last one of the two pilgrims took out of his pocket an

old worn portfolio, and approaching me, examined its contents. It only contained four Turkish francs, of which he decided to spend one and a half for the miraculous water. I would willingly have paid the money for him myself, but did not dare propose it. The poor fellow gave his franc, and in return grasped the phial with a look of intense delight. Who knows whether to-morrow he will not have to go without bread, and, overcome with exhaustion, be obliged to lie down under some hedge on the road to Nazareth? This elixir, excellently made from the balm which grows hereabouts, is unsurpassed in cases of nervous prostration. To the poor Russian, who believes so thoroughly in the supernatural, it will no doubt prove to have miraculous power, for, having sipped it, he will gain renewed energy, strength and patience, and will accomplish his pious pilgrimage without dying of fatigue or hunger by the way.

Our Lady of Carmel will surely watch over the good man and intercede with God for his safe return to his distant home.

V.

ON THE ROAD TO NAZARETH.

I was, no doubt, asleep and still dreaming of a certain dear little face with tip-tilted nose and great solemn eyes, when a heavy step, which made the wooden staircase of the Mount Carmel Hotel creak, wakened the echoes, and stopped before the door of my room. After two sharp raps, a voice announced, in unmistakable Teutonic accents: "It is five o'clock, madam."

My own most trustworthy of travelling clocks, which no change of temperature or vicissitudes of circumstances could impair, also marked the hour of five to the minute, as George Suss, the German driver, informed me that it was time to get ready for my journey to Nazareth.

ON THE ROAD TO NAZARETH.

Used as I was by this time to Oriental unpunctuality, I had specially impressed it upon the said George Suss that I did not wish to be late, as it would take six hours to reach Nazareth from Haifa by carriage, and if we delayed our starting, the heat would be quite intolerable by eleven. Now, however, the exactitude of the worthy Prussian annoyed me. Instead of going to bed at half-past nine like a reasonable person, as was my custom, I had foolishly remained on the terrace of the hotel until midnight, watching the Bay of Acre and the fantastic effects of the electric light which came from the British squadron exercising in the night. I had lost three hours' sleep, and was vexed at being waked from delightful dreams. Moreover, it was very cold, the sun having only just appeared behind Mount Carmel. Presently the harsh German tones of George Suss were heard again:

"Madam, it is half-past five."

The moment I opened my door he entered, and taking luggage and umbrellas, carried them down himself and placed them under the seat of the vehicle. As I was drinking my cup of tea I studied my coachman and his carriage. This German was a tall, thin, lank individual, with a short, mahogany-coloured beard, who wore a cork helmet pulled well down over his eyes: it appeared that he was the owner of three conveyances, but when he had to do with a *personage*— a prelate, a lady, or a rich Englishman—he himself drove the best of the three. This consisted of an immensely high four-wheeled *char-à-banc* with four seats, screened by an awning. It stood so high from the ground that we had to mount on a chair to reach the lowest step. Later during the journey, Suss explained in very Teutonic Italian that it was necessary the vehicle should be raised high off the ground, as it had often to descend into gullies and to cross the beds of rivers, and other marshy stretches of ground. For twenty francs (and two for *pourboire*), this lofty and imposing vehicle, which could easily have held ten persons, became my property during the journey to Nazareth. The Father Custodian of Jerusalem and Head of the Franciscans of the Holy Land had recommended me specially to his magnanimous care, so that George Suss became not only my driver, but my protector, guide, and friend. He occasionally observed me with an expression in which gentleness, patience, and perfect trustworthiness were blended. Perhaps he felt some curiosity with respect to a woman who was neither English, American, nor German, but only Italian, belonging to a country whence no one ever came to visit the Holy Land. Of what consequence could she possibly be?

We started off at a good brisk trot along the principal road of Haifa. By this time I had quite got over my feeling of sleepiness and annoyance. The carriage stopped before the door of the Franciscan Convent to take up Father Marcello of Noilhac, Superior of the Franciscans of Nazareth, who was returning to his home after a month's absence in Jerusalem. He was remarkable among the many strange types of Franciscan friars. Bony and thin in the face, with a rather sparse brown beard, he wore a great straw hat covered with a silk handkerchief, the usual head-covering of the monks of Palestine. He was very polite, but somewhat taciturn, and had melancholy-looking eyes, full of a certain expression of spiritual mysticism which I had not hitherto connected with monks. He was a Frenchman, and knew not a word of Italian. A slight hectic flush on his cheeks probably accounted for his presence in the mild climate of the Holy Land, which it was hoped might effect a cure, or, maybe, he had elected to come here to die in peace near the Holy Sepulchre. Further along the road we overtook a Turk going towards Nazareth, who asked me the favour of a lift, which, of course, I willingly accorded him. What a strange medley of people we were in that great, high, lumbering coach, driven by a Prussian from Magdeburg! The pious follower of St. Francis, who had come from a far-distant region of France, the Italian lady from Naples, and the Turk from Haifa. Thus as we drove towards the land where Jesus passed His happy childhood and gracious adolescence, we crossed the immense plain of Esdraelon in the fresh morning air. The light breeze swayed the tops of the grasses and the great wheels of the carriage crushed the daisies and bright yellow celandines. Father Marcello meanwhile with a serene expression recited his rosary and read his breviary. George Suss glanced lovingly at him

ON THE ROAD TO NAZARETH.

from time to time, for he adored the Franciscans of Nazareth, who brought him all his custom and prosperity. The fact that he was a Lutheran made no difference. He believed in Christ as completely as did the friar, whose eyes were bent on the yellow page of his book, and he asked no more, neither did he argue, but seemed to follow with the movement of his whip the slow turning of the sacred pages. The Turk smoked his cigarettes, dozing occasionally, his fez tumbling over his eyes at every jerk of the coach. He smoked even when he was asleep. I, meanwhile, gave myself up entirely to the enjoyment of the scene, and studied the beautiful landscape, so clear in the morning light, cultivated in plots of yellow and green. The morning breezes wafted off the fumes of the Turk's cigar and those of the short pipe of George Suss, who had craved permission to smoke also. Father Marcello pointed out from time to time some object of interest.

"That is the great Hermon," he said.

Hermon, the highest mountain of Galilee, is always covered with snow, its white crest lost in the sheen of the Oriental sky. Now our road lay entirely through pathless fields, and the air was filled with fragrance. We talked of the Kishon, a river the carriage had to ford where and when its waters were not too swollen. Father Marcello, having finished his prayers, told us in his thin, weak voice how he had been obliged one winter to remain shut up in Nazareth for two months, as he could not get to Jerusalem by way of Haifa, and the road through Samaria was still worse. The Kishon was certainly not easily fordable, and the Sultan has been in no hurry to construct a bridge across it. The Turk either did not, or pretended not to hear our remarks about this ; the Sultan is a long way off, invisible, and inaccessible, but Mahomet is another affair. If Mahomet is spoken of disrespectfully in the presence of a Turk, the scoffer is at once denounced to the police and sent to gaol. At last the Kishon came into sight—a great bed of a stony torrent, with a tiny thread of water meandering through ; but, oh ! such jolts and shakes, as to necessitate our clinging to the poles of the awning to prevent ourselves from being thrown out. The good Franciscan laughed, for he had been fifteen years in Palestine, and although he had only lately been made Guardian at Nazareth, the journey was not new to him. He had often performed it on horseback, in carriages, and even on foot.

I could scarcely believe he had really done it on foot, and said so ; to which he replied, " And why not, madam ? I was somewhat indisposed after it, but not seriously so."

We were now surrounded by verdant hills far and near.

" Is that Mount Tabor ? " I asked ; " and can you take me there, Suss ? "

" No, madam," replied the German, " I should not advise your going ; it is a horrid mountain."

Finally we reached a wide road shaded by tamarind trees, where we made a halt. We were now halfway, and it was about a quarter past eight o'clock. George Suss jumped down and attached two bags of hay to the horses' noses ; for they, too, must breakfast, poor beasts ! We, also, decided to eat. There was cold meat, with cheese, little native apricots, and English pastilles, the two latter being an offering from Father Marcello to the company, whilst the rest were supplied by me. Suss took a piece of bread and meat, but, as he remembered he had to drive, he could not be induced to touch any wine. The sun was already ardent, but the tamarind trees had thick branches ; a feeling of peace stole over us in this fruitful land of Galilee. Who would object to passing an hour under these trees ? The Turk slept on profoundly, his cigar between his lips.

" Are there many Turks here ? " I asked the friar.

" Luckily, no," he replied, in a low voice.

The hour passed, and the sun grew fiercer. The horses looked round anxiously at the bags of hay which were fast becoming empty. Suss talked consolingly to them in German. The wide expanse of country appeared longer instead of shorter as we went on our way, jolted and shaken all the time. The second half of the road was much the worse. We passed Nain, where the miracle of the widow's son took place ; and in the distance we could make out the road of Samaria, along which Christ went every year to Jerusalem, passing through the magnificent Naplousa.

ON THE ROAD TO NAZARETH.

The courteous monk now pointed out the mountains of Gilboa.

This name called up childish memories of Biblical history and the tragic story of Saul, as well as the lines of the Italian dramatist, beginning :—" *Di Gelboè son' questi i monti ?* " It always seems strange when one finds something as really existing which one has been in the habit of regarding as a mere figure of speech. Who has not smiled on hearing the words, " *Bell' alba è questa ?* " And yet on just such a morning as this, at about the same hour, in this sacred region, occurred the awful death of the Israelitish king and general. Father Marcello of Noilhac had surely never read Alfieri, and so I took good care not to speak about him. He continued to look before him, longing for a glimpse of Nazareth. Jerusalem is all very well for those who struggle and pray, but not for those who pray only. The eyes of the monk lit up at the name of Nazareth. He hoped, if it were God's Will, to pass the rest of his days there, and to die at the appointed time within its walls. The name, Nazareth, had attracted him from his earliest youth, when he was still in his father's distillery.

" Your dream is now realised ? "

" It is indeed," he answered with a happy smile, " and the reality is better than the dream."

Here, then, was a man who had not suffered illusion ; and now as the road which leads to the hills of Nazareth stretched out before us, and we beheld the landscape which inspired the Divine words, he seemed to have attained the acme of his earthly desires. Suss urged on his horses. Time flew as we hurried on. The Turk at last awakened.

" There is Nazareth," said the little friar, as the town appeared in the great declivity on the hill-side, with its red and white houses, its gardens and its orchards, stretching to the top of the hill to meet the azure sky so peaceful and happy-looking. Father Marcello's eyes were dimmed with tears. Indeed, what Christian can look upon Nazareth and not feel overcome with emotion and touched to the depths of his heart ?

VI.

THE STORY OF THE MADONNA.

Two villages of Palestine, Sepphoris and Cana, dispute the honour of being the birthplace of Mary. Tradition assures us that Anne and Joachim were in easy circumstances, possessing not only a small property in Cana, but also some land on the confines of Galilee, on Mount Carmel, where they went every year with their little daughter. It is true that Mary had many relatives living in Cana of Galilee, but it is not proved that this was her birthplace, and it must be content with the renown it won as the place where Christ performed His first miracle. It appears fairly certain that the Virgin Mary was born at a large village called Sepphoris about halfway between Nazareth and Tiberias, though nearer the former. Sepphoris, like most towns in Galilee, is built upon a hill, and the humble dwelling of Anne and Joachim stood on its summit. The name Mary, in all its variations of Miriam, Marian, and Mara, is most common in this part of Palestine, and it appears strangely frequent in connection with the life of our Saviour. First, Mary, His sweet, gentle mother, then her cousin, His aunt, Mary of Cleophas, so well known for her devotion and fervour : there was Mary of Bethany, the sister of Lazarus, whose greatest happiness was to sit at His feet and listen to His words, in the days which He spent in their quiet home : then Mary of Magdala, the impassioned penitent who so nobly expiated her sins. Tradition describes the childhood of the Virgin as a period of placid happiness, and speaks of her as a fair brunette, laying particular stress upon her wonderfully small hands and feet. She loved solitude, and in her own quiet home was ever industrious and reserved. Whenever her aged parents undertook the long tedious journey to Carmel, which they did on foot, stopping frequently by the way, the child always accompanied them. It is also said that she often ascended the

THE STORY OF THE MADONNA.

mountain overlooking St. John-of-Acre, and delighted to contemplate sky and sea from its summit: so that Carmel was blessed by her sweet presence, her pure thoughts and dreams. She always, however, gladly returned to the tranquil home at Sepphoris, and only left it at the age of thirteen and a half, when she went to Nazareth as the spouse of Joseph, the carpenter.

Those who are acquainted with the East will not be astonished at the early age at which the Virgin was bestowed in marriage, as it is a most common occurrence in these hot climates. Nor will it be matter of wonderment that so young a girl should have been given to a man of mature years, indeed almost an old man, for to an Oriental woman the disparity of age would increase her respect for one who, we are assured, she greatly venerated. Their little house was just at the entrance of Nazareth, and looked over a part of the blessed valley: it was built against a rock, like most of the houses in Galilee, and consisted of two rooms, one of masonry and one cut out of the natural rock; there was also a third room, which goes by the name of the "Madonna's Kitchen," and which has a small door leading into the garden. This little doorway opens upon a pathway leading across the fields which connected the house with St. Joseph's workshop.

Thus did Mary live until the day when she became the "Chosen One of the Lord," occupied with her household duties and surrounded by her family. Like the women of Nazareth, she wore the usual dark red skirt tied round the waist with a cord, over which hung an ample blue woollen cloak, also fastened at the waist, covering her head and falling over the dress, but thrown back from the brows. Like so many of her fellow-citizens, she also went barefoot. Each day she traversed the road leading to the fountain to fetch fresh water, which she carried in a jar, either on her head or poised against her hip: and thus the waters often reflected that sweet face on their clear surface. The road that leads to the well, which is almost outside the boundaries of Nazareth, is long and stony: but she must have fetched water every day, and later on, no doubt, in company with other fair Nazarene women, she washed the garments of the Infant Jesus in that same pool.

The life of Mary, the spouse of Joseph, was passed entirely in work and in prayer. She was in the inner room of the house on her knees, praying, when the Messenger paused at the threshold of the outer one. In the actual room where the mysterious scene was enacted, it is easy to conjure up the whole event; and as one recalls, in the twilight, the sacred words, one almost hopes to behold a vision of some celestial being! Hail, Mary! full of Grace, the Lord is with thee.

Later on, with her Infant clasped in her arms, she fled from those perils by which His dear Life was menaced. She dwelt in exile with St. Joseph in far-away Egypt, only reached after many months of weary travel, sleeping in fields or in the trunks of trees, their food herbs and fruit found by the way. After years of exile, when the fury of persecution had ceased, Mary returned to her humble home in Nazareth, to take up the thread of her former obscure existence. Now, whenever she visited the fountain, her little feet bruised by the stones on the way, she led a tiny Child by the hand : in the morning, when she left the house by the door which gives on to the fields, she carried Jesus to the workshop, that He might learn with His foster-father, Joseph, to become a carpenter. These years of gentle motherhood were so wonderfully tender and peaceful, and her life so free from anxiety, that this surely must have been for her the happiest period of her existence. She may, of course, have had from time to time during this quiet epoch a presentiment of the dreadful future in store for her Son, and the anguish of despair and death may have torn her heart when she considered His divine mission ; but, with Him by her side, she was easily consoled. His beautiful pale face, with its great blue eyes, framed in an aureole of fair hair, smiled at her, and each night, before He nestled to sleep, she held His little hands clasped in her own, and blessed Him. Thus did she enjoy to the full the holy happiness of being the Mother of the Divine Child. These were peaceful years, full of moral well-being, the result of a virtuous life spent among deeds of tenderest charity.

At last he grew to be a young man. His eyes were strangely fascinating in their sweetness and His words full of dignity and eloquence. The Nazarenes, astonished at His boldness, loved Him not, and looked upon Him as a rebel. The mother trembled for the safety of her beloved one. Joseph by this time, his holy mission accomplished, had died full of years. Jesus now desired to leave Nazareth, where He was not understood, and His mother, therefore, abandoned the home of her brief happiness and settled at Cana, where she had many relatives, whilst her Son began His wanderings in Galilee, and preached in the country around Tiberias. At times she felt anxious, and, fearing for His safety, followed Him : at others, perceiving the veneration in which He was held, she became more resigned. As the Son of Man approached His thirtieth year, the Madonna's life was filled with boundless anxiety. The time of peace was over and her martyrdom had begun. From henceforth she was the Mother of Sorrows.

She it was who solicited His first miracle. They were at a wedding feast together at Cana, and more wine was needed. Seeing that the host was greatly troubled and knew not what to do, Mary whispered to her Son, " They have no wine." He, however, lowered His eyes as though unwilling to manifest His Power, but His mother's supplicating expression decided Him, and He ordered the six jars which were standing outside the door to be filled to the brim with water, and the water was forthwith turned into wine. Thus His miraculous powers were revealed to the Madonna, but with their manifestation began the first step towards the Cross, and she followed Him, trembling in silence, whilst overwhelming joy and bitter martyrdom fought for supremacy within her heart. We find His mother among that group of women who, enthralled by Christ's sacred words of tenderness, could not leave Him, but surrounded Him, serving and adoring Him. The name of Mary will ever be connected with those holy women who had the joy of hearing the noblest words that have ever fallen upon human ears. They were consumed with sublime spiritual love, and lived, suffered, and died to possess it. The Madonna followed Jesus in all His wanderings round the Lake of Tiberias, where He preached to the fisher-folk, the tillers of the ground, the women, and the children. She also stayed at the same time that He did at Bethsaida, on the left bank of the Lake of Genesareth, in the house of the Apostle Peter, who, besides his wife and children, had his mother-in-law dwelling with him. His modest abode sheltered the Prophet of Galilee and Mary of Nazareth. Now Bethsaida is but a handful of ruins, having been cursed for its want of faith, and, like Capernaum and Chorazin, has fallen, so that, of all the villages along the lake, only Magdala, the birthplace of that other Mary, remains standing. The Virgin, though she feared for her Beloved, would not place any obstacle in the way of His Divine Mission, but meekly and unostentatiously followed Him on His perilous journeys to Jerusalem, where the people, fierce in their obstinacy, would not believe in the Prophet of Nazareth. This was, indeed, a tremendous task for the adoring mother, who hid her bitter suffering, and who, though she saw the glory, endeavoured to conceal the thorns which pierced her heart—who, whilst she smiled at the praises, foresaw with terrible clearness the Passion, the Agony, and the Death. In that torture of a mother's heart, Mary suffered the Agony of the Cross even before her Son !

On that never to be forgotten Palm Sunday when Christ was filled with the most perfect joy of His life, as the crowd proclaimed Him the Son of David, the Elect of God, and He passed through the Golden Gate which the Jews have never since opened, the Madonna was among the throng. All through the night on which Jesus was betrayed and arrested she watched in the house of the Apostle Thomas, where Mark had also taken refuge from the persecution of Pilate's soldiers, and had warned her of the terrible events taking place. Then, seeking her Son, in company with the other holy and silently-weeping women, they passed the night of Thursday to Friday outside the house of Annas, the High Priest, within whose walls Jesus was imprisoned. The women only knew that the young Prophet had been taken by His enemies, but the Mother knew He was doomed. She wept in silence. In the hour when His Passion began, when He was condemned in Pilate's Prætorium, and when He came forth laden with the Cross, His Mother advanced to meet Him. Jesus, seeing her, raised His head and saluted her with the words, " Hail, Mother." But she remained silent and as though turned to stone. A supreme anguish wrung her heart, and she leant against the other women. Barefooted, with her hair flowing beneath her blue mantle, her face drawn with suffering, she walked behind her Son. Her expression was that of one who expects no reprieve. She neither groaned nor complained, but the world has never witnessed a sorrow like unto her sorrow. Think of it, ye mothers who have loved your sons, and who have held the terror of death in your hearts as you watched beside your children's bed of sickness!

What painter has fittingly portrayed the face of Mary while she followed her Son along the " Way of the Cross," from the Prætorium to Golgotha, or has ever properly delineated her inexpressible, immeasurable grief? No one, surely. Artists have, indeed, depicted her under all her aspects of purity, chastity, and sweet tenderness, but no one has shown her face at that moment when it was convulsed with an unparalleled sorrow. No artist has ever been bold enough to realistically render on canvas this tragedy of a mother's heart. We can only picture the spectacle of that horror and desolation in our imagination. When she reached the spot where He was to die, they would not allow her to approach nearer and embrace the foot of the Cross. Nothing could distract her tearless gaze from her Son's awful Agony. All who have suffered should kiss the mound of earth on which the Mother of Sorrows stood at the supreme moment, as she watched her Son slowly dying. At last, with a loud cry, He gave up the Ghost; the heavens were darkened, the earth was shaken, and the veil of the Temple rent in twain. Towards evening Joseph of Arimathæa and the disciples came and took down the Body, which was placed in the Mother's arms, and she clasped It to her breast and pressed her lips to the beloved Face!

Martha, Mary of Cleophas, Mary Magdalen, and some of the disciples left Jerusalem in fear of persecution, on board a fishing-boat which conveyed them from Jaffa to the coast of Provence. The Madonna, however, remained in Jerusalem: she could not tear herself away from the tomb where they had laid Him. She visited it every day.

Her Son is risen and the Faith is beginning to spread on all sides, but she cannot leave the spot where Jesus suffered and died. The flowery land of Galilee will see her no more! Her light footstep will never press its paths again, nor will she again carry her jar to the fountain. The small house at Nazareth, with its orchards, the humble dwellings at Cana, and Sepphoris, where she was born, will never again shelter her. She will never revisit either the friends or the relatives of her youth. The Virgin remained where the great tragedy of Christ had its terrible fulfilment. She desired not to forget, but lived in prayer and sadness. The lovely fountain of Siloam, outside the walls of Jerusalem, sometimes reflected a woman's face as she bent over its mysterious waters—it was worn with age and grief. The fair girl who received the message of the Archangel Gabriel was a slender, bent woman now, on whose countenance life had imprinted its furrows. She continued to live in the house of the Apostle Thomas, who surrounded her with filial devotion in memory of his Master until her death. Finally, one day, she ascended the Mount of Olives, and the Angel Gabriel reappeared to her. He bore a palm branch in his hand and announced to her that her course on earth was run, and that her Son awaited her in His glory. Cheerfully she welcomed death and longed for heaven: the Celestial Messenger found her ready in Jerusalem, as she had been, long years before, in the dwelling at Nazareth. She was lifted up into Heaven, and as she rose she let fall her white girdle that Thomas might pick it up to hold in remembrance.

Her great yet humble history on earth thus ended in Heavenly glory.

VII.

A DAY IN NAZARETH.

ONE evening in June, as I was passing along the corridor of the Franciscan monastery, pausing occasionally to look out of its windows over the valley of Nazareth, wrapped in the shades of night, I was possessed by a feeling of intense sadness. I felt anxious and nervous at being so far from home, amid unfamiliar surroundings. There are such moments, when the fascinations of distant lands, scenes, and peoples, with all that is new and wonderful, are apt to pall. Several times of late I had experienced such moments of home-sickness and depression: but on this particular night even the stars appeared unfamiliar, perhaps even hostile. I walked along slowly with bent head, feeling quite unwilling to enter the little cell which formed my lodging, lest I should experience too great a sense of loneliness. The monk-hospitaller of Nazareth, Friar John of Rotterdam, a colossal Dutchman with the heart of a child, and who had a special devotion to the Mother of our Lord, of whom he constantly spoke to me when not conversing about his own mother who lived in Rotterdam, having finished his daily duties, presently came to bid me goodnight. Mine must have been a bewildered expression, for he immediately understood that something was wrong with me, and asked whether I were ill. I answered in the negative, and he said that I certainly must be entertaining some sad thought; and as he insisted so gently and kindly, I did not deny the impeachment, but was obliged to own to what, until then, I had scarcely been conscious of myself, the real cause of my trouble. I told him that the following day, the thirteenth of June, being dedicated to St. Anthony, was the name-day of my eldest boy, which I had never passed away from home before. He understood me at once, and looked at me so kindly that tears came into my eyes. Whereupon he attempted to console me in odd French with a strong Dutch accent, telling me that in the Church of the Annunciation close by there was an altar dedicated to St. Anthony of Padua, for whom he entertained great veneration, and that the following morning, before daybreak, he would offer a Mass for my little son, at which he invited me to be present. I thanked him, and felt at once much comforted.

When I awoke at half-past four the sun had not yet risen ; a faint light, however, appeared in the east, and the fresh landscape, still in the lingering shades of night, gradually became better defined. Before my door I found a lighted lantern, prepared for me by the kind forethought of Friar John of Rotterdam before going to the church. I left my room with a heart full of peace, feeling as though I were bound on some mysterious errand, and crossed the whole length of the Franciscan monastery before reaching the door leading to the church. There were some three or four pilgrims in the building, besides myself, but they were probably asleep. As I traversed the square in front of the Hospice, a slight breeze stirred the tops of the three or four pine trees growing in the enclosure, and I felt quite chilly. The Church of the Annunciation is about a hundred yards from the convent, perhaps not quite so far. I turned and looked upon the city of Jesus and Mary wrapt in profound silence, only broken by the clear, vibrating sound of the bell tolling for Mass. The church was empty, save for one lay-brother who was lighting the candles at St. Anthony's Altar, and who was to serve Mass. By the time he had finished clanging the bell, shadows were lifting all around : outside, on the town and on the hills Jesus loved so well, and inside the church which has been erected on the site of the house of Mary, where the Angel appeared to " the handmaiden of the Lord." I was here alone, to hear that Mass which was to call down the blessings of Heaven upon the head of my little son, and I prayed for him, for his happiness and health. Even from afar he must have experienced that blessing, and felt the help of my supplications. The monk, wearing his priestly robes, advanced from the sacristy, absorbed in the thought of the Holy Sacrifice which he was about to offer up. On my right hand, behind the High Altar, stands all that remains at Nazareth of the house of Mary, the rest being at Loreto : behind the High Altar, gleaming in the dawn, stands the column that records the spot where stood the Angel Gabriel. The vast, silent church was beginning to receive the faint light that announces the coming of day. Meanwhile, Friar John repeated with the utmost fervour the beautiful and suggestive words of the Mass, from the Introit to the first Gospel, and thence onwards to the Elevation and the last Gospel. I, too, felt myself alone with my Maker, humble, trembling, and full of faith, whilst the beloved image of my child, with his sweet, honest gaze, rose before my mental vision. Often had I felt that stirring emotion at the moment when Christ descends upon the Altar, and had bowed my head in solemn adoration : but never before had I experienced it so forcibly as I did in this church of the " Holy Apparition."

At the season of the year in which I visited Palestine, during the hours between eleven in the morning and four in the afternoon, the heat of the sun is so great, the light so dazzling, and the air so heavy, that it is quite impossible to venture out of doors, and one is constrained to remain at home, employing the time as best one can, resting and trying to keep cool until after four o'clock. I, therefore, did not begin my round of inspection of the town of Nazareth, with its green hills and sweet-scented breezes, until about five o'clock. The previous day I had carefully visited the Sanctuaries : those of the Annunciation, of St. Joseph, and of the Holy Table : but now I proposed to see the town itself, with its inhabitants ; to listen to their voices, to endeavour to understand their customs. To study the real life of a country, nothing is better than to ramble about, walking slowly and examining carefully without seeming to do so : to talk with a woman here and smile at a child there, and to make some small purchases. In this manner, pictures of a simple, delightful kind, compared with which superb monuments and magnificent palaces are as nothing, become engraved on the mind. Nazareth, though far smaller than Jerusalem, and not at all impressive, has, nevertheless, a peculiar charm of its own. It is not even so large as Bethlehem, but has a greater number of gardens, orchards, and cultivated fields, and above all there are scarcely any Mohammedans, Jews, Schismatic Greeks, Copts, or Abyssinians. Within its boundaries it belongs, as do the Holy Places, exclusively to the Latins, represented by the Franciscans : there is, therefore, no sectarian discord, no anger, or Oriental fanaticism, fierce disputes, or bitter revenges ; but it is a place of perfect peace and faith in Christ, where the Franciscans are free to exercise their piety and charity. The little town is built on the sides of two hills, and all its paths are on the slope, and are good on the whole, though stony in places. The high road leading to the market is even paved. The people of Nazareth are mostly agricultural ; but in the town they work at various trades, and are masons, blacksmiths, shoemakers, and weavers. I observed their shops, which, though small, are clean : they are excavated in the hill-side itself, the frontages being built of masonry. I particularly noticed the carpenters' shops, as Joseph, the foster-father of our Lord, must have had just such a one. Even where civilisation has most freely penetrated, ideas and customs have kept so stationary in Palestine for hundreds of years, that, in the interior of Galilee, they may be said to have remained exactly as they were 2,000 years ago, when Joseph used the plane, and Jesus helped him, His Mind filled with Its own Divine secret. The Nazarenes are good, worthy people: from one of them I bought a net made of string, ornamented with red and blue tassels, which formed the trappings of a donkey. This kind of work is made rather prettily here. A Nazarene with laughing eyes and dazzling teeth, who, having been at the Franciscans' school, spoke Italian, sold it to me. In a narrow lane I was surrounded by a perfect tribe of children, amongst them being one tiny little fellow, with the brightest of bright eyes, who chattered away in Arabic as fast as he could. He was a Christian, however, and Father John of Rotterdam told me he was learning his catechism. I gave him a few pennies, and the good monk told me he could never refuse these children, for he fancied the child Jesus must have been like one of them.

The sun was setting as I reached the great fountain of

Nazareth, which is situated a little beyond the town, in the direction of the Church of the Annunciation, or about 500 yards from where stood the house of Mary. I sat down on a stone bench beside it. The waters well up from three springs, that fall into a large stone basin : but the bowl is broken, and the water rushes away in every direction, forming wide pools and a rivulet further on, in which the women wash their clothes. It was now getting quite dark, but women still kept coming by the various lanes which lead to the fountain, to fill their jars with water for the night. They all wore, with innate elegance, the dark blue skirt, tucked up at the waist and held in place by a deep blue cord; the great blue cloak which, protecting their heads, falls a little over the forehead, and hanging in long, graceful folds, entirely covers them, only the small, bare feet, slender hands, and oval faces being visible. Truly they made a charming picture in the sunset glow, crossing with swift, soft step, scarcely touching the ground, putting their jars to the stream, as they bent their flexible bodies, and then quickly raising their amphoras to their heads, with a quick, easy movement, they walked silently away. The air was sweet : the sky grey, almost violet at times. The water gurgled at the springs and flowed, rippling onwards. More women came and went. I lost all sense of time as I watched these blue-clad figures, with their bare white feet, coming and going in the mists of evening—one, holding a little child by the hand, might have been the Madonna herself.

VIII.

ON MOUNT TABOR.

MOUNT TABOR dominates the lovely landscape of Galilee like a beacon, and its rounded cone and verdure-clad slopes are visible from every point. The nearer it approaches, the more charming appear its delicate curves and richly wooded sides. When I first beheld this sacred hill I was seized by an irresistible longing to ascend it and revel amidst its verdure, even to the spot where He appeared to His amazed disciples, arrayed in dazzling white garments, and His face resplendent with light. I could not believe that it was very difficult to reach the top of Mount Tabor; it looked so easy, and I felt sure the view over Galilee from the summit would be glorious! When I proposed this expedition to my dragoman he made no objection to accompany me, but, on the other hand, he displayed no great enthusiasm over it. The horseman inquired if my saddle were comfortable, and they both remarked that I might *perhaps* be able to go up on horse back, though they were agreed that I should certainly have to come down on foot. On my inquiring if the road was very steep they assured me it could not well be more so. After all they would not hear of my making the ascent on foot, saying a sure-footed horse that knew the ground perfectly afforded by far the safer means of progress. When I asked whether it were possible to descend on horseback, the dragoman shook his head ruefully, saying that the animal would inevitably tumble together with its rider. Notwithstanding these discouraging reports the expedition from Nazareth was decided upon. The horses started off steadily; the dragoman smoked; the horseman hummed an Arab song, while the little dog, Filfel, or Pepper, pranced around. For a full hour the path, though narrow, was good, and traversed fields of brick-red earth; Tabor, as we advanced, seemed to approach nearer and nearer, and at last towered above our heads. The ground now began to rise. When we reached a large olive-tree the dragoman stopped, got off his horse, and examined the straps of my saddle and stirrups to see if they were secure; before remounting he did the same to his own harness. Then he slowly started off again; meanwhile, the horseman riding close by my side kept his hand on my pummel.

Then began the strangest and most alarming ascent that ever was made, and unto which Vesuvius and Etna are mere trifles. It was no longer a path, but a more or less deep furrow filled with sharp cutting stones, which

ON MOUNT TABOR.

rolled down or barred the way as we mounted, and the horses constantly slipped as their feet struck them. The track rapidly became so steep that the horses looked as though standing upright on their hind legs, and the leader of our cavalcade warned me at every moment to bend my head well over the horse's neck, and if I neglected to do so he reminded me very sharply to obey his injunctions. On one side was a sheer precipice scarcely concealed by a few small trees which bent over the abyss; on the other were the boulders of the mountain. The path made wide curves, and at every turn the furrow looked more unsafe. As the horse could scarcely find a foothold and the stones rolled down so fast, I could with difficulty control an alarming sense of dizziness. A hundred times I regretted I had not come up on foot, and then again, as I considered the condition of the ground, I was glad enough I had not done so. And still up and up we went, the plain of Galilee receded further and further in the distance and looked like a moving sea of grass, while the poor horse, white with foam, struggled up bravely the last bit of ascent, which was like scaling a wall, and thus the summit of Mount Tabor was reached at last!

All white and sparkling in the sun stood the little Hospice belonging to the Franciscans, together with the small church, which bears the name of the "Gate of the Wind," in Arabic Bab-el-Auoa, so called because a strong wind blows here continually, sometimes turning to a very hurricane. A monk conducted me first to the church, whence, after I had remained in prayer a short time, he led me to an Alpine height covered with rare sweet-scented shrubs. This was the place of the Transfiguration and the scene of the transcendent episode which Raphael has depicted with so masterly a hand in that famous picture in the Vatican in which his intuitive genius, both as true artist and Christian, are so wonderfully blended. The transient light between the clouds which meet and part with such rapidity in the brief but constantly recurring whirlwind, for which the region of Tabor is famed, must have illumined with its refulgent brightness the Face of Christ at the moment of the Transfiguration. The broad plain of Esdraelon seemed to vibrate in the stormy breeze, whilst shining white in the far distance I could discern Sepphoris, the birthplace of St. Anne and of the Madonna; Cana, the land of the wedding feast and the scene of Christ's first miracle; and Nain, the town where lived the widow with her sick son; and yet nearer the horizon, but barely visible, stretched the road leading to the Lake of Tiberias. How greatly must the Son of Man have rejoiced when He ascended these heights to commune with His Heavenly Father! Only three of the Apostles were with Him at the time of the Transfiguration—Peter, James, and John; the rest had remained in the plain at a little Arab village called Daburieh, in memory of Deborah. Only these His most faithful followers accompanied Him to the summit, and witnessed the sublime vision. While I was thinking of all these things the voice of the Spanish friar, Father Augustin of Saragossa, recalled me from my meditations. It was the hour for refreshment and time to go. Before I mounted my steed, the monk handed me a visitors' book that I might write my name therein. Alas! how few ever ascend Tabor! During the year from February till June at least three thousand pilgrims had visited the Holy Land (without counting the tourists, who are nearly all English and personally conducted by Cook), but only eighty-two came to see the site of the Transfiguration. The road must have been execrable in the time of Christ, and no doubt this was the reason why the less energetic of the disciples remained behind at the foot of the hill. Thus only Peter, James, and John, the most devout and enthusiastic of the twelve, surmounted the difficulties of the ascent, and were rewarded by the wondrous sight. I signed my name at the eighty-third place in the visitors' book, immediately after that of Paul Bourget, who had been here a month earlier.

It took forty-five minutes to make the ascent alone, without counting the time wasted in the plain below; but they were forty-five minutes the bones of the traveller are never likely to forget! Before beginning the descent, I asked the dragoman anxiously whether it would take as long to go down as it did to come up. He shook his head, smiling, and assured me it wouldn't take half the time. Heaven be praised! As I approached my horse to remount, the dragoman, amazed at my audacity or laziness, prevented me, saying: "Are you going down on horseback? *No one* descends Tabor on horseback." The horseman took hold of the reins of the two horses and started off, whistling in order to attract the little dog Filfel. I began my descent on foot. Descent! I was precipitated downwards with a headlong rush! To go slowly and cautiously was impossible. I was swept along against my will and taken, like a flag that is furled and unfurled in the wind, like the frenzied whirl of a firework, twisting and twirling, down the rocky, uneven track. Forty-five minutes, indeed! The movement, so rapid as to be almost mechanical, hurried me down, amid dangers to right and dangers to left, till faint and giddy, I at last reached the plain. After a few minutes' halt to recover my breath, during which time I wondered whether I was alive or dead, mangled or whole, I mounted my saddle and started for the Lake of Genesareth and the erstwhile glorious city of Tiberias.

IX.

TIBERIAS.

IT required fully six hours on horseback to perform the journey between Tabor and Tiberias, to which must be added half an hour's rest for the horses on the road; thus, starting from Tabor at mid-day, it was impossible to reach the end of the journey until nearly seven o'clock, a late hour in Palestine, where the evenings are treacherous on account of the heavy dew. Six good hours of hard riding, during which the dragoman, Mansour, pulled up at times to allow me to get ahead of him, as he became aware of my impatience. The poor man, a most intelligent and courteous Nazarene, tried his best to shorten the way by relating all sorts of anecdotes, which I cannot, for the life of me, remember. The part of Galilee which stretches from Tabor to Tiberias is exceedingly arid, monotonous, and uninteresting, whereas the road which connects Tiberias and Nazareth passing through Loubieh, Sepphoris, and Cana, is quite delightful. The road taken on the outward journey is a series of immense desert steppes, gently sloping downwards, one after another: and, as each seems to end with the horizon, one fancies all kinds of strange and interesting lands and scenes may lie beyond, whereas, in reality, when we reached the spot we thought would be so fascinating, we discovered nothing new; indeed, owing to the very gradual incline, we were not even aware when we had reached its limits, and another wide stretch of plain spread out before us, so exactly resembling the last that the effect produced was one of utter weariness! Sucrie Mansour, the good-tempered dragoman, after we had been travelling four or five hours, cast furtive glances at me as he noticed my ill-humour and extreme fatigue, and repeated encouragingly at intervals, "A little while and we shall soon be there." I did not, however, believe him, knowing full well it was a six hours' journey at least, and not a minute less. Extreme fatigue made me very irritable, and as I looked back upon the previous day's journey from Nazareth to Tabor, even its perilous ascent and precipitous down-coming seemed to me quite pleasant when contrasted with this long, dreary journey in the afternoon glare across endless wastes, where neither tree, man, nor beast could be seen, and which overcame me with weariness and impatience.

At last Mansour announced: "In half an hour Tiberias will be in sight."

And this time I believed him! At a certain distance, behind the last piece of plain, something extremely blue and which was not sky now came in sight. It was Lake Genesareth or Tiberias. I breathed a deep sigh of relief as the dragoman pointed it out.

The little Roman city, with its grey fortified walls, could be discerned on the shores of that exquisite blue hollow with its steely reflections. But its immediate vicinity was all an illusion, for though seeming to be just below us, nay at our very feet, we took more than an hour—seventy terrible minutes—to reach it, during which time it appeared to recede further and further. More than seventy minutes of a continuous, perpendicular, breakneck descent on horseback down interminable steps apparently leading to the very bowels of the earth! When I finally reached the entrance to the Hospice at Tiberias I was in a high fever from sheer fatigue.

This Franciscan Hospice contained only two monks and three or four servants to attend upon visitors. What was once a really imposing Roman city, in the midst of beautiful scenery, on the borders of the lake, is now but an unimportant place, with a hot, damp, unhealthy climate, scorching, stifling wind, and, moreover, infested by the most venomous of gnats. To a Franciscan, going to Tiberias means enduring punishment with patience, the seeking after a self-imposed penance, or else the accomplishment of some religious vow. Many have been taken ill, and not a few have met death here. The guardian, Father Benedict, had resisted for two years, and had, moreover, retained both his health and his amiable temper. Of the two monks who were his companions, one had died the previous week. When he became seriously ill they wanted to remove him elsewhere, but he begged so hard to be allowed to remain to die on the shores of the lake rendered memorable by the incomparable teaching of Jesus, that they had not the heart to refuse his request. This monk had been very devout, and was reputed quite a saint.

The moment I arrived, throwing myself upon a couch, I asked whether I could have a room overlooking the lake; but this, it appeared, was not possible, as there were none on that side. The building was large and had long, rambling, empty, echoing passages, lighted only by flickering oil lamps. I proposed going to bed at once, but Father Benedict would not hear of my doing so until I had partaken of some refreshment. Soon after I reached my chamber the second monk brought me a tray with tea and eggs. He was a thin, old man, with a deeply-furrowed face and a reassuring smile. He was much concerned at my making such a very frugal repast, but I was almost too tired to eat.

"Are you alone with the Superior?" I asked, for the sake of saying something.

"Yes," he sighed, "alone. My companion died."

Was there not a tremulous light in his eyes as he said this, or was it only my fancy? Perceiving how sleepy I was he at once left me to myself, after first wishing me good-night. I then made my customary tour of inspection before retiring to rest. The door of my room, like all the others, opened on to a long, dark corridor and shut very badly, and from time to time the wind would blow one of them open, dimly disclosing a white, empty bed, and then bang to again. Having drawn my bolt I threw open the window, which was very low, and looked out into the courtyard facing the church. Reclosing it and putting out the light I retired to rest. I might have been asleep half an hour when I awoke, feeling terribly hot. I was feverish and breathed with difficulty, so I opened the window and returned to bed. I could not have been asleep long ere I again awoke with a start. This time I distinctly heard footsteps, that seemed actually in my room. What should I do? I looked hopelessly towards the window, which was just discernible and appeared like a misty square of light, across which I saw something black—the silhouette of an ancient Roman tower. Then a cock crowed: there was no other sound. Perhaps after all I had been mistaken. These strange surroundings, this deserted monastery, with the wind whistling down its gloomy passages, had evidently given rise to some sort of hallucination. Besides, I comforted myself with the thought that I had a revolver on the table close at hand. Though of what use would that be? I had never used a firearm in my life; and, notwithstanding its very diminutive size and innocent appearance, I lived in constant dread of its going off by itself in the portmanteau, and always kept it shut up in its case. Still, wherever I went I ostentatiously took it out and placed it on a table within reach.

Again I heard steps, this time so close that I sat up trembling and called out "Who *is* there?" But no one answered. Then lighting the lamp I looked round the room ; it was empty and silent. Realising that there was no chance of my going to sleep again, I got up and dressed and laid down on the sofa and tried to read. Once more I heard the step, now near and now further off, so going to the window I looked out into the courtyard below, which was in complete darkness. Yes ! close to the wall there was something moving with a dragging, cautious step. As my eyes became more used to the darkness I was able to distinguish a human form with bent head and arms hanging down, though I could not make out whether it were man or woman. Suddenly it vanished, and again it reappeared in the same mysterious manner. At this moment, as it raised its head, I distinguished the rugged face of the monk who had brought me my supper. Now he would throw himself down on the ground and then get up again. Anon, rising quickly, he would pace round and round the small courtyard. At times he would beat his head with his hands, and a deep sigh would escape him. Spellbound and unable to tear myself away from the window, my eyes being by this time accustomed to the darkness, I could see him much more clearly, and, moreover, I could distinctly hear his groans. I felt inclined to speak to him, but dared not. The air was heavy and damp, and so suffocating I could scarcely breathe, and the gnats stung most viciously.

As I leant on the window-sill watching the shadowy, restless form of the monk, I experienced a strange sensation of combined astonishment and anxiety. What could he be doing ? Was he ill or out of his mind ? And why those heartrending sighs ?

Presently I lost all sense of fear and felt more than ever a prey to intense curiosity, and tears even came into my eyes at the thought of this poor lonely old monk and his mysterious vigil. Indeed the whole scene impressed me like a dream. My limbs ached from the effects of my long ride, my nerves were unstrung and my brain was in a whirl. The monk at times appeared almost delirious, and would raise himself to his full height and toss his arms above his head. Then again I could hear his convulsive sobs. I wondered why he suffered thus : he, who no longer remembered fatherland or family, and had given up all human ties and desires, to live retired in this deserted, out-of-the-way corner of the Holy Land.

At daybreak I found myself still leaning on the window-sill where I had fallen asleep, breathing in the unhealthy, relaxing air of Tiberias. The friar had not gone away, but lay full length on something white. Worn out by his vigil, he was sleeping upon the stone which covered his dead brother.

I afterwards learnt that the poor old fellow had never recovered the loss of his companion, for whom he entertained a great affection and a boundless veneration. Each night he would feel compelled to visit the spot where his friend had been laid to rest, and passed the hours in prayer, often calling upon him who was no more. The Superior, deeply concerned for the health of his only surviving monk, sought advice from Nazareth, and in the meantime gently urged him to remain quietly in his cell. But this he could not do. Something stronger than his own will drew him to that grave which he could not forsake. As to myself, between the unhealthiness of the air and the swarms of mosquitos, I caught the germs of malaria, which declared itself a fortnight later in Constantinople, and the effects of which lasted for three years.

X.

ON THE LAKE.

As I have before said, it is not a road or a pathway which leads to Tiberias, but merely a track worn in the stony, thorn-covered ground by the hoofs of the horses and mules, and the feet of the men who accompany them. It is a long, steep, rugged descent, which taxes the strength and courage of the most intrepid of riders. When you do happen to meet, on your downward course, men and animals returning, you

ON THE LAKE.

begin to feel slightly uneasy concerning your own journey back. We chanced to meet a herd of goats making their way up the steep incline : they were obstinate, and determined to block our way so pertinaciously that they had to be driven off by sheer force, whilst we waited patiently watching them, before continuing our way. It was evening, and already half-past seven. The sun was just setting over the City and Lake of Tiberias, producing a vision of beauty which would have induced anyone, however preoccupied with personal cares, or worn out with fatigue, to pause and contemplate it. When I first perceived the Lake of Tiberias from the hillside, my eyes tired with gazing for seven long hours at monotonous brown scenery, I was completely entranced by the sublime beauty of Genesareth, as it lay stretched in all its length and breadth before me, and I uttered no further complaints to my long-suffering dragoman, whom I had so taxed by my impatience throughout the journey.

He, no doubt, was well aware of the effect that Genesareth would produce upon me, and that I should be thankful I had undertaken the journey that June morning, spite of all its trials and discomforts. Well do I recollect the broad smile upon his face as he led my horse down that rough path which leads to the Roman Gate of Tiberias, and watched my delight at the sight of the lake, lighted by the last rays of the sinking sun. How many people had he, probably, conducted from Nazareth to Tiberias, by way of Mount Tabor, and had patiently borne their increasing ill-humour, well knowing what a change that entrancing sight would work in them. How many sunsets had he witnessed over the waters of that wonderful lake, observing the changes wrought in the tired and irritated travellers as they became calmed and comforted and lost in spiritual rapture on beholding that view. The Oriental intelligence sympathises readily with the silence of mystic contemplation, a frame of mind in which it is itself so wont to indulge. Forgetting all material miseries and fatigues, I gazed upon the sea that had witnessed the miracles of Jesus, where His Words had been heard, and whose furious waves were stilled as His Divine Foot touched them.

It was evening: and I decided to sit down quietly on the balcony which overlooked the orchards of the Hospice and the Lake. The night was wonderfully clear and bright (as when the moon is about to rise), and the waters looked singularly dark and blue. The Lake was silent and deserted, with here and there a bright star reflected on its smooth surface. It appeared absolutely motionless: no murmur even of lapping wavelets reached the ear. The town of Tiberias, which two thousand years ago was built to attest the greatness of the Roman Empire, is to-day a thoroughly Jewish city, given up to the most hierarchical Judaism. Within it the lights were being extinguished one by one. In order the better to abandon myself to the impressions of absolute solitude, I watched impatiently for the last of them to disappear, so that every sign of human life and activity might be obliterated by the shadows surrounding me. Thus, lost in uninterrupted contemplation, I felt the nearness of the Divine Spirit to my own Soul. Here, Jesus once walked upon the verdant shores of the Lake, or sat in the boats of the fishermen He had made " fishers of men." In the small orchard beneath me, among the tamarind trees, no leaf stirred. No weird hum of night insects broke the deep silence that lay over all. When the last light had disappeared in the great Roman tower erected by Herod Antipas in memory of Tiberias Drusius—then was the moment to see the Lake of Galilee, by whose shores He passed three most active and happy years of His Life. As witnessed in the dimness of night, the Lake of Tiberias looked so vast that it indeed deserved to be called, as it is by the Evangelists, the Sea of Galilee, the name current at that time. As I gazed on those deep blue waters I readily recalled in imagination the events of the three years during which He wandered and preached.

Down there, to the left of Tiberias, stood Bethsaida, the birthplace of St. Peter, and Capernaum, where Christ performed so many miracles: both cities have now fallen to decay, but you can still trace their sites by the white round walls amid the yellow, scented genistas and fragrant lavender bushes. You may also picture the little town of Magdala, where the renowned penitent once lived: and as you watch the quiet surface of the lake and feel the soft breezes of Syria upon your cheeks, you call to mind that fragile boat in which Jesus loved to be rowed, that He might dream uninterruptedly upon the still waters; and whence, at times, He would lend a helping hand to the poor fishermen, His companions, silently blessing their labour, or repaying their kindly fidelity by miraculously filling their nets.

Then the day of the storm comes back to your memory, when, the Apostles being afraid, He calmed the angry waters by a word: and yet again, that other time, when He walked upon the troubled sea. Here, alone in the still night, at these recollections, an overwhelming tenderness fills the heart. Looking over these waters which were so dear to Him, you seem to feel the divine truth and to hear His words of love and charity, and you rejoice indeed that you have crossed broad lands and sailed over rough seas to gain this blessed glimpse of peace by the Lake of Genesareth. This is the reward of fatigue and discomfort, this the recompense of voluntary exile to a land so far from the well-loved home. In the silence of the night does He not come towards you, speaking to your heart and bidding you hope and trust in Him who is Hope itself? They say the age of miracles is past: but how can it be so, since a miracle is taking place in your very soul, as you try to fancy yourself one of the faithful band that accompanied Him whithersoever He went, and heard the echoes of the hills repeat His holy Words? Then you, too, feel impelled to follow in the steps of that beloved Presence, whenever He may come, and wheresoever He may lead.

XI.

THE MOUNT OF THE BEATITUDES.

ALL around this grey-blue lake of Tiberias the country is most charming, and the great draughts of fishes caught within its waters even now are proverbial among the fisher-folk. How many millions, in their unwavering faith, have believed and do believe that here, indeed, did Jesus wander for three years, followed by a crowd of fishermen, from among whom He chose His twelve Apostles, and that here He performed so many miracles. Within the boundaries of Galilee, Samaria, and Judæa, Christ passed the thirty-three years of His Life, never going beyond them: but from these narrow limits He was able to attack a whole wide world of customs, laws, and ideas, and to reconstruct another world of thought and feeling. In the limited scene of His activity Lake Tiberias may well be figuratively likened to a sea, nay, an ocean, so inconceivably vast and far-reaching were the consequences of the acts wrought and the words spoken by its shores. On a bright summer morning, when the dew of night still lingers, and the pilgrim wakes refreshed, the immense blue lake, misty amid the greyness of the fast disappearing shades of night, begins to glisten in the early rays of the sun. He used just such little boats as those we notice moored by the shore waiting for the fishermen, or the larger ones, with their folded white sails. The gently sloping green hills are mirrored in the peaceful waters disturbed by scarce a ripple. The fair mountains are all covered with flowers and grasses, and the tiny Syrian birds chirp, warble, and sing at dawn, among the sweet-scented bushes: whilst far away, towards Capernaum, the land of Peter, the wide plain looms in the grey distance, seeming yet another sea. Maybe, at that very spot by which I stood, among the reeds and grasses that grew by its margin, Christ's boat was moored.

About a quarter of an hour's journey from the ugly Jewish city of Tiberias, filled as it is with noble Roman remains, on the western shore of the lake, rises the most beautiful and most attractive of all the surrounding hills. It is slightly indented at the summit, where the white road crosses it amid fragrant grasses and yellow, violet, and grey flowers. The road by which you reach the top without much fatigue, in fifteen or twenty minutes, is a very gradual ascent. I particularly wished to obtain a view of the surrounding country from one of these elevations, whence I could take in at a glance the whole scene in which

THE MOUNT OF THE BEATITUDES.

Jesus preached, announcing the advent of the Kingdom of Heaven: though perhaps I should not have chosen this particular hill if my faithful dragoman had not, before setting out, told me—after waiting, with his usual quiet Oriental patience, that I should first question him—that the hill before us was Mount Hattine.

As this name suggested nothing special to me, I stood deliberating whether there was not some higher point of vantage; but the dragoman continued, in his phlegmatic way, " Hattine is the Arab name; the Christian one is the Mount of the Beatitudes."

At this I started and stood gazing at him fixedly; whilst he, supposing I had not understood, continued to explain, " It is the hill where Jesus preached the Sermon on the Mount, the Sermon of the Seven Beatitudes."

Turning my back upon the somewhat astonished dragoman, I hurriedly set out for Mount Hattine, he following behind at a short distance. It was an easy ascent, and from time to time I stopped to look back upon the Sea of Genesareth, above which the sun was now beginning to rise. When I reached the first level space I noticed some large boulders standing out among the grass; they were almost white, and looked like marble seats arranged in a semicircle. I observed that they were twelve in number. Always wishing to attain a still more extended view, I continued the gentle ascent until I had reached the last level ground which lay between the two peaks of Hattine. From here the Sea of Galilee looked even more extensive, and was entirely wrapped in sunshine. Tiberias, quite small from where I saw it, lay sparkling white upon the shore; and between the hills I could see Galilee, with its open plains and verdant fields stretching far away. Owing to the extreme clearness of the atmosphere the most distant objects were sharply revealed. I could distinguish in the distance the ruins of Capernaum and Bethsaida; and yet further on, those of Dalmanutha and Chorazin: all four cities where Jesus performed many miracles and yet was unable to rouse the lukewarm faith of their inhabitants. On the horizon towards the west I perceived a dark speck in the plain; it was the little town of Magdala, which was not destroyed for Mary Magdalene's sake. What a wonderful sight was this ! Just below my feet was the place where the miracle of the loaves and fishes was performed ; on the first landing stage, the twelve granite seats upon which the Apostles were wont to sit as they listened to Jesus when He promised that these rough stones should be exchanged for as many thrones.

With His love for height, where He felt Himself in closer communion with Heaven, whence He derived His strength, how often must He have come to this very spot. After His Baptism, for instance, did He not remain forty days upon that arid and dreary mount of Jericho where He prayed and fasted and was tempted of the Evil One ? Yes, He loved to come upon this Mount Hattine, surrounded by His faithful adorers, by His Apostles, and by the fascinated and spell-bound crowd of men, women, and children, all eager to listen to the sublime words that fell from His lips. On that sloping hillside the throng would spread, sitting down on stones or grass, forming groups, here happy and there thoughtful, waiting to hear the Master's Words of comfort or exhortation. Sometimes He would pause to converse, with that gentle benignity evoked by so peaceful a scene by which Nature herself helped to soothe the ardour of His fervent Heart. Thus did the hours pass, and the crowd, forgetful of all else, sat in awestruck ecstasy and silence at His feet. Then again would come days of admonition and prophecy : hours of solemn emotion, when that Voice was heard on the lower levels of the Hill of Hattine, and Christ proclaimed the near advent of the Kingdom of Heaven. Sorrow should vanish, and so too poverty, and Death itself should be conquered. Such were the Divine Promises. Then the multitude on the flowery slopes of Hattine shouted and wept for very joy, and mothers would raise their children high in their arms, begging that Jesus would bless them. A question from a disciple, a woman's exclamation, a child's tear, would be enough to call forth those refulgent truths from the Master's lips, truths which can never be obliterated. On a balmy day in spring, when the air was fragrant with sweet scents, and the six boats had landed, laden with fish, Jesus ascended the Hill of Hattine, followed by the people, who had abandoned

houses, huts and tents, emptying the surrounding villages, and the shores of Genesareth lay silent. The light was intense, and the air soft and caressing, whilst the grasses in the fields were gently swaying to and fro, for all Nature appeared to lend herself to heighten the joy visible on all the eager faces of those who awaited some great and wonderful event. For some time Jesus knelt in prayer, and when He finally arose the multitude felt that deep mysterious intuition of an impending wonder. Here, under the pure firmament of Heaven, with the wide expanse of sea and fertile land which God had blessed, this throng of fishermen and tillers of the soil, this swarm of women and children in their poverty and simple-heartedness, awaited those unparalleled words which were destined to stir the whole world to its very foundations, and which have been handed down to us under the name of the Sermon on the Mount. From here, then, were proclaimed the Beatitudes of the Spirit, which open the gates of Heaven. These are the words which have most consoled, liberated, and exalted those who suffer, giving comfort, faith, strength, and eternal hope—
" Blessed are they that weep."

Let us then stoop and kiss the ground of this most sacred hill—the hill of the Beatitudes !

XII.

MAGDALA.

THROUGHOUT the Gospels, sometimes clearly and sometimes vaguely, appears the figure of a sinful woman. The accounts of her meetings with our Lord vary both as to the time and the manner in which they occurred: so that, to the superficial reader, it might seem that several such women were intended, whereas to the more discriminating student it is evident that the facts recorded refer to one woman only. The penitent sinner whom Christ pardoned was Mary Magdalene and no other. The Old Masters, both Italian and foreign, have depicted her as marvellously beautiful, nearly always fair and graceful, with hair falling loosely over her shoulders: but all, without exception, have given her a countenance of purely material loveliness, in which there is no shadow of poetry or spirituality. In Palestine, however, where, especially among the lower classes, tradition plays so great a part in the preservation of historical events, it describes the Magdalene as a woman of the usual Hebrew type—tall and agile, most elegant and harmonious in her movements, with a dark, oval-shaped face, long, melancholy, proud eyes, a mouth red as the flower of a pomegranate, and masses of dark hair. Thus do the fishermen and agriculturists of Galilee portray Mary Magdalene, although Titian has presented her to us in quite another light, with fair hair and a dazzling complexion. It does not, however, really matter much, as in Art it is beauty that chiefly counts; but none the less these tillers of the soil round Magdala are perfectly right in describing her as they have learnt to picture her to themselves, as a woman of a flexible, seductive figure, full of womanly grace, large sparkling brown eyes, and a sweet, irresistible smile. But Titian may also be right, who knows?

It is not certain whether Mary Magdalene was living in Magdala when she first met the Saviour at the time He was preaching on the shores of Tiberias, or whether that meeting took place later, in Jerusalem itself. This luxurious woman, clad in rich draperies, her head leaning on her jewel-bedecked hand, covered by a white silk mantle, from which her scented tresses escaped, her whole person exhaling balsamic odours, may have been carried from her native city in a stately palanquin, across the country that separates Magdala from Nazareth, and from thence to Jerusalem. She may have travelled across that country, so rich in flowers and vegetation, to the great and glorious Zion, the City of the Law, and of luxury and pleasure. Also her heart, hardened by selfishness, was without a trace of tender feeling: no tear had ever dimmed the brightness of her cold pitiless eyes. She was hard and cruel, glorying in her charms, proud of her wealth, her jewels, her clothes, and her matchless beauty which called forth a murmur of admiration wherever she went. But the day came when the rose of Magdala began to droop : and the thought was terrible to her. She knew she was despised by all, and that on her conscience lay the burden of innumerable sins, and she was overwhelmed with horror of herself and of her past life. Thus, persecuted, scorned, insulted, she fled to the feet of the Saviour, expecting to be condemned. But lo ! Christ pardoned her ! At that supreme moment the Magdalene's heart overflowed and tears gushed from those eyes which had never wept before, effacing all the impurities of that guilty soul, which was henceforth filled with fervent hope and immeasurable love. Jesus had gained a soul equal to any of His Apostles in passionate devotion. This was no woman who followed from idle curiosity, led away by the whim of the moment, and He had with Him henceforth an ardent and ever faithful servant. Her tender feet, which had never been used to walking, were never weary of following in the wake of the small band that accompanied the Saviour, even along the most tedious and stony of roads : her hand, which had hitherto done no work, laboured untiringly now : her knees, which had never been bent in prayer, were now continually bowed in supplication to the Father in Heaven. She followed Jesus everywhere like a shadow, watching over Him ever so tenderly. She was the first to meet danger and bear suffering and fatigue without a murmur. Traces of Mary Magdalene are to be found wherever Jesus laid His weary Head, and wheresoever His voice was heard. In the city of Bethsaida, where so many of His miracles took place, and also on Mount Hattine : in the country places round Safed, where He preached to the poor tillers of the soil, as well as beneath the arches of the Temple in stony-hearted Jerusalem : along the wonderful road which leads down to Lake Tiberias, as well as in the Garden of Gethsemane—everywhere !

To Him she owed all. Lost in sin, He recalled her to new life : she, a stranger to affection, was moved by Him to boundless love ; all unconscious of the ennobling power of suffering patiently borne, she experienced within herself this purifying influence ; her moral regeneration resulted from that one word of pardon. Let us follow the steps of Mary Magdalene during the week of our Lord's Passion. She was in the acclaiming crowd on Palm Sunday. Then, when the betrayal took place in Gethsemane and the Apostles forsook Him, the impassioned Magdalene followed Him step by step, from the moment of His spiritual Agony in the Garden to the Palace of the High Priest : here she passed the night before the gate, awaiting the sentence. Her grief was nearest to that of Mary of Nazareth. Wherever Jesus suffered the heart of the Magdalene was torn with anguish. She went from the Prætorium to Golgotha, she stood at the foot of the Cross, she watched Jesus die—her cry of agony was heard, her sobs could not be repressed : she only dried her tears to help Joseph of Arimathæa and the good Nicodemus, when they fetched Him down from the Cross : she brought spices and ointments to embalm His Body. On the third day she was the first to visit the Sepulchre, early in the morning, whilst it was yet dark. She it was who found that the stone had been rolled away, and ran to warn the Apostles, and to her it was that Christ first appeared. Judas had betrayed Him, Peter had denied Him, Thomas believed Him not, all the Apostles were wavering and uncertain : Mary Magdalene alone had perfect faith. From the instant of her conversion her trust was never shaken, and her love never faltered.

I determined to visit the little town of Magdala. It was on a summer's evening, by the shores of the Lake of Tiberias, that I had a long discussion with a poor fisherman (who, by the way, may have been a descendant of St. Peter, St. James, or St. John) as to the cost of taking my dragoman and myself across the lake by boat to visit Medjdel, or, as we call it, Magdala. This I proposed doing at six o'clock the next morning, setting out for the village, which lies about five hundred paces inland from the shore. The fisherman asked twenty-four shillings for the expedition, to which I agreed. He said a rowing boat would take at least eight hours to go there and back. I suggested sailing as quicker, but he answered that this would be impossible, as there was no wind on the lake during the morning hours, and in the afternoon it would be against us. Then we went to examine the boat in which he proposed taking us. It was a great, flat, heavy, uncomfortable-looking craft, wherein I did not fancy having to pass eight or more hours. Most reluctantly I now began to feel I should be obliged to give up this fascinating way of viewing the lake, where once a hundred sailing and rowing boats were wont to ply daily, carrying provisions to all the villages round, lending animation to the scene, but where now all was silent, and the very fishermen seemed to have forgotten their trade. Regretfully I at last settled to go on horseback, my dragoman concurring in this decision. The poor boatman went off silently without protest. He must have been used to these disappointments, as very few go by water to Magdala, Bethsaida, and Capernaum. The arduous journey to Tiberias, that none but the most fervent of religious pilgrims undertake, has completely worn out the last remaining energy and strength of the traveller. We, therefore, started off on horseback. The morning was fresh and delightful, and all around looked bright and cheerful; my steed, a small Arab, nimble as a bird, having well rested, needed but a gently spoken word to make him fly along gaily. He was called *Aoua*, which means " The Wind." As we proceeded on our way by the shores of the lake, the base of the Hill of Hattine was disclosed, the Mount of the Beatitudes, where King Baldwin was so terribly defeated in a battle against the Mohammedans, whereby he lost the throne of Jerusalem, and the work of the Crusades was rendered unavailing. We crossed the cornfields where Jesus spoke the parable of the tares and the wheat, and just before us stood the hill where the miracle of the loaves and fishes took place. It was indeed a lovely morning, the whole air filled with balmy odours, and rendered still more lovely by constant glimpses of the beautiful silvery blue Lake of Genesareth coming into view. Our little steeds flew along as though they carried nothing on their backs, with rhythmic, almost musical, step; and we reached our destination in an hour and a quarter, instead of two hours, as we had been told.

Magdala is a miserable little village consisting of a few scattered houses built of basalt, which look dark and gloomy. Once upon a time a very fine Catholic Church stood here, but it was destroyed in 1300, and has not been rebuilt. I wondered if one of these sombre houses had been the one where Mary Magdalene spent her youth. Who can tell? I roamed about, trying to find something on which to feed my imagination, and came upon a great palm tree with some ruins close to it. Could this have been the spot where she lived at the time when she started for Jerusalem, in the fulness of her beauty and insatiable longing for pleasures and luxury? Perchance this palm tree may have been one of many in some fine garden! Further on, to the left, nearer the road and quite at the end of the village, are the remains of a great wall. Could this have been her dwelling? Who knows? All is wrapt in mystery. Still the place exists, the only one of the five towns along the shore where Jesus preached; Capernaum, Bethsaida, Dalmanutha, Chorazin, and Magdala. Everywhere hereabouts He exerted His Divine Power—speaking, preaching, teaching, and performing miracles of tenderness, mercy, and wisdom, though the heart of man remained untouched, hard, and cold as stone. Remember the terrible menace: " Woe unto thee, Chorazin! woe unto thee, Bethsaida! for if the mighty works had been done in Tyre and Sidon which have been done in you, they had a great while ago repented, sitting in sackcloth and ashes. But it shall be more tolerable for Tyre and Sidon at the Judgment than for you. And thou, Capernaum, which art exalted to Heaven, shalt be thrust down to hell!" Well the malediction of Jesus has fallen upon those cities! Chorazin and Dalmanutha are in ruins, and so are Capernaum and Bethsaida. Only one remains standing—little Magdala: and she will endure to the end of time, say the fishermen, for she was the birthplace of the woman who, though a sinner, was blessed by the Pardon of Christ which lasteth for ever!

PART VIII.
ST. FRANCIS IN PALESTINE.

I.

HOSPITALITY.

THE Grand Hotel at Jerusalem, situated in the city proper, can easily accommodate a hundred persons, and is well and elegantly appointed after the English fashion, to which has been appropriately added a certain Oriental tone which is by no means unattractive. There are in the new quarters, outside Bab-el-Khalil, two other hotels, very clean and comfortable, under English management, the " Howard " and the " Feil." Furnished apartments and boarding-houses are scattered all over the town, but more especially in the Catholic quarters. But the hostelry most sought after by pilgrims is the large and handsome hospice or *Casa Nova* belonging to the Franciscans, where, ever since St. Francis of Assisi visited Palestine, hospitality has been offered most cordially to all who seek it, provided they profess some form of Christian belief. The *Casa Nova* must not, however, be confounded with the Franciscan Friary, which is under the government of the Custodian of the Holy Land and Guardian of Mount Zion—the titles borne by the head of the Friary of San Salvatore—and which no lay person of either sex is allowed to enter. The Franciscans, however, perform their works of charity outside the walls of their enclosure, teach in the schools, superintend their various trades, and exercise hospitality. The *Casa Nova* is, therefore, quite a distinct institution, which faces San Salvatore, and where three or four Franciscan Friars, together with eight or ten lay brothers, attend upon the travellers during the pilgrim season. It is a large three-storied building, capable of containing at least three hundred people, and has even accommodated as many as five hundred. It is built round a central courtyard or cloister with four very long ambulatories, on to which open the doors of the cells allotted to the pilgrims, and all of them are whitewashed, very airy and clean, and contain a charming little white bed supplied with mosquito curtains, a night table, a writing table, a great chest, two or three chairs, and a rug beside the bed. Everything looks very comfortable and restful. There are three classes of cells or rooms, the first for the more important personages, the second for ordinary travellers, and the third for the poor. The latter often arrive broken down and in ill-health, suffering more or less from repulsive diseases. But there is scarcely any difference made between the three classes, and the chamber of the wealthy pilgrim or high dignitary of the Church differs but little from that of the poorest guest. For did not St. Francis found his hospices in Palestine especially for the poor?

The *Casa Nova* and its Friar hospitaller, Father Philip, of Castelmadama, a man of genius, refined and sympathetic, receives most cordially, for Christ's sake, whoever craves admittance, be he man or woman, rich or poor, Roman Catholic, Lutheran, Protestant, Copt, Armenian, or Greek. Beyond being requested to register your name and from whence you come you are asked no questions. This slight formality once complied with you are escorted to your room, and the lay brother tells you the hours of the meals and the time you must return at night. In the morning they give you coffee and milk; at one o'clock an abundant and well-prepared dinner, together with good wine of Jerusalem or Hebron; in the evening a hot supper. You are at liberty to do as you please; you are not compelled, either directly or indirectly, to follow any religious services; and they never talk about religious matters unless you yourself open the conversation on those topics. If you require a guide, they commend you to the care of a Franciscan Friar; and if you ask for the best guide-book to Palestine, they give you the excellent one in three volumes, written by the erudite Father Lavinio of Ham, an incomparably practical work, which, though full of mystic poetry, is precise and reliable. When you wish to go on an excursion, they find you a dragoman, escort, and horses, and they advise you about everything in a most sensible manner. In a word, they assist you in all your difficulties, and if you chance to fall ill they nurse you most attentively and kindly. In short, they know everything, undertake everything, and make everything as easy as possible for you, and this without any fuss, affectation, or intrusiveness. They speak every language under the sun, and have travelled all the world over ; belong to all nationalities, though for the glory of their founder, who was himself a native of Italy, they all speak Italian, teach it, propagate it, and defend it ; and if the name of Italy is still honoured in Palestine, it is entirely due to the followers of St. Francis and their patriotic, generous, and charitable works. How few are aware of this ! Some Italians even pretend never to have heard that it is owing to the Franciscans that the Holy Sepulchre is still in the possession of Latin Christendom.

The hospitality of the Franciscans is most strikingly manifested in the less important centres of Palestine, Samaria, and Galilee, where neither roads, inns, nor furnished rooms are to be found ! Wherever there is a spot connected with the lives of Jesus and Mary you are sure to find a Franciscan monastery and hospice. Bethlehem possesses only a small inn, but it has a beautiful Franciscan hospice ; Nazareth has a very poor little hostelry which is closed in May, but the Franciscans receive you at any time in their clean and comfortable dwelling, whose porch is overshadowed by a huge sycamore tree. Tiberias is a Jewish town, but on the shores of the lake the Franciscans have their hospice ; even in the small towns of Nain and Cana of Galilee, at Emmaus or Sichem, you are sure to find a hearty welcome from the followers of the poor man of Assisi.

On that never-to-be-forgotten day in May when I reached Nazareth, my eyes dazzled by the sun and my throat parched, I felt uncertain whether I might not be stranded by the wayside without food or shelter. The bell of the hospice had scarcely sounded, however, ere the door was opened and I was ushered up a flight of stairs and shown into a small parlour, where the good-hearted Father John of Rotterdam received me. In this quiet retreat at Nazareth, with its great shady trees, and in my delightful room cooled by the breezes from the hills, I passed some of the most peaceful and happy days I can remember, during which I was able to indulge in uninterrupted meditation.

Oh, dear and never-to-be-forgotten Franciscan hospitality, giving all and asking for nothing, procuring for the body rest and for the mind peace, and never demanding the least return. How well I remember the day we left Nazareth to begin the ascent of Mount Tabor. God knows how fatiguing it was; with its perpendicular ups and downs, and its dizzy precipices! Although only about 1,980 feet high, this mountain is as perilous to ascend as any glacier of over 13,000 feet. But it is Tabor! the Mount of the Transfiguration! and I, even I have accomplished it! But I cannot describe the state in which I reached the top, nor all the horrors I underwent to do so. I was in a state of nervous breakdown when I reached the door of the convent, and Father Augustin of Saragossa, the Spanish Friar, who lives alone with two other monks and two servants, came to my assistance, and, after having shown me my room, left me for a couple of hours to sleep the deep, dreamless sleep of utter prostration; later on he conducted me to the site of the Transfiguration, and here again he left me alone to meditate in silence and contemplate the extensive and noble view. Afterwards, he gave me my breakfast, and with kindly attention the cook, a lay brother, placed upon a piece of sponge cake a fresh crimson carnation.

II.

THE WORK.

ST. FRANCIS OF ASSISI followed in the footsteps of his Master and imitated Him in perfect humility and serenity of spirit. He was full of the same tender love for the simple-minded and the little ones. He possessed the same love of nature, of flowers, plants, and animals, and was, moreover, full of the same enthusiasm for social reform, in which he ever took the side of the poor, rather than of the rich, and of the weak against the oppressor.

When the Crusaders finally abandoned the Holy Land and the Holy Sepulchre fell into neglect, the Minor Conventuals or Minorite Friars established themselves close to the church erected in honour of the Last Supper. Later on, they were placed in possession of the Holy Places as representatives of Catholicism. Notwithstanding the terrible persecutions and frequent martyrdoms to which they were subjected by the Mohammedans, the Minorites of St. Francis have never ceased to safeguard the Holy Places. The Franciscans of the Holy Land, and particularly those attached to the Churches of the Last Supper and of the Holy Sepulchre, were cast into prison in the year 1395 by order of the Egyptian Sultan, who wished to avenge himself on Peter I. (de Lusignan), King of Cyprus, who had sacked the city of Alexandria. Five years later, however, thanks to the good offices of the Venetian Republic, they were set at liberty and reinstalled in their various Sanctuaries. In 1537, after Andrea Doria, Doge of Genoa, had destroyed the Turkish fleet at Lepanto, Sulyman I. ordered the Governor of Jerusalem to imprison all the Franciscans of the Holy City in the Tower of David. From thence they were eventually transferred to the prison of Damascus, but were presently liberated, thanks to the intercession of Francis I., and once more appointed Guardians of the Holy Places. Their rights were again contested in the seventeenth century, during the reign of Louis XIV., but France intervened in their behalf. Moreover, in 1673, a Convention was signed between Louis XIV. and the Sublime Porte, which declared in its thirty-third article that "the Franciscan Friars should in future be allowed to retain their Sanctuaries both in and out of Jerusalem." Twice Louis XIV. was forced to insist, even by threats, upon this Convention being duly respected. Finally, Leopold I., Emperor of Austria, who had vanquished the Mohammedans on several occasions, and more particularly in 1699, profited by his position as victor to insist that the Franciscans should be left in peaceful possession of their monasteries throughout the Holy Land without fear of interference from the local government. Since that time, the followers of St. Francis have not suffered any violent persecution at the hands of the Turks : all that they have endured, even to the shedding of blood, has been brought upon them, thanks to the fanaticism of the Schismatic Greeks and Armenians. These two sects are far more fanatical than religious, and are apt to forget the teachings of Christ in their eagerness for supremacy, and by dint of bribery, cunning, or even violence, have deprived the Franciscans as much as possible of their influence. But as the Friars are destitute of all worldly possessions, and live entirely on the alms they receive, these fanatical sects are powerless to obtain any great material advantage from them. Unfortunately, the followers of St. Francis no longer have the entire custody of the Holy Places. The Church of the Last Supper has been taken from them by the Turks, under the pretext that it contains the tomb of a Mohammedan Saint. They have been expelled from the Church of the Assumption by the Schismatic Greeks : and they are not allowed to say Mass in the Church of the Nativity at Bethlehem. A few years back they were deprived of the secular right of celebrating the Divine office on one day of the year in the Church of St. James, which belongs to the Schismatic Armenians, nor are they permitted to say Mass in the Church of the same sect built upon the spot where Jesus was brought before Caiaphas. It is true that the head of the Minor Friars in Palestine bears the title of Custodian of the Holy Sepulchre and Guardian of Mount Zion, and that the Order

THE WORK.

still possesses all the most important and interesting of the Holy Places, but their rights are often contested and their beneficial influence is thereby considerably diminished.

These Friars Minor of Palestine are also called the Fathers of the Holy Land. It is a name which has been bestowed upon them for having, during six centuries and a half, struggled unceasingly to hold the triple mission confided to them by St. Francis, and solemnly confirmed to them by the See of Peter. They must defend, preserve, and venerate the Holy Places which have been sanctified by the Life, miracles, and Death of the Saviour. They have to receive the pilgrims who visit the Holy Land, and give them all the spiritual and material help they can. They must preach the Gospel in the Land where Christ's Words were spoken. This triple mission they accomplish, more especially in those places where they have the care of parishes as well as of the Sanctuaries. At Jerusalem, for instance, they are not only Guardians of the Holy Sepulchre, but they are missionaries, curates, doctors, chemists, and hospitallers as well.

They direct the schools, where they teach in Italian only: they manage the workshops and laboratories: they take care of the orphans of both sexes, teaching them, and instructing them in various trades, giving them a thorough religious and moral training. They assist widows, sick persons, and the poor, paying their house-rent and giving them food and clothing, and they moreover teach them to work, so that they may render themselves independent. Their mother house is in Jerusalem, but they have a noviatiate at Nazareth: and a seminary at St. John-of-the Mountain, where the students of the Order of St. Francis finish their noviatiate. Their studies in philosophy are followed at Bethlehem, and those in theology at the convent of St. Salvatore at Jerusalem. The Franciscans have forty-three friaries, thirty schools, and thousands of pupils all over the Holy Land.

But how is it that the Franciscans in Palestine manage to carry on this stupendous organisation of faith, worship, propaganda, charity, and hospitality? How is it that they have erected friaries and churches and have maintained their imposing ritual: that they have kept up their homes and carried on their workshops : have helped the poor and cared for the pilgrims who pay nothing for their lodging ? How, in a word, have they been able to do this miraculous work through so many centuries ? All is paid for by the alms of the Faithful. For it is well known that the great rule of the Order of St. Francis is poverty: no Minor Friar, be he even Father Louis of Parma, the General of the Order, possesses more than two habits at a time. They receive abundant alms from all parts of the world for the custody of the Holy Places, South America being especially generous in this respect. Italy, alas ! though most Christian and the native land of St. Francis, as well as the seat of the Papacy, to her shame, sends less than any other nation ! One particular day in the year is set apart, when the alms in all the churches under the sway of the Roman Hierarchy are given to the maintenance of the Holy Sepulchre. The Christian who resides in Palestine is nearly always poor, for even when he does possess anything his contact with the Sacred Tomb broadens his sympathies and induces him to give all he possesses at the time in charity.

And you, dear reader, whoever you may be, if perchance this account of my journey has touched your heart, by awakening the memories of your childhood's faith ; if what I have described with the frankness and loyalty of a Christian, though without literary or artistic effect, as I saw and felt it myself, should have enkindled in your soul a sentiment of veneration for the Land of Jesus, I pray you, remember the followers of St. Francis in Palestine, pity their hardships, admire their courage, imitate their active faith, and love them in the name of Jesus Christ, and help them also, for His sake.

PART IX.
THE LAST DAY.

I.

ADVICE TO THE INTENDING TRAVELLER.

MANY travellers, even ardent Christians, as well as those who desire to visit the Holy Land for purely intellectual purposes, are deterred from undertaking the journey for fear of the expense, the distance, and the difficulties of travel. A few practical hints on this subject may not, therefore, be out of place here, especially as they come from one who has so recently undertaken a pilgrimage to the Land of Jesus. Palestine can be reached without much difficulty, and is so charming, by reason of the variety and beauty of its scenery and its intense historical interest, that it may well be described as absolutely fascinating. Those who will only get up at their usual hour and *will* eat only the same food they do at home, might just as well remain in their own dining-rooms : they are not travellers in the true sense of the word. If one wishes to thoroughly enjoy Palestine it is necessary to resign oneself to an entire change of habits, a topsy-turvydom, so to speak, of our ordinary mode of life, and this, after all, is not without its compensations.

Six weeks suffice for a tour through Palestine, though travellers who can afford the time and money can well remain there two months. The best season is from January to the end of May : the summer is too hot, in autumn it is not very healthy, and during the winter months the roads, in consequence of thunderstorms and the swollen state of the rivers, are indescribably bad. There are people, to be sure, who undertake the journey at any time of the year, even at Christmas-tide, but it is wiser to choose a more fitting moment. The fine weather begins at the end of January, and March and April are the most perfect months for visiting the Holy Land; May and June are still pleasant, though rather hot.

Every Wednesday an Italian boat leaves for Alexandria, reaching that port on the following Saturday evening or Sunday morning, an easy and pleasant voyage. Arriving on Sunday morning at Alexandria, it is usual to wait there for the boat for Jaffa until the following Thursday or Friday: thus there is ample time to visit Cairo. A four hours' railway journey takes you from Alexandria to the latter city, starting early in the morning and arriving in the capital at eleven o'clock. From Cairo you return to Alexandria in order to catch the steamer to Jaffa. There are good vessels on all the various lines: but on board the Egyptian steamers the food is bad and they are not over-clean: the sleeping accommodation is not particularly good on the French: and distinctly the best are the Austrian Lloyd, which are in every respect excellent.

The Lloyd steamer starts on Fridays at eleven o'clock in the morning for Jaffa, the only other places of call being Port Said, where there is a stop of seven or eight hours to load and unload, during which time you are able to take a small boat to see the Suez Canal. On Sunday morning you enter the port of Jaffa after less than two days at sea, and on the same day at half-past two you can take the train for Jerusalem. Were it not for the delay of four or five days at Alexandria it would only take about a week to go from Italy to Jerusalem by the same route as the mails. Between February and June the sea is invariably calm: and notwithstanding the somewhat ominous appearance of the harbour of Jaffa there is no real danger anywhere.

Most people remain at Jerusalem about a fortnight, which is quite long enough for seeing the sights of the city and its environs. Horses, donkeys, mules, carriages, and litters can be hired in the town. The most important excursions in the immediate neighbourhood of the Holy City are the Valley of Jehoshaphat and the Mount of Olives, both of which can be accomplished on foot or on donkey-back. You can walk to nearly all the places of interest

ADVICE TO THE INTENDING TRAVELLER.

within the city, but there are three or four places further afield, namely, Bethlehem, which is about an hour's drive, Solomon's Wells, the Sealed Fountain, and the Closed Garden, the last reached by carriage in about two hours. The excursion to Hebron, the city of Abraham, can be performed in the same way, as also that to St. John-of-the-Mountain, and is about an hour's drive from Jerusalem.

It takes three days to go to Jericho and the Dead Sea, and there is no carriageable road all the way : so you must either select a palanquin, which is less fatiguing, or else a horse. This latter mode of progression is by no means disagreeable, as the horses are surefooted and go at an easy pace. By leaving Jerusalem at two o'clock in the afternoon, you can reach Jericho by eight in the evening. Here you can dine and sleep, starting off again at four in the morning for the Dead Sea and the Jordan, a journey of three hours. With a further rest of two hours on the banks of the Jordan you are back again at Jericho at three in the afternoon, where you must spend the night, and return to Jerusalem the next day. No doubt this is a fatiguing expedition, but it brings its own reward, for an excursion to the Dead Sea and the Jordan is so fascinating that only the most indolent of people could possibly resist undertaking it. Occasionally there are brigands to be met with on the road between Jericho and the Dead Sea, but with a proper escort and a prudent dragoman any danger can be easily avoided. Strange relations exist between the escorts, dragomen, and the highwaymen, but, as a rule, the former are entirely in the favour of the traveller. Therefore, remember never to quarrel with your dragoman and Bedouin, for your safety lies entirely in their hands, and your purse also. By the time you have visited Jericho you have become so enchanted with the Holy Land that instead of six weeks you determine to remain two months. It is impossible to see all the sights of Jerusalem in less than ten days. I myself remained twenty-five days, only to leave it with a heavy heart and the deepest regret.

The second part of the journey to Palestine is to Galilee, the land where Jesus passed His Youth and which was the scene of His early preaching : a journey so replete with poetic interest that it would require a far more eloquent pen than mine to do it justice. The journey from Jerusalem to Galilee overland takes eight days on horseback across Samaria, which is tedious and uninteresting. It is preferable to go by sea. A train takes you to Jaffa in four hours, say on a Sunday morning. From here you take the Austrian steamer which skirts the coast of Syria and Karamania, and in eight hours you reach Haifa, the seaport of Galilee. Here you sleep and remain all day Monday to visit Mount Carmel. On Tuesday, at six o'clock in the morning, you start for Nazareth in a brake belonging to George Suss, the German I have mentioned. At midday you reach the village, where you ought to remain as long as possible, for it is a charming place and well worth seeing.

The principal excursions from Nazareth are Mount Tabor, Tiberias, and Cana, which take from five to six days, and as there are no carriages to be had, your choice lies between a horse's back or a palanquin. Leaving Nazareth in the morning, you reach Tiberias about midday, having taken about three hours, and here you remain until the following day. Six hours will take you from Tabor to Tiberias, and this may be called the real pilgrimage of your journey to Palestine, as it is the most tedious, fatiguing, and wearisome of all. Tiberias and its lake, however, repay you for your trouble a thousandfold. Remaining at Tiberias two days, you visit the shores of the lake, the ruins of Bethsaida and Capernaum, and the village of Magdala: the Mount of Beatitudes, the cornfields, and all the blessed region through which Christ preached. All this can be achieved either by boat, horseback, or on foot. It takes three hours to explore Cana and Sepphoris, and after five days' absence in a very land of dreams you are back again in Nazareth. Twelve days are barely enough to visit Galilee, and to a real lover of this most charming of lands, twenty days are certainly not too many. There are no brigands in Galilee, and the climate is delightful—maybe a trifle hot at Tiberias in June, but never oppressive. The Nazarenes are excellent people, and all their surroundings are quite enchanting. When you leave Nazareth you return to Haifa by carriage, and after spending a day or two more at Carmel

A HOPE.

you set out for Italy by an Austrian steamer which takes you round by Alexandria to Naples.

II.

A HOPE.

How much money is needed to visit the Land of Jesus? It is impossible to obtain a definite and satisfactory answer. There always lurks the feeling that only the very rich can afford such an undertaking; but surely the countless pilgrims from all parts of the world, Poles, Austrians, Germans, and peasants from the furthest parts of Russia and Macedonia, are not millionaires in disguise. They will tell you it is possible to visit the land where He Lived and Died even for a few shillings, let alone pounds. But, although the most numerous, they are, in a sense, exceptional pilgrims. The ordinary tourist, who wishes to see Palestine comfortably but without extravagance, can do so for between £100 and £140. I spent £140, but this included £40 which I spent in purchases of mementoes of the various places I visited as presents for friends, which are, needless to say, superfluous. Therefore, £100 will amply suffice to cover expenses of the journey, for mine included a short stay in Constantinople.

Let those who have visited the Higher Engadine, Saint Moritz, and Interlaken confess how much more than this they have spent on these most commonplace journeys. Living costs much less in the Land of Jesus than in most other countries, and if two or more people travel together the expense is, of course, greatly reduced. A second person would only cost a third extra, and three or four less in proportion. I should not advise going in a party of more than four persons, as it rarely ends pleasantly. On the steamers, whether Italian, Austrian, French, Russian, or Egyptian, the journey, with living included, costs between 24s. and 32s. a day, first-class; and I strongly recommend the Austrian

Lloyd Line of boats. At the Hôtel Jerusalem at Jaffa you pay 8s. a day, and at the New Grand Hotel at Jerusalem, 10s.; both are excellent, and much frequented by English people. A dragoman, who is quite indispensable, costs 6s. 6d. a day in Jerusalem, 10s. in the neighbourhood, and 12s. for distant excursions. An escort Bedouin, armed to the teeth, costs 16s. a day, but he is only necessary for the journey to Jericho, the Dead Sea, and the Jordan, a matter of three days; a good horse comes to 4s. a day each for yourself and your dragoman. Thus it is evident that several people together will save a great deal. A palanquin, for those who are too weak or too advanced in years for riding, costs 6s. 6d. a day. One must not, however, forget that the custom of backsheesh reigns supreme throughout the Ottoman Empire, though even to Mussulmans it is not necessary to give exorbitantly to satisfy them. Curiously enough, all over Palestine nearly everyone understands Italian, a fact no doubt due to the influence of the Franciscans; most people speak French, and a little English. One is much more rarely cheated in Palestine than in the West. The Consuls afford every assistance, but the Franciscans are your truest friends in the Holy Land, and have compiled the best guide-books, that by Father Lavinio of Ham being, as I have said, in every way admirable, well written, learned, and full of useful information.

It may be thought that only those who possess £120 to do what they like with can give themselves the treat of a journey to Syria, the Land of Jesus. But this is not the case, for by economy and forethought it can be managed for much less. Travel second-class on the steamer, which is by no means uncomfortable; on reaching Palestine try and find some people willing to share with you the expenses of dragoman, carriages, and escort; and £60 will suffice for six weeks' stay. Then, instead of going to hotels, make use of the Franciscans' hospitality, which you can repay by as much or as little as you like; the really poor need give nothing at all, and are none the less well treated. The followers of St. Francis never ask for anything and never observe whether you go to church or not, or to what nationality you belong—they welcome you in the Name of Christ.

A HOPE.

Backed by this wonderful organisation of Christian charity, your expenses are easily reduced to a minimum. It is almost impossible to say for how little people have visited the Holy Land, who, being resolved to do so, have studied the cheapest ways and means, and were prepared to bear hardships cheerfully in the accomplishment of their pilgrimage. The patient and taciturn Russian and Polish peasants, who set out with £4 in their pockets, tramping from hospice to hospice, and sanctuary to sanctuary, are never without their *samovars*, in which they brew tea several times in the twenty-four hours. The traveller by palanquin or horseback will pass many such on the high roads, carrying their pilgrims' staffs and bundles of clothes ; but they never so much as turn round to look at him, but tramp steadily on, taking three days to accomplish what the more fortunate travellers are able to do in six hours. They are often so weary as to sink asleep by the roadside. In the churches you will see them, their eyes so full of the ecstasy of their Faith as to make you feel ashamed of your own lack of fervour. Sometimes they fall sick and even die by the way. These poor souls are indeed the true pilgrims, and are there not some of other nationalities like them ?

I have written with one great hope in my heart, that this book of mine will be read, not for the sake of its writer, but on account of the sacred title it bears, by many who do not care for novels and stories. What I ardently desire is this : that some of my readers, after perusing these pages and having gathered information of a practical character as to the ways and means of reaching Palestine, will be prompted to follow my example and undertake the holy pilgrimage. Many a costly, uninteresting tour is made, from which the traveller returns weary both in mind and body : whereas a visit to the country of Jesus has an incomparable fascination and poetical charm all its own, the memory of which can never be obliterated. May I, therefore, hope that from some great city or little village of my own native land, or even from some foreign country where my book may be read in its translated form, I may have the joy of feeling that at least a few of the readers of my work will be inspired by its pages to see the cradle lands of Jesus.

Indeed, if I cause but one solitary pilgrim to visit the Holy Land I shall feel that I have not written my book in vain.

III.

ISSA COBROUSLY.

THE word "dragoman" means, literally, "interpreter": but in Egypt, Palestine, and Syria it assumes greater significance, and describes in one word all the qualifications of interpreter, *cicerone*, guide, escort, friend, and servant. Yes, even friend! I remained only three days in the company of the one-eyed Turk, Ahmed of the shrewd face, who acted as my dragoman in Alexandria : but never shall I forget his Italian-Marseillaise-Arabic jargon, or his profound silence during the numerous peregrinations which I made alone on the banks of the Nile, when I would get in and out of the carriage scores of times, whilst he held my flowers, field-glasses, parasol, or cloak with the most obsequious patience. Never shall I cease to remember the marvellous powers of intuition he displayed and the practical manner in which he carried out my orders. He exhibited, I remarked, quite wonderful acuteness of observation when he described Ramleh, the summer residence of the Khedive : in short, never had I met with a more intelligent automaton and respectful servant. When he accompanied me on board the Austrian Lloyd steamer, the *Apollo*, as I was starting for Jaffa, he asked whether I could take him with me ; and when I, in my turn, asked him whether he could act as dragoman in Palestine, he replied, with true Mohammedan frankness, "Oh, no." I explained as clearly as I could that under the circumstances it was impossible, but he was quite unconvinced, and shook his head dolefully : then, solemnly placing my hand on his heart and raising it to his brow in token of profound homage, he quietly left the deck and went off to his little skiff, and presently disappeared.

A true Turk was my old dragoman at Cairo, Hassan, a true Turk was he: not an Egyptian, but a Turk with the many-folded turban around his fez, with the long tunic fastened to his waist by a silken cord, and ample trousers. Hassan was old, very old, and slow in his gait, with a clucking voice, but of such noble aspect, that I felt ashamed to let him sit beside the coachman, and really thought it was my duty to ask him to take a seat beside me in the carriage. Hassan would knock regularly every morning at five o'clock at my window, which was on the ground-floor of the Hôtel du Nil, in order that we might be able to start on our various sight-seeing expeditions before the sun became too hot. When at last I appeared his wrinkled old face would light up with a bright smile, and then off he would start before me, clearing the way with his little ebony stick. At times, when mounted on the box seat, he would address, at rare intervals, a word to the coachman, or occasionally turn round and explain something to me. I could not understand a word of his French, which was considerably worse than that of Ahmed in Alexandria. One word, however, constantly recurred in his conversation, and that was *Piramillo*, which I made out to mean " Pyramids." Notwithstanding all obstacles, we really understood each other perfectly. I can't say how! One thing Hassan may pride himself on, and that is, having been through a course of Neapolitan dialect : whilst I may flatter myself on having mastered so complex and complicated a dragoman jargon that I shall, I believe, experience no difficulty in understanding any dragoman I may ever come across in the future. A wonderful man was the imposing and aristocratic-looking Hassan, who, with a simple wave of his wand, could clear the road of men and beasts, and with a couple of words silence the most impertinent of cabmen, or settle a dispute over the price of a velvet cushion or piece of gold embroidery with an Arab vendor of curiosities. He was especially tactful when he visited a mosque, on entering which he would address the custodian in his deep-toned voice with the usual salutation, *Eleik salaam*, the latter answering gravely, *Salaam eleik*. He cautioned me to supply myself with small coin " for these common people," as he called them. Inside the mosque he would carefully select for me the best pair of slippers, and his grave salutation to the Prophet was a sight to see and never forget. Whenever I wanted an explanation he would give it: otherwise he was correct, solemn, and taciturn, though a flash of humour would occasionally light up his wrinkled countenance. He told me he had three sons, concerning whose beauty, talent, and virtues he would deliver himself of quite a panegyric, declaring that he only continued to act as a dragoman at his age on their account, because he did not intend them to follow his calling, but (if such was the will of Mahomet) to keep a shop in the bazaar and become rich men.

"And what does Mahomet think of it?" I asked, solemnly.

"Mahomet is good and great," he answered, as he bowed his head low, with an expression of intense satisfaction.

I also told him about my own four little sons, for it was a comfort to speak of them even to an old dragoman. He would listen, silent and apparently unmoved, occasionally, however, smiling benignly on me. This good Turk was no decrepit old fellow, but still hale and hearty. How well I remember the morning when we visited the Ghizeh Pyramid together. All along the road he never ceased warning me against the rapacity of the Bedouins, the keepers of the Pyramids, calling them thieves, liars, and assassins; but when we reached the borders of the desert and those delightful brigands surrounded us, he quickly perceived my admiration for them, and never ventured again to deride their abominable rascality, though when I was allowing myself to be quietly pillaged by them, he flew into a terrible outburst of fury and launched every sort of frightful Turkish imprecation on their heads. A little more and, old as he was, he would have come to blows, single-handed, with the agile acrobats of the Pyramids! On the way back, however, he joined in the merriment the adventure had excited in me, though he would occasionally turn round and shake his fist at the retreating groups of Bedouins and at the Sphinx rising mysteriously out of the yellow sand. He called it *Le sfunx,* under the impression he was speaking the most perfect Parisian French. Just before I left he pulled a small Egyptian charm out of his pocket, bidding me present it to my favourite son. The quick-witted old rascal was so preternaturally intelligent that he actually understood things I never intended him to comprehend !

Never, never shall I forget my dear, faithful friend and companion in Syria, Dragoman Issa ! Forty days we passed together, and they may surely count for something even if the most perfect of dragomans, Issa Cobrously, had not combined in himself every possible sympathetic and endearing qualification. I must explain more fully the reason for my enthusiastic and tender admiration for this pearl of dragomans : for whereas in Egypt it is quite possible to do without one, in Palestine he is an absolute necessity. No one, however intelligent, brave, or rich, would think of dispensing with a dragoman in the Holy Land. In Jerusalem itself he may only act as guide and *cicerone,* but once you are outside the city gate of Solima he becomes of paramount importance. Before the time of Cook, the dragoman was quite a gentleman and a power in the land, and possessed horses, palanquins, tents, beds, kitchen utensils, and even all the necessary apparatus for serving a dinner, so that the traveller had to bargain with him for so many days and so many people and he would answer for his comfort and safety. What the all-powerful Thomas Cook now undertakes on a vast and well-organised scale, at great expense, but greater comfort, the dragoman of old would do for less money, but much more agreeably. Now their business is almost ruined, for the English and other tourists, " personally conducted " by Cook, need bargain no longer with the dragomans, who are now merely guides and *ciceroni*. Occasionally the poor fellows rebel against their fate, but Cook always ends victoriously. Issa in his time had earned a good round sum. He was only fifty-five years of age, during forty of which he had been a dragoman. He had travelled all over Asia eight times, had been twice to Africa with Gordon Pasha ; twenty-seven times to Damascus, and twenty to Bagdad, besides visiting every part of Arabia—Arabia Petræa to Moab, from Samaria to Galilee, Ascalon to Beyrout, and Rosetta to ancient Phœnicia. Small in stature, dried up and thin, he appeared much older than he really was. Constant riding had bowed his legs, and his face was dark, fleshless, and wrinkled. His moustaches were iron-grey, but his eyes were still bright and sparkled with intelligence. He was a Christian of Jerusalem, and spoke Italian, French, and English fluently. His long journeys in so many lands, with people of such varied nationalities, who were, for the most part, persons of refinement and culture, had done much to quicken his intelligence, and had given him an insight into many things, a keen observation, and a fund of anecdote with which to enliven the interminable tracts of road, traversed either on horseback or in a palanquin. At first I was so impressed with his knowledge that I followed meekly all his directions, and they were usually far the best and most practical, but by degrees I asserted my own will, and he yielded to the caprices of one who invariably wanted to write when she ought to have been eating, and to sleep when it was time to move ! Now and then, under the pretence of consulting him, I would propound one of my freaks, when he would look doubtfully at me; but if I insisted, he would say, meditatively :

"Very well, don't trouble about it. I will arrange all."

When he said he would arrange a thing, whatever happened, arranged it was. How well I remember his kindness, devotion, and courage during the journey to Jericho. We were five : myself, Issa, the escort, the muleteer and his boy. If during that long, tedious, and dangerous journey I felt neither fatigue nor weariness, and was unaware of danger, I owed it all to my good Issa. He kept close to my palanquin during the first stage of six hours, riding on horseback : having chosen the freshest and least dangerous hours for the journey. When at last we arrived at the mysterious and uncanny house kept by those two strange Russian women at Jericho, at seven o'clock in the evening, he himself settled me in my room, lighted my candles, and without resting a moment set to work to cook my dinner—and an excellent dinner it was, consisting of rice soup, roast meat, and fowl, finishing up with dried fruit and biscuits, which he had brought with him. After dinner he even made me a cup of tea.

Noticing that he himself ate nothing, I asked him the reason. He informed me he was never hungry in dreadful Jericho. And in truth the atmosphere of that place is so heavy and suffocating that it had a curious effect even on me. The weird house and strange noises frightened me more terribly than I had ever been before in the whole course of my life. I was possessed with the idea I should be murdered. Unable to remain longer indoors I went into the garden, where I could see the light in the kitchen and Issa washing up the dinner things and preparing the coffee for next morning. When I told him of my fears, instead of going to sleep on the divan in the dining-room, he threw himself down upon the mat outside my door like a good and faithful dog! During those three days he served me in like manner, anticipating my every wish, leaving me to enjoy my meditations in peace, but coming at the least word to help me pass the time by recounting interesting anecdotes. The height of his devotion was reached the night we came back to Jerusalem. We had returned to Jericho on the third day at midday, from the Dead Sea and Jordan, and having dined at two o'clock we were to have remained until four o'clock in the morning to rest the men and beasts. Another reason for not starting earlier was that the moon did not rise until midnight and that the first part of the road, after leaving Jericho, was the most infested by brigands. Should we meet with twenty such, what could we five do, although armed? It was evident, therefore, how unwise it would be to start before the hour Issa had determined. By five o'clock in the afternoon I was so thoroughly weary of the place that I felt incapable of remaining another hour—therefore, summoning Issa, I told him so.

He was much amazed at my decision and said it was useless to think of starting; the animals wanted rest and so did the men. Determined not to be thwarted, I told him to give more food to the beasts, and more money to the Arabs, but that go I would and that immediately. Again he tried to reason with me, by saying that by nine o'clock the road would be perfectly dark and unsafe.

"Are you not afraid?" he asked.

I replied, "No," feeling remarkably brave. Then I asked whether he himself was afraid.

"No," he answered, quickly, "only I have your safety to think of—you must remember my responsibilities."

"Never mind me," I urged, "you can say I insisted. Moreover I am sure I shall be ill if I remain. You don't wish to leave me here a corpse, I suppose?"

Noticing that I really was suffering, the good creature did his best to persuade the Arabs. This was not to be done in a hurry, notwithstanding the brilliancy of the offer made them. The men protested, urging the unsafety of the roads as well as their own fatigue. At last the matter was arranged in this wise: we should start at half-past six, arriving at the half-way resting-place a little before ten o'clock. Here we were to stop for a couple of hours and not continue our road till the moon rose. To this arrangement I was obliged to submit, otherwise there was no moving them to do anything; but to get out of loathsome, suffocating Jericho I was prepared to undergo any risk and trouble. We therefore set off; until eight o'clock it was still light, but very soon afterwards it suddenly became so dark that our company assumed the appearance of phantoms moving along the road. Issa remained close to my palanquin with his hand on the window ledge and left me to the enjoyment of my meditations. Occasionally he would ask me if I had everything I needed, and when I answered affirmatively he seemed content.

On we went through the darkness, my palanquin swaying from side to side, nothing audible but the dirge-like song of the muleteer's boy. Occasionally a great black shadow would rise up in front of us—it was the mounted escort turning back that he might not leave us too far behind. The night was deliciously fresh. Suddenly we came to a halt: the khan was reached, and the owners came out and spoke excitedly to Issa in Arabic whilst the palanquin was being lowered to the ground. The men and beasts entered the shed, and Issa and I remained outside, I still resting in the litter, he stretched on a carpet close by.

"What were those men saying?" I asked.

"Nothing."

"But I wish to know."

"Nothing, I assure you, but nonsense."

As I insisted, he owned that they thought us both mad to undertake the journey in the darkness. People had been attacked only the previous night.

"And what did you say to them?"

"I said I had obeyed my orders and that you were not afraid."

"And what if something had happened, Issa?" I queried.

"They would have had to kill me first, and that is not so easy."

"How good you were to come, Issa," I said.

"I only obeyed your commands," he answered simply.

Then we began to talk about other things in the easy manner of the East. He abused Mahomet, who was his particular detestation. Issa was no bigoted Christian, but Mahomet he declared to be a muddler, a scurvy fellow and vicious thief, like all Ottomans for that matter. What particularly attracted him in the history of Jesus was His being the Son of Mary, the pure angelic Virgin: whereas, according to Issa, Mahomet's mother was no better than her worthless son. He railed more and more excitedly against the muleteer of Medina, who had had the audacity to found a religion in opposition to his own.

"Do you speak thus to the Turks?" I inquired.

"Certainly, I tell them what fools I consider them to be—they and their precious thief of a Mahomet!"

"And how do they take it?"

"Oh, sometimes they laugh, and at others they wish to fight me."

"What then?"

"Well, we fight."

"For Mahomet?" I queried.

"Horrid old intriguer," he murmured.

So the night quickly sped away, Issa amusing me with his chatter while he attended to all my wants, forgetting nothing for my comfort or safety, even going on before we reached a hotel to see everything was prepared for my reception.

He was always delightful. If we visited a church in Jerusalem or Bethlehem he would never intrude on me when he saw I was praying, for he was a truly religious man and full of sympathy for the devout. In a shop or bazaar he was most useful in putting down the Turks or Hebrews who tried to cheat. He told me he had a wife and two sons, but he had lost a little daughter three years before and could scarcely speak of her without tears. He was most devoted to his wife and to his profession, for he was never tired of travelling. I wondered whether he would go on working till his legs were bent into the shape of a hoop and his shoulders had become like a note of interrogation! Certain it is that he was never tired of suggesting journeys, describing their beauties and attractions. Thus he proposed our going to Asia Minor, Damascus, Bagdad, the very city of the "Arabian Nights." And I had not courage to disappoint him by saying it was impossible: but the present journey had, indeed, drained my resources so that I had no hope of undertaking another, however entrancing. He had a love for perpetual motion, for eating and even sleeping in the open air: possessing the true poetic spirit of the explorer he was always in search of new and far-off horizons. For Gordon Pasha he entertained a profound veneration, and, like all those who greatly loved the mystic English general, he could not believe in his death, and, doubting all the accounts, hoped he might meet him once more before he himself passed away.

Someone must have told him that I wrote books, which rather vexed me, as he persisted in asking me questions about my work and telling me how he had once acted as dragoman to an English authoress. Thus my *incognito* was done away with, though I did all I could to make him believe I only wrote for my own amusement and that no one ever read my books. He only smiled and looked sceptical, and suggested I should write an article against his arch enemy, Cook, whom he called the slayer of the dragomans of Palestine as he had robbed them of their means of livelihood. The obnoxious Cook was horribly rich. Issa hated his name all the more as he had heard that Queen Victoria had knighted him. I promised to do what I could to thwart the fell purpose of this dread personage, although, to be sure, I felt it would be most unjust. But how could I refuse to oblige so delightful a dragoman! He served me admirably to the very last minute, and implored me to send him my husband and all my friends, as he had no intention of giving up a profession he loved so well for long years to come. He was not grasping, however, for he did not want to accept the little present I made him in grateful return for all his care and attention, and also for his excellent company. He ended by accepting it, however, but I perceived he was really moved. And so was I at the thought of quitting Jerusalem, the Holy Sepulchre, and Nazareth: and I felt a pang, too, at leaving my faithful, friendly Issa Cobrously, whom I might never meet again! This evidently did not occur to him, as he fancied I should certainly take another journey with him to purchase turquoises at Damascus or pearls at Golconda: and he said, "*Au revoir*," whilst I in my heart knew it was "Good-bye." In trying to describe this simple and valorous-hearted man, so full of kindness and fidelity and of poetic charm withal, I have done what little I can to make him known to those who can appreciate the really noble and true, the only qualities that are worthy of being recorded.

IV.

LEAVE-TAKING.

THE evening before my departure I took an affectionate farewell of Cavalier Mina, the sympathetic Italian Consul at Jerusalem, and his charming wife, thanking them for all their kindness and hospitality during my stay in Palestine. I was to leave next day at eleven o'clock for Jaffa, whence I was to take the steamer for Constantinople, and they expressed a wish to come and see me off; but this, with many apologies for my seeming ingratitude, I begged them not to do, having always had the strongest objection to taking leave of my friends at a railway station, where, in the hurry and confusion of departure, one is far too much preoccupied to enjoy their company.

So this was, indeed, to be my last evening, and to-morrow my happy trip to the Holy Land would be ended! After my visit to the Consulate I went to the *Casa Nova* to bid farewell to my good friends the Franciscans, and to thank them for all their helpfulness to a lone woman during her sojourn in a strange land. These excellent men are usually calm and cheerful under all circumstances, however trying, and observing my sadness at the thought of leaving these holy surroundings, they did all in their power to raise my drooping spirits, and pressed all kinds of little presents such as rosaries, medals, &c., upon me, declaring cheerfully that they would be sure to come and see me whenever any of them came to Italy. One, however, an old man, only gave me his blessing, knowing full well that at his age there was little likelihood of his ever again leaving Palestine. The others, seeing how moved I was, spoke hopefully and made me promise that the next journey I undertook to the Land of Jesus I would be sure to come and see them. The next journey! They also gently reproved me for not having stayed at their hospice that time instead of going to the crowded hotel. I was to be sure and let them know beforehand. I promised vaguely and sadly all they wished, being well aware my promise could never be fulfilled. One very old monk, when the others had done talking and our next meeting had apparently been settled, said in a low voice: "If I am still alive, send me a copy of your book when you have written it."

I could not answer him, and turned away that he might not see my distress. Then I returned to the hotel, preceded by a *cavass* with a lighted lantern, as the streets of Jerusalem are left in total darkness after nightfall.

There exists among the travellers who come to this sacred city a pious custom, that the first thing to do on arriving and the last before leaving is to visit the Holy Sepulchre. Next morning, therefore, feeling more than usually nervous and agitated, I went for the last time to the church which contains the most venerated Tomb in the world. It was a glorious day and the streets of Jerusalem looked bright and full of life in the clear sunshine. The birds twittered, even as they had done six weeks before when I first beheld the great windows of the façade of the church. Inside there was the same going and coming of priests of all nationalities, monks, visitors, and mendicants. Suddenly all my enthusiasm seemed to leave me and I became cold and unmoved. In vain did I try to collect my thoughts with my brow pressed against the cold marble of the Holy Sepulchre and lose myself in prayer. It was useless: a thousand and one foolish commonplace details about my journey crowded into my brain. The closing of boxes, telegrams to send, what hotel to go to in Constantinople, &c., &c. Impossible to excite the least feeling of interest and emotion, I remained untouched—frozen. Thus did I kneel for some time, asking for grace to feel at least some sorrow at parting. This was not the first time I had experienced such stagnation and incapacity to raise my spirit in fervent prayer, and thereby conquer my horrible and sterile indifference. Sometimes it comes after a period of much fervour and entreaty for spiritual communion. I had, of course, been lately through a time of great excitement during my stay in the Land of Jesus, and I had been much agitated by mystic impressions, so that perhaps I was now incapable of bearing any more. Rising from my knees, I left the Holy Sepulchre and walked out of the church as coolly as if I were leaving a commonplace telegraph office. Then I returned to the hotel like an ordinary tourist who is pleased at the thought of having plenty of time in which to make all the final arrangements for departure. All went smoothly, without a hitch—my luggage was packed, my bill paid, I had not forgotten the servants, and my good friend Issa was beside the carriage which was waiting to drive me to the station, standing a little way off outside the great stone archway Bab-el-Khalil. Everything was complete. I took a last look round my room to see that I had left nothing behind, counted my packages, felt that I had my keys—yes, everything was in perfect order: but still I could not get over the impression that I had forgotten something. What could it be? I turned over in my mind all that I should have done—my passport was *visé*: I had telegraphed to the hotel at Constantinople: my place was booked on the steamer. A still silent voice in my heart seemed to whisper, " You have forgotten something, you have forgotten something." Slowly and troubled I descended the staircase, amid the salutations and farewells of everyone, and was just about to enter the carriage, when lo! I suddenly remembered that I had forgotten to take a *real* farewell of the Sepulchre of our Lord; and I therefore returned to the great church for a few last moments of meditation and prayer.

Thus, hurried and agitated, did I re-enter the Church of the Holy Sepulchre, only a few moments before the train was to start, driven thither as by some irresistible force. As I approached the Holy Tomb I felt all the anguish of separation, and as, prostrate beside it, my lips pressed the cold marble with passionate kisses, my arms stretched across it, and my eyes rained tears upon it, I recollected that I should never return again; after all, one only goes to Jerusalem once in a lifetime, and I realised that my feet would never again pass beneath its gates, or my heart be filled with such an anguish as this. Only once before had

I experienced anything approaching this emotion, and that was when, during the most terrible and desolate night of my life, I had thrown myself, sobbing and inconsolable, upon the body of my dead mother ; and thus now I was torn and heartbroken at leaving the place where He had lain. I may have excited surprise in some who were witnesses of my grief, and others, on the contrary, may have sympathised with my emotion at parting from this sacred spot, and may even have joined their tears to mine : but I neither looked at nor noticed them. When I reached the threshold I looked back as one does at the body of some one who is greatly beloved, and then the thought came to me that this great church would endure when I was no more ; this Tomb, like a living thing, would continue to watch over Christian souls and hearts : but I should never behold it again. Then, with bowed head, I slowly went out. I can recall nothing more, neither how I reached the station nor how I left the city : this only I remember, that I was silently weeping and my heart was very, very sore within me.

As the train was carrying me away I looked back upon the high hills of Zion. I was glad indeed that I was alone with my grief, and that I had had the courage to refuse to allow anyone to see me off. In the carriage with me were some English people who evidently thought me either ill or demented, for their words came back to me long afterwards. At the time, however, I did not heed them, for I was trying to impress the last view of Jerusalem upon my mental vision and to carry away with me every line, colouring, and detail, that I might recall it all when far away. The noise and bustle of the station did not disturb my thoughts: the faces around me looked like phantoms : yet the sun was shining brilliantly and the atmosphere was clear as crystal. I endeavoured to impress the picture, just as it was, upon my brain. At last we were off. Jerusalem disappeared from before my eyes, 'though I still continued to try and catch a last glimpse of the Holy City as the train rolled swiftly on. It was indeed all over now. The Tower of David was the last object I perceived, and as it faded into nothingness I made a vow. I swore that for

Jesus' sake, and for that of this Land made blessed by His Life and Death, I would write a book: not the best or most artistic perhaps, but the most human and sincere. I promised to write it with the faith and humility of a true Christian for other trusting and hopeful Christians to read. My vow is now fulfilled. To-day I lay my work at the foot of the Cross, and as I stretch out my arms towards it I murmur for myself and for those dear to me, the words so often uttered by the early Christians: "*Ave Spes Unica.*"

THE END.

PRINTED IN GREAT BRITAIN AT
THE PRESS OF THE PUBLISHERS.

A FEW OF THE RECENT ISSUES IN NELSON'S EXTENSIVE LIST OF GENERAL LITERATURE.

FROM FIJI TO THE CANNIBAL ISLANDS.
      Beatrice Grimshaw.
THE PATH TO ROME. Hilaire Belloc.
THE PEOPLE OF THE ABYSS.
       Jack London.
A LODGE IN THE WILDERNESS.
       John Buchan.
THE GREAT BOER WAR. A. Conan Doyle.
THE LAND OF FOOTPRINTS.
      Stewart E. White.
WILD LIFE IN A SOUTHERN COUNTY.
      Richard Jefferies.
THE DESERT GATEWAY. S. H. Leeder.
A BOOK ABOUT ROSES. Dean Hole.
THE ALPS FROM END TO END.
      Sir W. M. Conway.
UNVEILING OF LHASA. E. Candler.

T. NELSON & SONS, LTD., London, Edinburgh, & New York.

A FEW OF THE RECENT ISSUES IN NELSON'S EXTENSIVE LIST OF GENERAL LITERATURE.

COLLECTIONS AND RECOLLECTIONS—
Second Series.   G. W. E. Russell.

LIFE OF GLADSTONE.   Herbert W. Paul.

MARSHAL MURAT.   A. H. Atteridge.

THE PSALMS IN HUMAN LIFE.
R. E. Prothero.

MY FATHER (W. T. Stead). Estelle W. Stead.

NEWBOLT'S POEMS.

THE GOLDEN AGE.   Kenneth Grahame.

SIR HENRY HAWKINS'S REMINISCENCES.

NAPOLEON: THE LAST PHASE.
Lord Rosebery.

FROM A COLLEGE WINDOW.
A. C. Benson.

SELF-SELECTED ESSAYS. Augustine Birrell.

A MODERN UTOPIA.   H. G. Wells.

NELSON'S HISTORY OF THE WAR.

By JOHN BUCHAN.

Price 2s. 6d. net per vol. All volumes are sold separately. A Standard Work. Everywhere recognized as the Authoritative Narrative of the War. Everywhere praised as a Brilliant Military History.

ALREADY PUBLISHED.

Vol. I. From the Beginning of the War to the Fall of Namur. With Preface by the EARL OF ROSEBERY, K.G. 23 Maps and Plans.

Vol. II. From the Battle of Mons to the German Retreat to the Aisne. 19 Maps and Plans.

Vol. III. The Battle of the Aisne and the Events down to the Fall of Antwerp. 23 Maps and Plans.

Vol. IV. The Great Struggle in West Flanders, the Two Attacks upon Warsaw, and the Fighting at Sea down to the Battle of Falkland Islands. 43 Maps and Plans.

Vol. V. The War of Attrition in the West, the Campaigns in the Near East, and the Fighting at Sea down to the Blockade of Britain. 25 Maps and Plans.

Vol. VI. The Campaign on the Niemen and the Narev, the Struggle in the Carpathians, Neuve Chapelle, and the Beginning of the Dardanelles Campaign. 21 Maps and Plans.

Vol. VII. From the Second Battle of Ypres to the Beginning of the Italian Campaign. 27 Maps and Plans.

[*Continued on next page.*

T. NELSON & SONS, LTD., London, Edinburgh, & New York.

NELSON'S HISTORY OF THE WAR
(Continued.)

ALREADY PUBLISHED.

Vol. VIII. The Midsummer Campaigns and the Battles on the Warsaw Salient. 17 Maps and Plans.

Vol. IX. The Italian War, the Campaigns in Gallipoli. and the Russian Retreat from the Warsaw Salient, 17 Maps and Plans.

Vol. X. The Russian Stand, and the Allied Offensive in the West. 38 Maps and Plans.

Vol. XI. The Struggle for the Dvina, and the Great Invasion of Serbia. 20 Maps and Plans.

Vol. XII. The Retreat from Bagdad, the Evacuation of Gallipoli, and the Derby Report. 16 Maps and Plans.

Vol. XIII. The Position at Sea, the Fall of Erzerum, and the First Battle of Verdun. 29 Maps and Plans.

Vol. XIV. The Fall of Kut, the Battle of Jutland, and the Second Battle of Verdun. 32 Maps and Plans.

Vol. XV. Brussilov's Offensive, and the Intervention of Rumania. 22 Maps and Plans.

Vol. XVI. The Battle of the Somme. 34 Maps and Plans.

Vol. XVII. From the Opening of the Rumanian Campaign to the Change of Government in Britain. 26 Maps and Plans.

Vol. XVIII. From the German Overtures for Peace to American Declaration of War. 14 Maps and Plans.

Vol. XIX. Spring Campaigns of 1917. 35 Maps and Plans.

Vol. XX. Summer Campaigns of 1917. 28 Maps and Plans.

Vol. XXI. The Fourth Winter of War. 34 Maps and Plans.

Vol. XXII. The Darkest Hour. 27 Maps and Plans.

Vol. XXIII. The Dawn. 38 Maps and Plans.

T. Nelson & Sons, Ltd., London, Edinburgh, & New York.

A FEW OF THE RECENT ISSUES IN NELSON'S EXTENSIVE LIST OF POPULAR NOVELS.

SALUTE TO ADVENTURERS. John Buchan.
MARRIAGE. H. G. Wells.
RODNEY STONE. A. Conan Doyle.
THE WITCH OF PRAGUE.
　　　　　F. Marion Crawford.
THREE MISS GRAEMES.
　　　　　Miss S. Macnaughtan.
PRESTER JOHN. John Buchan.
PAUL PATOFF. F. Marion Crawford.
TRENT'S LAST CASE. E. C. Bentley.
THORLEY WEIR. E. F. Benson.
THE RIDDLE OF THE SANDS.
　　　　　Erskine Childers.
THE WILD GEESE. Stanley J. Weyman.
THE OLD WIVES' TALE. Arnold Bennett.

T. NELSON & SONS, LTD., London, Edinburgh, & New York.

A FEW OF THE RECENT ISSUES IN NELSON'S EXTENSIVE LIST OF POPULAR NOVELS.

JIM OF THE RANGES.	G. B. Lancaster.
FORTITUDE.	Hugh Walpole.
A ROLLING STONE.	B. M. Croker.
THE SEA HAWK.	Rafael Sabatini.
MARRIED OR SINGLE?	B. M. Croker.
THE RED COCKADE.	Stanley J. Weyman.
THE MANXMAN.	Hall Caine.
THE LOOT OF CITIES.	Arnold Bennett.
SAILORS' KNOTS.	W. W. Jacobs.
FOUR FEATHERS.	E. A. W. Mason.

T. NELSON & SONS, LTD., London, Edinburgh, & New York.

www.ingramcontent.com/pod-product-compliance
Lightning Source LLC
Chambersburg PA
CBHW021406230426
43666CB00006B/659